Indigenizing Movements in Europe

Indigenizing Movements in Europe

edited by

Graham Harvey

SHEFFIELD UK   BRISTOL CT

Published by Equinox Publishing Ltd.

UK: Office 415, The Workstation, 15 Paternoster Row, Sheffield, South York-
      shire S1 2BX

USA: ISD, 70 Enterprise Drive, Bristol, CT 06010

www.equinoxpub.com

First published in Volume 9.2 of the *International Journal for the Study of New
Religions*

© Equinox Publishing Ltd 2019

First published in book form 2020

© Graham Harvey and contributors 2020

British Library Cataloguing-in-Publication Data

A catalogue record for this book is available from the British Library.

ISBN-13: 978 1 78179 790 7 (hardback)
ISBN-13: 978 1 78179 791 4 (paperback)
ISBN-13: 978 1 78179 792 1 (ePDF)

Library of Congress Cataloging-in-Publication Data

Names: Harvey, Graham, 1959– editor.
Title: Indigenizing Movements in Europe / edited by Graham Harvey.
Description: Sheffield, South Yorkshire ; Bristol, CT : Equinox Publishing Ltd.,
   2019. | Includes bibliographical references and index.
Identifiers: LCCN 2018059177 (print) | ISBN 9781781797907 (hb) |
   ISBN 9781781797914 (pb)
Subjects: LCSH: Europe—Religious life and customs. | Religion, Prehistoric—
   Europe. | Indigenous peoples—Europe—Religion.
Classification: LCC BL695 .I54 2019 (print) | LCC BL695 (ebook)
   | DDC 200.94—dc23
LC record available at https://lccn.loc.gov/2018059177

LC ebook record available at https://lccn.loc.gov/2019981432

Typeset by Queenston Publishing, Hamilton Canada

Contents

Contents

— I —

Indigenizing Movements in Europe

Graham Harvey

Comparisons are at the heart of this book, some more or less explicit than others. This introduction devotes significant space to comparisons between religions that are often categorized as "new" and those often labelled "Indigenous." It does not forget that these ways of grouping some religions are, in various ways, integral to or parasitic of the questionable practice of comparison that is indicated in the phrase "World religions." Thus, this book also offers some data for the consideration of the *practice* of comparison. However, as terms in the title indicate, there are two more central comparisons at issue here. Most obviously, there is a comparison between religious movements that are "European" and others that are "Indigenous." An explanation for capitalizing "Indigenous" will be offered soon but the relevant comparison hinges on the question of whether *European* movements which are not Indigenous in a particular sense do, nonetheless, *indigenize* in ways that might be comparable with practices of Indigenous peoples. This is already to point to the second key comparison. Drawing on Paul C. Johnson's (2002) coining and discussing of the term "indigenizing," this book compares and contrasts practices in which people either indigenize or extend their repertoires of ideas, practices and/or discourses.

Indigenizing

Johnson's use of "indigenizing" arose in his reflections on processes among the Garifuna and practitioners of Candomblé in South America and the Caribbean. He contrasted it with processes he labels "extending." He writes,

> Both [indigenizing and extending] are present among all religious groups, but are balanced and mobilized differently by each. *Indigenizing* discourses and practices have as their objective the configuration, at least imaginatively or

1

discursively, of a pure group performing traditional practices on its original homeland. When outsider signs, symbols and practices are relied upon, they are quickly indigenized—given a culturally specific form that makes the outsider symbol "ours," even traditional. *Extending* discourses and practices take as their objective the lowering of social boundaries, the circulation of religious knowledge and symbols into wider availability, and the overt assimilation of new forms acknowledged to be from outside. (Johnson 2002, 312)

Johnson's terms recognize tendencies to emphasize resonance with and relevance to local and ancestral traditions (indigenizing) and tendencies to stress universal relevance or global engagement (extending). These exist on a continuum and are more likely to be matters of emphasis rather than opposites. Those who conceive of themselves and their cultures as maintaining, enhancing or purifying discrete ethnic, cultural or religious communities may represent one trajectory. Others not only assert that they have something to say to the rest of the world but may also seek to revise "local ancestral" traditions in the light of more global traditions. Often, the two trends are activated in phases or in varied encounters with "others." At times, people might draw in practices and ideas from elsewhere to enhance their received or current lifeways, practices of knowledges. At times (and possibly simultaneously) they might share or offer what is theirs to the wider world.

The first question generative of this book is whether these processes are visible among members or practitioners of European religious movements. The second question is whether comparing processes among European and Indigenous religions increases understanding. Before we approach those questions, it will be helpful to consider the practice of comparison and some of the terms drawn into our consideration of the potential (a) for observing and (b) of observing indigenizing processes among European religions.

Comparative practices

Although people are sometimes told that they are not comparing like with like, or that they are wrongly comparing chalk and cheese or oranges and apples, comparison can, at least sometimes, be helpful in refining understanding. Clarifying what is distinctive and what is shared between phenomena can lead on to the asking of further questions. Comparison can also be immensely helpful when we test the value of an idea or theory. It may lead us to check not only whether, or to what extent, an interpretation or thesis might apply elsewhere but also how productive or even predictive a proposal might be prove more generally or globally. This book arose from a double panel at the 2018 conference of the European Association for the Study of Religion in which the authors considered the possibility that the term "indigenizing" might (or might not) enrich analysis, interpretation, theorization and/or discussion of movements and practices beyond those which lead to its coining.

So then, this book focuses on a selection of European religious movements which are typically the kind of movements labelled "new religions" or "new religious movements." They are not usually the focus of scholars interested in Indigenous religions. Similarly, members of the groups we have chosen to discuss only rarely identify their religions as Indigenous. Nor do they usually lay claim to being Indigenous themselves. They certainly do not do so programmatically, definitively or with any great emphasis. This is important because some Europeans (like some Hindus) certainly do attempt to assert their indigeneity and use such language as a plank of their nationalist, regionalist or ethnic self-assertion. Religion can be an element of such efforts and we could have devoted space to the kind of groups which identify themselves as, for example, "Native Faiths" (see, e.g., Rountree 2015). Our goal here, however, has been to see how the term "indigenizing" might reveal or develop better understanding of processes that are comparable to those implicated in Paul C. Johnson's coinage but occur among a quite different array of religions.

A further possibility is raised and debated in a final chapter. This asks whether the testing of the wider applicability of "indigenizing" (which *might* be imagined as the indigenizing of the term by a different scholarly community and/or as expanding its reach to other movements) might also feed back into discussion of its Indigenous originating contexts and interpretations. Among other matters, this additional comparison of scholarly practices raises significant questions as to the relation between nationalist, romantic and anti-colonial modes of indigenizing. Before we get to this and other chapters, some further consideration of the comparative terms "new," "Indigenous," and "World" is offered.

Comparisons: "New"

It will have been noticed that in the previous paragraphs there is an evident contrast between the capitalized "Indigenous" and the lower-case "new religions." If "New" were to be capitalized it might have suggested that novelty is the defining characteristic of religions to which this label is attached. However, not only do many adherents of such religions assert the antiquity of their roots, but there is no scholarly consensus as to when "new" began. When "new religious movements" first entered the scholarly arena, the label "new" was often applied to movements founded or first organized in the nineteenth century. More recently, the term's reference has been restricted to post-World War II or post-1950s movements. In each case, a movement's claims to be a contemporary expression of, for example, Buddhist, Christian, Hindu or Muslim traditions was or is often of less scholarly interest than the "newness" of its social organization. However, the putatively recent origins of such groups are not the only attractor of scholarly interest. In addition, questions have been asked about the fit or resonance between these "new religions" and the contemporary era. Is there something specifically modern, late modern or post-modern about these religions in contrast with others? Are the dynamics of consumer or supply-chain capitalism more relevant to the practice of new religions than they are to other religions? Is there a relationship between a group's ideology or practices and climate catastrophe, political crises or other contemporary phenomena.

A broader sense of contemporaneity is conveyed in the website of the *International Journal for the Study of New Religions* (IJSNR). This notes that it and its parent society, the International Society for the Study of New Religions (ISSNR), have chosen to adopt a broad definition [of "new religions"]. Articles with subject matter as diverse as conversion to Satanism (Lewis 2010), children in new religions (Van Eck Duymaer van Twist 2010), ecumenism and religious dialogue among Jehovah's Witnesses (Chryssides 2012), new ideas of food taboo in some contemporary Jewish and Muslim communities (Theobald 2012), as well as gender and spiritual therapy in Japan (Gaitanidis 2012) have been published in *International Journal for the Study of New Religions* since its inception (Equinox 2019).

In short, the putative novelty of some religions has not proved to be of enduring interest or of interpretative or theoretical value. Other matters have attracted more interest and generated more recent—and more critical —debate. Nonetheless, "new" continues to label a swathe of religions and remains a comparative term. But with what should such religions be compared and on what basis?

Comparisons: "Indigenous"

Indigenous religions present themselves as a possible category for comparison with new religions. Before offering a short summary of what an "Indigenous religion" might be, let's return to the capitalization of "Indigenous." It is notable that not all authors in this book follow this practice. Indeed, in coining the term "indigenizing" Paul Johnson does not do so either. Why is "Indigenous" capitalized here and elsewhere? What does the capital letter gain and offer?

The capitalized "Indigenous" and the lower-case "indigenous" might be synonymous in some contexts. Both can be used to refer to communities which self-identify in ways that the United Nations Permanent Forum on Indigenous Issues (UNPFII) indicates in its "working definition."

Indigenous communities, peoples and nations are those which, having a historical continuity with pre-invasion and pre-colonial societies that developed on their territories, consider themselves distinct from other sectors of the societies now prevailing on those territories, or parts of them. They form at present non-dominant sectors of society and are determined to preserve, develop and transmit to future generations their ancestral territories, and their ethnic identity, as the basis of their continued existence as peoples, in accordance with their own cultural patterns, social institutions and legal system (UNPFII 2004, 2).

It is the self-determination recognized in this statement that is marked by the strategic capitalization of "Indigenous" elsewhere by many (but by no means all) Indigenous people.

Matters could be put this way: "indigenous" is more broadly applicable than "Indigenous," pointing to the origins (e.g. of persons, oranges or chickens) in particular places at some point in time. In contrast, the capitalized "Indigenous" can indicate more specific projects of community or world construction in which colonialization, marginalization and the extinguishing, distancing and other manoeuvres of so-called "Modern Western cultures" are contested. ("Modern" and "Western" are also capitalized here for strategic, polemical or heuristic purposes—which could be expanded on by reference to Latour 1993, 2013). Such modes of Indigeneity are not merely reactive (let alone reactionary) but involve creative exploration of the contemporary value and use of customary practices, processes and protocols (see Allen 2012, building on Jahnke 2006).

That such exploration takes place surrounded by settler States and other continuing colonialisms is just one aspect of the relationality of the term "Indigenous." (The same is true for terms like "indigenous," "native," "aboriginal" or any of the myriad specific terms for particular Indigenous nations and other communities when used of people for whom the capitalized Indigenous is employed here.) Relations and challenges work both ways and it is not only those who claim to be Indigenous who distinguish those so labelled from other kinds of person. Distinction and differentiation can involve significant violence against Indigenous people (individuals or communities). These are matters to be tackled. However, the fact being focused on here is that of the relationship between those people, communities and concerns which are (or can be said to be) Indigenous and those which are nonindigenous. As the Peruvian anthropologist Marisol de la Cadena argues in relation to Andean world-making (2015, 188), the Indigenous and the nonindigenous emerge together, inseparably even when they seek separation. These are necessarily comparative terms, relations not boxed identities, and, as is the case with all relations, their entanglement leads to their exceeding what they might be alone. Like two threads in a tapestry, it is their embraidedness that shows us more of the picture than we would see were the threads alone.

One more element of the contrast at issue here is raised by the Indigenous botanist Robin Kimmerer's struggles with the question of whether people (specifically North American settlers) can *become* Indigenous. She writes,

> Against the backdrop of [settler] history, an invitation to settler society to become indigenous to place feels like a free ticket to a housebreaking party. It could be read as an open invitation to take what little is left. (Kimmerer 2013, 211)

She is clear that "Immigrants cannot by definition be indigenous" but (drawing on her botanical expertise and vocabulary) she argues that while some settlers remain invasive, others *can* "naturalize" (2013, 213–214). While the focus of this book is not on settlers but on Europeans still in Europe, Kimmerer's "naturalizing" might have some kinship with the key term at issue here: "indigenizing." Before committing ourselves to a discussion of "indigenizing" there are other comparisons and comparative terms that require attention.

What makes a religion indigenous?

In the essay from which the term "indigenizing" is drawn Paul Johnson proposes that Indigenous religions may be defined "as the religions of those communities that imagine themselves in indigenous style—as organically bound to a land site" (Johnson 2002, 306). This is a good starting point. Indeed, it serves as such for the final chapter of this book: Bjørn Ola Tafjord's powerful response both to Johnson and to the chapters between this introduction and his afterword. The emphasis on land and peoplehood (sometimes conceived of as relationships with specific ancestors and/or what they handed on to current generations) is a common but not uncontested feature of many other discussions of what makes a religion "Indigenous." It is important to be clear that the phrase "Indigenous religions" is more specific than the phrase "the religions of Indigenous people." Such people might identify (even to the exclusion of other possibilities) as Baha'is, Christians, Muslims, Rastafarians, or any of the myriad other religions available to them. However, it is equally important to note that indigenizing processes might not only be observable among those thoroughly committed to enacting religious traditions inherited from "traditional" ancestors but also among those Bahais, Christians, Muslims, Rastafarians and others. They too are able to learn from others and to adopt and adapt what seems helpful to them.

Significant recent collections that debate such matters include Greg Johnson and Siv Ellen Kraft's (2017) *Handbook of Indigenous Religion(s)*, Christopher Hartney and Daniel J. Tower's (2017) *Religious Categories and the Construction of the Indigenous*, and the four volume set of readings presented by Graham Harvey and Amy Whitehouse (2019) as *Indigenous Religions: Critical Concepts in Religious Studies*. These and other publications demonstrate that the question of the meaning or reference of the term "Indigenous religions" remains unsettled and challenging. However, something about the centrality of land and locatedness are clear enough to offer a contrast with religions that emphasize other-worldliness or transcendence. Again, then, we are confronted by another comparison—albeit one that is frequently debated by those involved in the study of Indigenous religions. It is, at any rate, employed strategically here to enable a discussion to continue.

Comparisons: "World"

A more widespread debate and a more prevalent contrast involves noting that academics who study religion(s) have vociferously contested the term "World religions" for some decades. This is invaluably surveyed and developed by contributors to Chris Cotter and David Robertson's (2016) *After World Religions: Reconstructing Religious Studies*. The labelling of particular religions as "World," "new" or "Indigenous" is not innocent—it is rarely merely descriptive but generally argumentative. Privilege and prejudice is at least implicit in the claim to own the label "world" (as in "world class"). "World religions" is, after all, not contrasted with "Martian religions" but with "minority religions," "folk religions," "ethnic religions," "syncretic religions," "popular religions," and other alleged errors of belief or practice. For this reason alone, I have capitalized "World."

Any claim that "World" *is* in fact simply descriptive actually distorts matters and conversations. Particular approaches, methods and positions are embroiled in its usage. It is arguable that studies of new religions and Indigenous religions have reinvigorated the academic study of religions in recent decades. They have certainly challenged the dominance of a focus on those so-called "World religions" and, more significantly, they have contested the approaches and attitudes that have infused the study of those religions. It is usually the case that those "World religions" are approached theologically— or at least from an assumption that normative teachings and institutions define the real or proper version of any religion (or of the only versions worthy of study). Meanwhile, "new religions" have more often been approached sociologically and "Indigenous religions" have largely been approached anthropologically. In both cases, the questions asked and the issues explored are often about the doing of religion in diverse and changing ways.

It is, then, the contrast between an approaches which is important. The "World religions" approach imagines that the proper topic of study is a formulation of correctly believed or practiced religions. In contrast, most scholars of religion prefer and promote approaches to that get to the lived, vernacular and material realities of religions. In view of our interest in indigenizing practices, these contests between approaches might also be evoked in the contrast between the terms "syncretism" and "compositions." The first indicates that it is wrong to mix proper beliefs and practices from one place or community with those from elsewhere. This can only result in confusion and the need for corrective lessons. Some colleagues contrast this with "hybridity," which indicates that combinations of different ideas and practices generate interesting new combinations. However, in the different context of studying animal-human relations Vinciane Despret argues that

Hybridization remains a matter of "combination," thus of the reproduction of certain characteristics of the two "parent" species… Metamorphoses, conversely, retranslates "combinations" into a system of "compositions," a system that remains open to surprise and to the event: "other things" can arise that profoundly modify beings and their relations. (Despret 2016, 190)

The great advantage of Despret's "composition" is that points to open ended, on-going processes and to the anticipation of surprise in our studies of what happens. It is this that emboldens us to wonder if indigenization can tell us anything new or interesting about European religious movements.

Indigenizing in European religious movements

Since the mid-twentieth century, members of religious movements identified as Paganism, shamanism, native faiths and others have experimented with at least three forms of indigeneity (or "being indigenous"). These might overlap and reinforce one another. The first is seen in claims to be reviving or re-presenting religious practices from ancestral, pre-Christian or pre-Modern times. The second form of indigeneity is found in lessons learnt (directly or indirectly) from Indigenous peoples (especially Native Americans, Siberians and/or Amazonians). A third form, of increasing prominence since the late twentieth century, has been an emphasis on localizing rather than on universality. In line with broader European cultural trends, some of the rhetoric of these claims to indigeneity have been implicated in the construction of identities (putative ways of being distinct from others). However, arguably they are more helpfully understood as practices, projects or processes. It is the recognition of the performative character of discourses and practices related to indigeneity which led Johnson (2002) to encourage examination of processes of indigenizing. This book tests the interpretive and methodological value of this approach in relation to selected European religious movements and phenomena.

The following chapters present seven case studies. These involve Irish Paganism (Jenny Butler), British animist spirituality (Graham Harvey), Glastonbury Goddess devotion (Amy Whitehead), British Druidry (Suzanne Owen), European powwow enthusiasts (Christina Welch), Italian shamanism (Angela Puca) and Lithuanian Anastasians (Rasa Pranskevičiūtė),. They have been selected so as to enable a range of different relations between European movements and (other-than-European) Indigenous cultures. Presentation of relevant data will orientate readers to these movements, and explore the varied processes by which such Europeans have learnt from or among Indigenous peoples, or from the scholarly or popular literatures presenting these for consideration. Authors are also attentive to the possibility that less than respectful practices of appropriation from Indigenous people underlie any apparent similarity between European and Indigenous practices. (It is significant that Johnson published about appropriation and shamanisms some years before he developed his argument about indigenizing, see Johnson 1995.) A response by Bjørn Ola Tafjord focusses on the theoretical and conceptual value of the panellists' reflections and arguments. It considers important questions for the practice of the study of religions—whatever category of religion is in view. In these ways, this books aims to enhance understanding and enrich debate both about evolving European movements and also about the concepts and practices of Indigeneity, indigenizing and of scholarly practices in relation to such phenomena.

References

Allen, Chadwick. 2012. *Trans-Indigenous: Methodologies for Global Native Literary Studies*. Minneapolis: University of Minnesota Press. https://doi.org/10.5749/minnesota/9780816678181.001.0001

Astor-Aguilera, M. and G. Harvey. 2018. "Introduction: We have never been individuals." In *Rethinking Relations and Animism: Personhood and Materiality*, edited by M. Astor-Aguilera and G. Harvey, 1–12. New York: Routledge. https://doi.org/10.4324/9780203709887

Cotter, C.R. and D.G. Robertson, eds. 2016. *After World Religions: Reconstructing Religious Studies*. London: Routledge. https://doi.org/10.4324/9781315688046

Chryssides, George. 2012. "Ecumenical with the truth? Jehovah's Witnesses and dialogue." *International Journal for the Study of New Religions* 3(1): 5–26. https://doi.org/10.1558/ijsnr.v3i1.5

de la Cadena, Marisol. 2015. *Earth Beings: Ecologies of Practice across Andean Worlds*. Durham, NC: Duke University Press. https://doi.org/10.1215/9780822375265

Despret, V. 2016. *What would animals say if we asked the right questions?* Minneapolis: University of Minnesota Press

Equinox. 2019. Website of the *International Journal for the Study of New Religions* https://journals.equinoxpub.com/index.php/IJSNR/

Gaitanidis, Ioannis. 2012. "Gender and spiritual therapy in Japan." *International Journal for the Study of New Religions* 3(2): 269–288. https://doi.org/10.1558/ijsnr.v3i2.269

Hartney, C. and D. J. Tower, eds. 2017. *Religious Categories and the Construction of the Indigenous.* Leiden: E.J. Brill. https://doi.org/10.1163/9789004328983

Harvey, G. and A. Whitehead, eds. 2018. *Indigenous Religions: Critical Concepts in Religious Studies.* New York: Routledge.

Kimmerer, R. W. 2013. *Braiding Sweetgrass: Indigenous Wisdom, Scientific Knowledge, and the Teachings of Plants.* Minneapolis: Milkweed.

Jahnke, Robert. 2006. "Māori art towards the millennium." In *State of the Māori Nation: Twenty-first Century Issues in Aotearoa*, edited by Malcolm Mulholland, 41–51. Auckland: Reed.

Johnson, G. and S. E. Kraft, eds. 2017. *Handbook of Indigenous Religions.* Leiden: E.J. Brill. https://doi.org/10.1163/9789004346710

Johnson, P. C. 2002. "Migrating bodies, circulating signs: Brazilian Candomblé, the Garifuna of the Caribbean, and the category of indigenous religions." *History of Religions* 41(4): 301–327. https://doi.org/10.1006/reli.1995.0015 Reprinted in *Indigenous Diasporas and Dislocation*, edited by Graham Harvey and Charles D Thompson, 63–81. London: Routledge.

———. 1995. "Shamanism from Ecuador to Chicago: A case study in ritual appropriation." *Religion* 25: 163–178.

Latour, B. 2013. *An Inquiry Into Modes of Existence: An Anthropology of the Moderns.* Cambridge, MA: Harvard University Press.

———. 1993. *We Have Never Been Modern.* New York: Harvester Wheatsheaf.

Lewis, James Roger. 2010. "Fit for the devil: Toward an understanding of 'conversion' to Satanism." *International Journal for the Study of New Religions* 1(1): 117–138. https://doi.org/10.1558/ijsnr.v1i1.117

Rountree, K. ed. 2015. *Contemporary Pagan and Native Faith Movements in Europe: Colonialist and Nationalist Impulses.* Oxford: Berghahn. https://doi.org/10.2307/j.ctt9qctm0

Theobald, Simon. 2012. "Doubtful food, doubtful faith: A comparative study of the influence of religious maximalism on new ideas of food taboo in some contemporary Jewish and Muslim communities." *International Journal for the Study of New Religions* 3(2): 245–268. https://doi.org/10.1558/ijsnr.v3i2.245

UNPFII. 2004. "The Concept of indigenous peoples." www.un.org/esa/socdev/unpfii/documents/workshop_data_background.doc

Van Eck Duymaer van Twist, Amanda. 2010. "Children in New Religions; Contested duties of care." *International Journal for the Study of New Religions* 1(2): 183–206. https://doi.org/10.1558/ijsnr.v1i2.183

About the author

Graham Harvey is professor of religious studies at The Open University. His recent research largely concerns "the new animism," especially in the rituals and protocols through which Indigenous and other communities engage with the larger-than-human world. He was a member of the international research project, "REDO: Re-assembling democracy" (funded by the Norwegian Research Council). For this, he focused on the Sámi organized Riddu Riđđu festival in Sápmi and the London based ORIGINS Festival of First Nations in which Indigenous performers present their cultures and knowledges to metropolitan and global audiences. Harvey's research interests contribute to his broader, long-term engagement with material- and lived-religion. His recent teaching related work has involved a focus on foodways and associated "purity" practices. His publications include *Food, Sex and Strangers: Understanding Religion as Everyday Life* (2013), and *Animism: Respecting the Living World* (2nd edition 2017). He is editor of the Equinox series "Religion and the Senses," the first volume of which, *Sensual Religion: Religion and the Five Senses* (2018), he co-edited with Jessica Hughes. He is also the founding co-editor of the Routledge series "Vitality of Indigenous Religions," a multi-volume research level monograph series aiming to enhance engagement with the lived realities of Indigenous religions.

2

Entering the Magic Mists:
Irish Contemporary Paganism, Celticity and Indigeneity

Jenny Butler

This chapter explores the ways in which contemporary Pagans in Ireland engage with traditional culture, as well as with notions of the Celtic, in forming identities that are regarded by some practitioners as being indigenous identities. This cultural process at work in the Pagan movement is examined against a backdrop of contested constructions of "Irishness" in different political and sociocultural milieus. Drawing from ethnographic research on the Irish Pagan community, the examination includes examples of mechanisms used by modern Pagans to engage with ancestral and historical cultures. In entering the "magic mists" to search for symbols and ideas to help connect to the "old religion," modern Pagans create something new and unique while taking inspiration from the past. This overview of Pagans' utilization of cultural forms, and their use of tradition, aims to communicate why this creative approach to the past, and resulting formation and maintenance of identities, is culturally significant in the Irish context.

Introduction

Contemporary Paganism manifests in Ireland in a variety of forms, many of which are influenced and inspired by the ancient world of the Celts. Druids, Wiccans and other Pagan Witches in Ireland today engage with traditional cultural forms—popular practices and folklore—as well as with notions of the Celtic in forming identities that are regarded by some practitioners as being indigenous identities. The sense in which "indigenous" is generally used by Pagans in the Irish context is almost synonymous with the concept of "old religion," as a type of spirituality which has origins, or at least roots, in a religious tradition that preceded it.

Marian Bowman remarks that

> the Celtic mists are swirling once more, and in the twilight can be glimpsed an assortment of images of the Celts. Pagans, New Agers, Christians and society at large are reclaiming the Celts, and while there have been various periods of fascination with Celts and Druids in the past, they have not had such spiritual significance as we are witnessing now. (2000b, 242)

In claiming a lineage to ancestral cultures now shrouded in the mists of time, contemporary Paganism in Ireland involves interesting mechanisms for relating to the past and for entering into the Celtic mists to reclaim symbols and images of special significance for the here and now. The historicity of religious or cultural concepts, ways or customs are located in the popular religious practices of the pre-modern era or the extant sources that tell us something about the pre-Christian Irish world; contemporary Pagans reference both historical frameworks, with more emphasis on one or other depending on the particular "path"[1] or type of Paganism. Historical detail is knitted together with ideas originating from various sources—Romantic writings, antiquarian folklore collections, fantasy art and literature, global Pagan discourses—and meshed together with particularized conceptions of what "Celtic" means.

This chapter aims to show how contemporary Irish Paganism forms a "style of imagined community," in the sense that Johnson (2002, 305) describes, with emphasis on particular features of the environment, i.e. modern-day Ireland. Various forms of cultural capital are employed in establishing Paganism as something home-grown and embedded in "Irishness," including conceptualizations of native land, ancient monuments, language, mythology and folklore. Given the broad information base from which modern Pagans draw, and the fragmentary nature of the information that is utilized, "indigenous Irish Pagan" identity can mean many things. Paul C. Johnson's use of "indigenous" as an abstract tool or ideal type in the Weberian sense, and his concept of an "indigenizing movement," are employed here in an analysis of the ways in which contemporary Paganism is "made local" or vernacularized and embedded into Irish cultural tradition, as well as made legitimate (in terms of cultural capital and social status) by evoking a Celtic past as a foundation it is reattaching to.

Indigeneity and Ireland

Indigenous, in the sense of what is native to a place or in the signification of the original inhabitants of a given region, is contentious and contested in

---

1. The term "path" is used in Paganism to mean the type of Paganism a practitioner belongs to (for example, Druid, Wiccan, or Shaman), rather like the different forms of Christianity are referred to as "denominations."

the Irish context for a number of reasons. Claims about native or intrinsically Irish identities, defined against foreign or imported identities, can be emotive. Ireland's political and sociocultural history have culminated in an environment in which there is a sense of unease around claims to indigeneity. In the Irish milieu and the identity politics that operate within it, there are complexities around the political status, and concurrent cultural potency, given to ethnically-defined identities and entitlements that might belong to "native Irish culture," particularly if such cultural, social or political privileges are to be contrasted against the identities of groups that have settled, occupied or colonized the country in the past.

Anglo-Irish identities, those of mixed English and Irish parentage or lineage or, more usually in its usage, those of English descent but born or resident in Ireland, make sharp distinctions around "Irishness" problematic and definitions and discussions of "Irish indigeneity" even more problematic. "Irishness," "Englishness" and "Britishness" have been implicated in such a tumultuous and emotive history on the island of Ireland that all applications of these terms will probably be contested by some sector of society. Even present-day Ireland, with its melting-pot of cultures, in part due to the influx of people from around the globe during the Celtic Tiger,[2] the core definition of Irish national identity is that it is not British, and similarly political and cultural discourses underscore the Republic of Ireland's independent status and its distinctiveness from Britain, which makes the position of the United Kingdom (the political and territorial union of Britain and Northern Ireland) complicated and identities must be negotiated in relation to symbolic boundaries and physical borders. Johnson remarks on this situation:

> Granting a degree of post-modern hyperbole in the contemporary characterizations of the world as sheer unbounded flux and flow, it is nevertheless clear to even the most sober observer that territory and boundaries are a central concern of our time. (2002, 302)

Tensions in relation to territory and boundaries are clear when it comes to designations for the islands of Ireland and Britain as viewed together. The term "British Isles," once used in a seemingly unquestioned convention as a geographical label for the archipelago in the North Atlantic Ocean that consist of the islands of Great Britain, Ireland, the Isle of Man and numerous smaller isles scattered around the coast, 1,000 or 5,000 depending on which

---

2. The "Celtic Tiger" is a term that refers to the economy of the Republic of Ireland from the mid-1990s to the late-2000s, in which there was a period of rapid economic growth and prosperity for some sectors of Irish society, before the economic crash which led to a recession and the introduction of a series of austerity measures.

body is enumerating them.[3] As a topographical descriptor found on many historical maps, the British Isles includes two sovereign states, the Republic of Ireland and the United Kingdom of Great Britain and Northern Ireland. Though the definition is based on geography, there is no escaping the political wrangling around the territory it encompasses and as a consequence has no legal status and is not used in official governmental capacities. There is no single unproblematic term to refer to the inhabitants of both islands of Britain and Ireland despite their close physical proximity and close cultural connections and interrelations "across the water" with diasporic communities in both directions.

There are other diasporic identity issues that arise in the negotiation of relationships between Irish-born people and Irish-Americans in particular. Oftentimes people whose birthplace is in the United States claim that they are "Irish"; this claim is particularly associated with descendants of those who emigrated to America during the nineteenth century, largely as a consequence of the Great Hunger, a series of famines from 1845–1849. This is normally well received by the tourism industry and commercial concerns, but is not always received so well among the general public on the ground in Ireland and the claim to Irishness might be disputed or challenged. In fact, the term "yank" is still prevalent in Ireland to refer to Americans, a term which in the past was used mostly in a light-hearted way or as a term of endearment, as a "name given to family members, relatives or neighbours who had emigrated to the United States, when they came home on holidays" (McMahon and O'Donoghue 2004, 860), but which nowadays can often be used in a derogatory fashion to refer to a particular type of (usually gullible) tourist, and the culture of Americans can generally be viewed as quite alien to Irish society.

There are some among the Irish Pagan community who view American-based forms of Celtic Paganism with suspicion or even disdain. While there are many close connections in the contemporary Pagan milieu between Britain and Ireland, both in relation to the composition of groups and networks (i.e. Irish and British practitioners based in both locations), and events and gatherings at sacred sites in Ireland and Britain, there seems to be something of a disconnect between the Celtic Paganisms of Ireland and America.[4] Due

---

3. For example, the official blog of the British Ordnance Survey maintains British Isles as "purely a geographical term" which refers to the islands of Great Britain and Ireland (including the Republic of Ireland) and the 5000 or so smaller islands off the coasts (see https://www.ordnancesurvey.co.uk/blog/2011/08/whats-the-difference-between-uk-britain-and-british-isles/).

4. For instance, numerous Irish informants made reference to the Order of Bards, Ovates and Druids (OBOD), a contemporary international Druidic organization founded by Ross Nichols in England in 1964, but Ár nDraíocht Féin (ADF) (meaning "our own

to the hyper-awareness of the cultural sensitivities involved in the relationship between Britain and Ireland, perhaps there is more wariness of the potential for cultural misappropriation by Celtic Pagans in America when it comes to the Irish context.

Assertions about "native religion" or "original religion" can likewise be provocative within Ireland. As the "island of saints and scholars," Ireland has a time-honoured and enduring association with Christian religion, missionary endeavours, and religious scholastic traditions. Roman Catholicism has long held a privileged and special status in the Irish State and its governance and in the population's culture and people's everyday life. Due to responses to colonization and sectarian divides, being Catholic became a symbol of Irishness as Protestantism became associated with Britishness, specifically Englishness; in this way, as John Coakley (2011, 96) describes "'religion' may constitute a form of social labelling." During the foundation of the nation-state, Roman Catholicism became inextricably linked with Irish national identity, to the point where there was a co-stereotyping process whereby all Irish people were assumed (or expected) to be Catholic and the assumption was made within and outside of Ireland. To dislodge the status of Catholicism and Christianity more broadly by the re-emergence of Paganism, with contemporary groups contending it is the indigenous (i.e. the oldest known) religion would perhaps cause a social and political backlash. Celtic Christians might argue that there is an indigenous form of Irish Christianity. As Alan Gailey points out, "it is clear that different social groups adhere to different corpuses of tradition in defining their identities or in ascribing their identities to themselves" (1988, 65), and a contemporary Pagan push to be given the status of indigenous in a religious sense would likely be met with criticism from both organized religious authorities and other new religious movements who are also basing their legitimacy in the distant past.

There is a difference, however, between the Irishness of a person—which, as a characteristic of an individual, is the status of belonging to a particular nation by birth, being raised there, or by the granting of citizenship from the state authorities—and the Irishness of a tradition, which can rest on other factors. Cultural continuity in terms of customs, social attitudes and worldview, and ways of doing things, is shared between people but doesn't "belong" to anyone in any strict sense. In this way, an individual can share in cultural traditions whether or not they hold a particular nationality. Thus, non-Irish Pagans

---

Druidry" or, literally, "our own magic"), founded by Isaac Bonewits in 1983 in Ohio only came up once in an interview. There are various factors at play, not least the closer physical proximity of OBOD members across Britain and Ireland and the type of correspondence course training offered by OBOD.

resident in Ireland can practice Irish Pagan traditions and engage with the same cultural resources without this being problematic or provocative. With contemporary Paganism, the process of engaging with cultural traditions associated with place is perhaps easier since the new religious movement involves mechanisms of melding together disparate cultural elements in any case. It is possible to identify a shared corpus of traditions—characteristic features of worldview and ritual and festival practices—of contemporary Paganism globally, but there is always a vernacularizing process at work and Paganism in different places takes on local flavour and absorbs cultural aspects out of the context it is manifesting in. In the case of contemporary Irish Pagan traditions, much relies on the land and on history, and the combination of the two in the understanding of the land as something tangible that has existed since ancient times and holds upon it the archaeological heritage, Celtic and pre-Celtic, that connects people in the modern day to their ancestral forebears.

Paganism and Irish cultural traditions—A new indigeneity?

Through formations of a unique worldview and through various externalizations of that worldview—ritual activities, ritual dress and general personal adornments such as jewellery and tattoos with spiritual meanings, the creation of artwork and other items of material culture—Pagans in Ireland connect with history and traditional cultural forms. The historical and pre-historical materials that are linked to are those of the earliest known cultures, particularly those of Europe. For the Irish Pagan community, the eras with most relevance to modern identities is the time in which Celtic peoples inhabited the country and also early modern Ireland, as well as the period—nineteenth century and early to mid-twentieth century—in which the folklore collections were compiled, which provide information on continuing folkways, customs and especially popular religious practices and festival celebrations. The combination of details from both periods is used, in often a de-contextualized way, to inform Pagan ritual creation and relationship with the land and local places which are deemed sacred sites. The process of blending disparate ideas, creative forms, and cultural elements is characteristic of contemporary Paganisms in general, but local inflections are always involved; Paganism manifests uniquely in every country or region where it appears, taking on ideas about national and local identity and engaging with local sites and land.

Within contemporary Pagan movements on a global scale, there is a strong desire to restore older ways of life, especially symbolic practices connected with forms of religion that pre-date Christianity. Examples of this include reconstructions of ancient rituals (especially in Nordic and Germanic Paganisms), a continuation of traditional religious festival observances (with a disregarding or de-emphasizing of Christian observances) by combining information about festival celebrations in different time periods. Many Pagans of different paths make a conscious effort to live in accordance with natural rhythms like changing seasons, buying food that's in season or growing one's own food, and perhaps using traditional methods of cultivation or creation of objects or clothing. In the Irish context, relatively little is known about the pre-Christian world and scholars must rely on archaeological sources and early Irish literature, which was largely compiled by medieval Christian scribes meaning that any information on Pagan deities and religious practices has already been mediated through a Christian worldview. While academics are limited to such sources, Pagans often incorporate other materials and influences in creating a picture of the Celtic world, including eighteenth and nineteenth century writings and artworks arising from the Romantic movement, fused together with fantasy art (paintings, literary works) and also marketing images produced by the tourist industry. In this way, inspiration comes into play in a creative approach to connecting selectively with the past. This approach is also due to a reflexive awareness among Pagans that it isn't possible, in the Irish case at least, to reconstruct precisely what the old religion was, so instead people use whatever historical detail is available as part of a spiritual relationship to the past.

Thus, various cultural resources are employed in garnering information about native Irish cosmology and practices, and particular details are amalgamated within an already existing framework of meaning. Global Pagan movements share much with regard to conceptualizations of the past, and ways of engaging with historical and contemporary cultures, but there is also much to be said about local distinctiveness and there are qualities and forms of Paganism that are unique to the Irish milieu. The native Irish cosmology and practices are often presented in tandem, within Irish Pagan discourse, with the lifeworlds and cosmologies of native peoples around the world, and this is an interesting approach to the concept of indigeneity. In the Irish setting, the indigenous or native peoples, when understood as the Celts are part of the distant past. Since there are no indigenous groups in Ireland in the sense of tribal peoples living in forests or on reservations alongside "mainstream" society, and therefore none of the issues of marginalization and concomitant struggles that such peoples face, it is perhaps a lot less controversial to engage with a "native" identity that is so detached from modern Irish everyday life.

The Old Religion and the New Religious movement

Claims about the "original religion" may well be aggravating for some Christian groups in what is still a hegemonically Roman Catholic society. In early

Christian Ireland, aspects of the older religion blended together with the one that superseded it. Diarmuid Ó Giolláin (1997, 203) describes the process of "pre-Christian phenomena being Christianized and of surviving non-Christian phenomena taking on a Christian frame of reference," which resulted in a syncretic form of religiosity that continued to hold both pre-Christian and Christian elements within it until its present form of "popular Catholicism." In contemporary Paganism, there is a tendency to strip away the Christian elements from popular religious practices in an attempt to reclaim the "pagan" parts, by incorporating the latter into ritual practices. From the Pagan perspective, the integration of popular religious traditions into one's worldview and practices is part of retrieving survivals of the old religion.

Kathryn Rountree, in her comparison of Irish and Maltese Pagans, remarks on how

> in both countries some neo-pagans incorporate Christianity into their personal spiritual paths and identities. Overall, Irish and Maltese Pagans are perhaps less antagonistic towards the prevailing Catholicism of their societies than many of their counterparts elsewhere are towards Christianity.
>
> (Rountree 2010, 4–5)

It could be posited that, in the Irish context with its syncretistic religious background, Pagans are less hostile towards the Christianity they encounter most, Roman Catholicism, precisely because it is so ritualistic and in its popular form features strands of the ancient religion which preceded it. In fact, Pagans incorporate ritual elements commonly found in Irish popular religion that may well be identified by others as popular Catholic traditions, for example the circumambulation of holy wells and sacred stones. As mentioned above, Catholicism became wedded to Irishness in such intricate ways that it can be difficult for Irish people, or those with Irish heritage, to reject it outright. In a much broader sense, Christianity is nevertheless viewed as a threat to indigenous modes of being because of the world's history of missionizing, mistreatment of native peoples and disregard—oftentimes disdain—for their lifeworlds and traditional religions. Thus, the new religious movement of Paganism is driven more by an impulse to "re-Paganize" and repackage folk religion than to connect with Catholicism.

Since Irish Paganism tends to be influenced by Romantic Nationalism, and since Pagans are negotiating all of the aforementioned identity-politics around "Irishness," they tend not to entangle themselves in political debates or to try to create a political standing for Paganism in Ireland (see further Butler 2015). Though some groups refer to themselves as "temples," more as a demarcation of a sacred space in which to freely gather together, there haven't been overt attempts to build physical Pagan temples in Ireland or to have particular sites given official "sacred site" status. It is important to note, however, that there was a Pagan-led campaign to protect the Hill of Tara in County Meath from being damaged by the construction of the M3 Motorway and in this controversy, the sacred site status was firmly claimed by Pagans.

Celticity and Irish Pagan cultural expressions

As outlined previously, Pagans merge historical materials with artistic and other inspirational materials in a creative approach to the past while giving certain periods of time a greater significance because of what can be gleaned about religious practices or traditional customs that are of most relevance for Pagan identities in the present. Many contemporary Pagans draw spiritual strength from the past by the orientation of their own spiritual expression within a fabric of meaning that takes up strands from history and the ancient world, and by situating their ritual activities in a meaningful framework which also references that past even if it cannot be reconstructed. Bowman (2000a, 88) explains how "a variety of spiritual seekers consider that the Celts are providing inspiration, motivation and exhilaration in their religious lives" and states that "the "spiritual Celt" is real, whether or not he or she exists/existed."

Pagan individuals and groups innovatively use symbols associated with the Celtic and pre-Celtic world. For example, the images and motifs in stories belonging to the corpus of early Irish literature are referenced by Pagans in ritual, whether explicitly where a ritual re-enacts a particular story theme or where the motifs from the story hold significance for some part of the ritual, or for a pathworking (within Pagan usage meaning a type of meditative practice often involving visualization following along with spoken-word storytelling). Ireland's pre-Celtic archaeological heritage is also referenced by Pagans, with symbols found in petroglyphs being incorporated into Pagan jewellery, artwork and ritual objects. The triskelion and spiral are the most common for Irish Pagans to use and these are found on sites like Newgrange, a passage tomb in County Meath dating to circa 3,200 BCE. Though it is not definitively known who erected these monuments or what exactly they were for (with Newgrange, speculations abound due to the illumination of the passage and chamber by the rays of the rising sun on the winter solstice), Newgrange and the Hill of Tara, also in County Meath are mentioned in the Irish mythology, which is designated as "Celtic mythology" by academics and popularly.

During Ireland's colonization when the population was forcibly made to switch from their native language to speaking English, the native language terms were also translated. This involved linguistic transitions but also cultural translations, and terms with spiritual meanings were re-contexted and reconceptualized by English speakers. It is important to note that the history of the

Irish language, and the cultural trauma surrounding its use, resonates with many nationalist causes and also has complex associations with different group identities and iterations of "Irishness" through time and in the present day.

There are medieval accounts of the *aos sídhe*, an Old Irish language term for a mythical race of beings, the "people of the mounds," later translated as "fairies." The mythical people called the *Tuatha Dé Danann* ('people of the goddess Anú) are also associated, in later folklore, with the fairies. The word *sídhe* (also *síth*) has distinct but related associations in that it can refer to the spiritual beings themselves as the "fairy host" of the otherworld, to an "otherworld hill or mound," and to "peace" (*síocháin* in modern Irish) (Ó Cathasaigh 1978, 137). The Old Irish terms for spiritual beings and abodes are not directly translatable and the use of the English "fairies" and "fairy realm" brings with it many different cultural and linguistic associations. As mentioned in relation to semantic usages, the term *sídhe* can refer to the otherworldly beings of Irish mythology and also to the mounds which are above and below the level of landscape that humans see, adding to their liminal associations. In the native language, reference can be made to both, whereas in English different conceptualizations are involved with the words "fairy" and "fairy realm." The mythological chthonic realm of the *sídhe* is accessible via the mounds, some of which are ringforts (colloquially known as "fairy forts") and also is associated with particular caves, rocks and trees (especially hawthorn).

Traditions connected with the *sídhe* can be found in the early Irish literature, in the folklore collections of the nineteenth and early twentieth century, and in contemporary cultural manifestations and popular discourses. Similarly, information about the Pagan gods derives from archaeological sources and from the corpus of medieval texts, mainly eleventh and twelfth centuries. The Irish materials are the most extensive in what has been preserved of Celtic mythology and, despite being filtered through a Christian worldview in their compilation by Christian scribes, contain information about deities and the spiritual world as understood by the Celts. The otherworld, deities, pagan kings, and mythological battles are interconnected with old place-names, sacred hills, and areas of the Irish landscape. Therefore, for contemporary Pagans the land remains an access point to the otherworld of native Irish cosmology, both in a palpable way as a loci for ritual practice, and in an imaginative way when employed in discussions of the past and the old religion.

Fairies are significant in contemporary Pagan discourse and in ritual practices and are generally regarded as spirits of place, which is exemplary of Pagans' utilization of indigeneity since the ways of engaging with fairies are often similar to the ways that indigenous peoples in different cultural settings engage with ancestral or nature spirits. This is part of a cultural mechanism of "indigenizing" in how contemporary Pagans are taking concepts and practices from indigenous cultures and religious traditions, for example African and South American traditional religions and their conceptualizations of, and relationships with, the spirit world, and re-framing them as part of a new nature religion in the Irish context. In this way Pagans in Ireland "imagine themselves in the indigenous style" (Johnson 2002, 303).

Fairies are conceptualized within a cosmology inspired by indigenous religions elsewhere in the world, and this understanding of local nature spirits is projected back not just onto the pre-Christian context but onto more recent time-periods such as the folklore collections of the nineteenth and early twentieth century and legend motifs and recorded traditions are reinterpreted. For example, some Pagans leave things as offerings for the fairies at ringforts or at "fairy trees" (hawthorn). This is part of Irish traditional culture, as with the tradition where farmers would throw the "beestings," the colostrum or first milk taken from a cow after a calf was born, in the air for the fairies or pour a drop of *póitín* (illicitly distilled whiskey) on the ground in honour of the fairies. While Pagan activities connect with the traditional practices, there are also new practices and conceptualizations of the fairies involved. For instance, some Pagan groups, such as a Druidic group called the Owl Grove, sometimes call on the *sídhe* to take part in their rituals and create a portal by magical visualization through which the beings are welcomed to come (for more on the rituals of this Grove, and the Hibernian Order of Druids, see Butler 2005). In this way, concepts and ritual actions from indigenous cultures that exist in the present day are re-contexted in modern Ireland.

The native Irish-language term for "magic" is *draíocht* which literally means "druidry," or *draíochta* meaning "magical," and so modern Druids have a backdrop into which they can set their magical "workings" (in Pagan discourse a technical term for conducting a ritual). There is no native Irish term for the spell-casting type of witch familiar to us today, only the word *cailleach* which has more a connotation of "hag." Pagan Witches in particular connect with traditional "witch" figures of pre-modern rural Ireland such as the *bean feasa*, which can be translated as "wise woman" or "woman of knowledge," whose role was of local healer and advisor on otherworldly matters, particularly related to the fairies, and who were credited with curative and often psychic abilities; as Nancy Schmitz notes, "the curative powers of the wise woman are directly related to the fairy world" (1977, 172). Depending on the path of Paganism a practitioner affiliates with, Witch or Druid or "Pagan" as a generic self-identification, connections will be made more to ancient times or to specific historical time periods.

Ancestors and Old Gods: Being indigenous in a sacred landscape

Given Ireland's historical and cultural background, Contemporary Paganism emerged as a movement that connects with an indigeneity that is located in the distant past, and this Irish Pagan indigeneity could be described as being filtered through a cluster of notions of the Celtic. As discussed above, some of the meanings connected with the Celtic are from scholarly sources—Celtic Studies and archaeology—while others are spiritual ways of knowing that often belong to the domain of personal experience in ritual. Recourse can be made to this framework of Celticity in order to transcend contemporary political debates as well as to evade being embroiled in historical cultural sectarianism and partisan divides.

One way of circumventing the religious and cultural divides and fraught manoeuvring around identities in historical and contemporary Irish society is to look to the land as the locus for spiritual connectivity since Paganism is a nature religion. Generally in the Irish Pagan discourse, romantic notions of the spiritual landscape are employed rather than nationalistic or exclusionary rhetoric of "homeland." For many contemporary Pagans, the land is imbued with a special spiritual quality, conceptualized by some as the magic it holds from rituals conducted upon it hundreds or even thousands of years ago, by others as the energies of the land itself, whether emanating from ley lines or the spirits of the plant and animal life within or from the spiritual beings it is believed to contain, such as fairies. The land, and the ancient structures upon it, are associated with the deities of pre-Christian Ireland, with the ancient Druids and Pagan kings, and with entranceways to the otherworld or spiritual realm. The lack of detail about life on the island prior to Christian influence has allowed space for more romantic and idealized envisioning of pre-Christian populations and associated lifeways. Mythic history and modern projections are united in these portrayals into what Donald Meek might describe as "a glowing portrait of the "Celts" and their spirituality" (2000, 4).

Johnson states that "indigenizing discourses and practices have as their objective the configuration, at least imaginatively or discursively, of a pure group performing traditional practices on its original homeland" (2002, 312), which in the context of Irish Paganism involves the connection being made between the Celts and Irish people in the modern day, along with an emphasis on the land and the built heritage upon it as the nexus of connection between that age and now. Johnson (2002, 312) adds that "when outsider signs, symbols and practices are relied upon, they are quickly indigenized—given a culturally specific form that makes the outsider symbol 'ours,' even traditional." An example of this process at work in Irish Paganism is how Wicca, a form of witchcraft founded by Englishman Gerald Gardner, is localized in the Irish cultural milieu as "Celtic Wicca."

"The unique significance of pagan witchcraft to history," says Ronald Hutton, "is that it is the only religion which England has ever given the world" (2001, vii) and Wicca is strongly associated with the British magical milieu. In fact, the term "British Traditional Witchcraft" has come to differentiate Gardnerian Wicca and Alexandrian Wicca (founded by Alex Sanders) from the subsequent forms of Wicca, especially those that developed in the United States. As a type of Witchcraft that could be denunciated as an "English import" to Ireland, or as alien to Ireland, Wicca is thus "Celtified" by drawing in the local aspects of culture that are perceived by practitioners as being Celtic. Interestingly, Janet and Stewart Farrar, influential figures in the Wiccan community, who, after relocating to Ireland in 1976, co-authored books, such as *Eight Sabbats for Witches* (1981), in which they used the traditional Irish festival names for the Witches' Sabbats, thus popularizing the use of the Irish names[5] in Paganism more broadly. In his discussion of "extending discourses and practices," Johnson (2002, 312) identifies the process whereby religious knowledge and symbols are "circulated into wider availability" and the community "endorse the extension of the meaning of beliefs or practices beyond territorial limits and previous social boundaries, such that what was once a local truth is now presented as a more broadly applicable, even a universal one." The globalized contemporary Pagan "Wheel of the Year" structure with its division of the year according to Celtic cosmology, and often use of Irish names for the festivals, being made accessible to the international Pagan community is a good example of this process even though in the Paganism case it is the movement of ideas, largely via the internet and popular literature, rather than migrating people that is spurring it on.

Wicca, in Ireland, engages either explicitly with the romanticized notion of the Celtic or to some extent with native popular magical practices. Again the local landscape, as well as the island of Ireland with all of its mythological associations, becomes significant. Emphasis is placed on sacred sites and recorded rituals and events at these places prior to the introduction of Christianity. The land is both a material and ideological connector to the past. The notion of spiritual permanency, religious traditions that connect to the land and particular territory, become all the more important in attaining a secure position culturally and socially in the present day. The work of Eric Hobsbawn (1983, 12) reminds us that "all invented traditions, so far as possible,

---

5. The traditional Irish names for the festivals are *Samhain* (traditional beginning of winter), *Imbolc* (traditional beginning of spring), *Bealtaine* (often anglicized as Beltane, traditional beginning of summer) and *Lughnasadh* (traditional harvest celebration).

use history as a legitimator" and when it comes to the creation of indigenous identities, it is a particular historical narrative combined with ideas about pre-history that lays the foundations for identity-building. Identifying as religiously Celtic is a relatively recent phenomenon, as James Lewis notes:

> An aspect of the present [Celtic] revival that sets it apart from its predecessors is the extent to which Celtophiles are appropriating Celtic identities and, as part of this appropriation, engaging in religious practices perceived to be Celtic. (2009, 480)

Irish belongs to the Celtic language family and in both forms of Old Irish and modern Gaelic gives the older (prior to colonization and the anglicization of place-names) and traditional place-names that are interconnected with mythology, legend and local and regional folklore. Ireland has a strong tradition of literary achievement and poetic expression is highly valued, and is also associated with the bardic poetry and druidic systems of ancient times. Some Pagans contend that modern Irish (and/or Old Irish) is the appropriate language to use when communicating with deities or spirits of the land. Spiritual lineages are interwoven with place and also with an emotional sense of belonging for many practitioners. Again, it is perhaps easier to utilize language on spiritual, poetic and romantic levels, in relation to a distant past, than it is to implicate oneself in more recent debates about Irish as a "native language" of Irish people when English is the mother-tongue of the vast majority of the population and when English has been the predominant language in Ireland since the eighteenth century when it first started to displace Irish.

Notwithstanding the current issues with the Irish language and whether it can or should be used to denote Irishness, Pagans in Ireland—interestingly whether native Irish speakers or not, and whether or not they are Irish-born or of Irish nationality—often incorporate Irish (modern Irish or Old Irish) into their rituals with some going to great effort to learn phrases or passages in Irish to incorporate in a ritual. This most often relates to honouring the ancestors or specific deities. Particular conceptualizations of sacred landscapes and perceptions of appropriate behaviours in communicating with spiritual beings combine in Pagan activities and understandings of how the land, myth and language relate to the Celtic past. Such conceptualizations are evoked in legitimizing current identities and spiritual lineages while also evading nationalistic rhetoric and the cultural baggage attached to more recent history.

Celticity is most often the backdrop for different Pagan groups of Witches or Druids when they are ascribing identifications to themselves and in asserting their place in the Ireland of the present day. Sense of place may be achieved by developing a connection to the "energies of the land," to the local culture, to the spirits or deities associated with the local area or the country itself. As explained previously, ancestry can be genetic, by birth, or spiritual and the cluster of meanings around Celtic is usually where the significance of contemporary identities is attached. Amy Hale notes that scholars now recognize that, rather than "focusing on the "inauthenticity" of contemporary Celtic traditions, the ambiguities and complexities surrounding the Celts and various expressions of Celtic identity are in themselves worthy of study" (2002, 157) and indeed it is of value to gain some insight into why contemporary Pagans in Ireland wish to ascribe Celtic identities to themselves and in which ways they do so.

Conclusion

Pagan culture involves various processes where tradition is used to construct identities and cultural prestige is maintained by utilization of the concept of indigeneity, which is usually articulated in Pagan discourse as being a follower of the "old religion," or "ancestral culture of the land." Indigenous, then, in Contemporary Pagan discourse could be understood as a synonym for "ancient" religious and cultural elements, but only those that pre-date Christianity. In the restricted demarcation of "indigenous" as something that connects to or continues a preceding longstanding culture, contemporary Irish Paganism could be understood as a new type of Irish indigeneity. The inventive formulation and articulation of such identities is of great cultural significance in gaining an understanding of the processes whereby cultural elements are selected as significant for modern Pagans and why. Ireland's history of colonization and Christianization, with the strong historical hold of Roman Catholicism over everyday life for the Irish population, has produced a climate in which claims to be "indigenous" yield various responses. The sociocultural landscape of the country, as well as its geographical landscape and architectural heritage, have together shaped a certain kind of Paganism that incorporates local cultural resonances. Thus, there are a number of "indigenizing" processes at work, with Irish Paganism taking direct influences as well as inspiration from pre-Christian practices of the Celts, with some claiming to be restoring an ancient religiosity. Simultaneously, there is another operational mechanism whereby a globalized contemporary Pagan culture and shared community finds its local expression, engaging with place, history, and sociocultural traits, customs and character.

In his discussion of Garifuna religion in Central and Brazilian Candomblé, Johnson describes "two distinct types of extension" (2002, 303), and both of these types can be identified as mechanisms at work in contemporary Irish

Pagan religion, albeit in quite a different context to the two he is comparing. One type of extension (as Johnson identifies in the practice of Candomblé), which involves the circulation of meanings globally, has led to "the participation of new practicing bodies" and "has brought a new ethnic constituency" (2002, 303), of non-Irish Pagans who are resident in Ireland who are practicing a form of Irish Paganism. The second type of extension (recognized by Johnson in Garifuna religion) is seen in how globalized contemporary Paganism, and the existence of an international Pagan community on the internet and in popular literature, allows new circulating symbols and meanings to be brought into the worldview of local groups and the rituals practiced in the native land. Johnson remarks that "we are challenged to shift attention from bounded religious arenas to the processes by which lines are drawn, crossed, and redrawn" (2002, 308) and contemporary Paganism as it is lived offers a fascinating example of such processes at work. The cultural dynamics of the global and the local, as well as the mechanisms of religious revival, resurgence and reinterpretation, all interrelate in the ways that people are "being indigenous" and "making place" in the contemporary Irish Pagan community.

Acknowledgement

The ethnographic research on which this chapter is based was supported by a Government of Ireland Scholarship in the Humanities and Social Sciences awarded by the Irish Research Council.

References

Bowman, Marion, 2000a. "Contemporary Celtic spirituality." In *New Directions in Celtic Studies*, edited by Amy Hale and Philip Payton, 69–91. Exeter: University of Exeter Press.

———. 2000b. "Cardiac Celts: Images of the Celts in paganism." In *Pagan Pathways: A Complete Guide to the Ancient Earth Traditions*, edited by Charlotte Hardman and Graham Harvey, 242–251. London: Thorsons.

Butler, Jenny. 2015. "Paganism in Ireland: Syncretic Processes, identity and a sense of place." In *Modern Pagan and Native Faith Movements in Europe: Colonial and Nationalist Impulses*, edited by Kathryn Rountree, 196–215. New York: Berghahn Book. https://doi.org/10.2307/j.ctt9qctm0.14

———. 2005. "Druidry in contemporary Ireland." In *Modern Paganism in World Cultures: Comparative Perspectives*, edited by Michael Strmiska, 87–125. Santa Barbara, CA: ABC–CLIO.

Coakley, John. 2011. "The religious roots of Irish nationalism." *Social Compass* 58(1): 95–114. https://doi.org/10.1177/0037768610392726

Gailey, Alan. 1988. "Tradition and identity." *The Use of Tradition: Essays Presented to G. B. Thompson*, edited by Alan Gailey, 61–67. Co. Down, Ireland: Ulster Folk and Transport Museum.

Hale, Amy. 2002. "Whose Celtic Cornwall? The ethnic Cornish meet Celtic spirituality." In *Celtic Geographies: Old Culture, New Times*, edited by D. C. Harvey, R. Jones, N. McInroy and C. Milligan, 157–170. London: Routledge.

Hobsbawm, Eric. 1983. "Introduction." In *The Invention of Tradition*, edited by Eric Hobsbawm and Terence Ranger, 1–14. Cambridge: Cambridge University Press.

Hutton, Ronald. 2001 [1999]. *The Triumph of the Moon: A History of Modern Pagan Witchcraft*. Oxford: Oxford University Press.

Johnson, Paul Christopher. 2002. "Migrating bodies, circulating signs: Brazilian Candomblé, the Garifuna of the Caribbean, and the category of indigenous religions." In *History of Religions* 41(4): 301–327. Reprinted in *Indigenous Diasporas and Dislocation*, edited by Graham Harvey and Charles D. Thompson, 63–81. London: Routledge. https://doi.org/10.1086/463690

Lewis, James. R. 2009. "Celts, Druids and the invention of tradition." In *Handbook of Contemporary Paganism*, edited by James. R. Lewis and Murphy Pizza, 479–493. Leiden: Brill. https://doi.org/10.1163/ej.9789004163737.i-650.135

McMahon, Sean and Jo O'Donoghue. 2004. *Brewer's Dictionary of Irish Phrase and Fable*. London: Weidenfeld & Nicolson.

Meek, Donald E. 2000. *The Quest for Celtic Christianity*. Edinburgh: Handsel Press.

Ó Cathasaigh, Tomás. 1978. "The semantics of síd." *Éigse* 17(2): 137–155.

Ó Giolláin, Diarmuid. 1997. "The fairy belief and official religion in Ireland." In *The Good People: New Fairylore Essays*, edited by Peter Narváez, 199–214. Lousville: The University Press of Kentucky.

Rountree, Kathryn. 2010 *Crafting Contemporary Pagan Identities in a Catholic Society*. Surrey: Ashgate.

Schmitz, Nancy. 1977. "An Irish wise woman: Fact and legend." *Journal of the Folklore Institute* 14(3): 169–179. https://doi.org/10.2307/3814072

About the author

Jenny Butler is based at University College Cork, where she teaches on contemporary religions in Ireland, Western Esotericism and New Religious Movements. She conducted the first ever ethnographic study of Irish contemporary Paganism and her book on this topic, *21st Century Irish Paganism: Worldview, Ritual, Identity*, is forthcoming from Routledge. She holds a PhD in Folklore and Ethnology and is a specialist on Irish folk religion. Her research has been supported by the Irish Research Council, the Royal Irish Academy, the Ireland-Canada University Foundation, and the Ireland-Newfoundland Partnership (Department of the Taoiseach). Dr Butler has been a Government of Ireland Research Scholar (2001–2004), a Dobbin Scholar (2010) and a Charlemont Scholar (2017). She is the Secretary of the Irish Society for the Academic Study of Religions (ISASR) and an officer of the Executive Committee of the European Association for the Study of Religions (EASR) and a member of the Executive Board of the International Society for the Study of Religion, Nature and Culture. She founded the Irish Network for the Study of Esotericism and Paganism (INSEP), which is affiliated with the European Society for the Study of Western Esotericism (ESSWE), of which she is currently a Board Member.

— 3 —

Bear Feasts in a Land without Wild Bears: Experiments in Creating Animist Rituals

Graham Harvey

Reception of academic debates about animism have led to an increase in the number of people who self-identify as "animists." Among Pagan animists, one example experiments with a midwinter Bear Feast to embed respect for the larger-than-human world in foodways and rituals. To do so they draw on Indigenous and scholarly sources in processes that might be "indigenizing" in several senses. Sources are drawn into an existing tradition, re-shaping it along more localized and more animistic lines. They also encourage the kind of personhood that is more often encouraged among Indigenous people—i.e. promoting "dividuation" rather than the individualizing of consumer capitalist Modernity. Simultaneously, ceremonies are developed that also draw on / in Indigenous knowledges (some mediated by scholars) as well as advancing a post-Protestant, un-Modern re-turn to ritual.

British Bear Feasts are experiments in developing an animistic ritual complex. They provide scholars of religion with opportunities to observe and consider both the continuing evolution and diversification of the new Paganisms and also matters that coincide with scholarly "turns" to performance, ontology, material religion, vernacular religion and more. In addition, as an increasing number of Pagans now self-identify as "animists," scholars interested in contemporary religion(s) are provided with an opportunity to study Pagan engagements with Indigenous people and with academic debates—e.g. about different modernities and about the reception and impact of research.

The specific question addressed here is whether the emerging Bear Feast tradition (and its wider Pagan animist context) exemplifies a form of indigenization. A contrast with another, coexistent trend—in which other Pagans promote a universalizing or globalizing vision of their religion—increases the value of exploring the notion of an indigenizing trajectory. Indeed, it will become evident that participants in Bear Feasts are not only aware of the tension between indigenizing and universalizing but are exercised by it in various ways. Although the motivations, experiences and reflections of Bear Feast participants are diverse and fluid, they closely match those tendencies which Paul C. Johnson (2002) identifies as "indigenizing" and "extending." In particular, they are more of a field of negotiation than an organized (albeit dynamic) continuum. The nub of Johnson's argument is that such tendencies, practices and lifeways are processes or projects rather than fixed identities. They contrast with Weberian ideal types in being everyday, dynamic and malleable rather than abstract, bounded and static imaginaries. The Bear Feast tradition attracts attention as a movement that allows us to test the analytical value of the term "indigenizing" in relation to phenomena beyond those which generated Johnson's concept and argument.

In the following section I offer an orientation to some key terms and their contrasts and varied uses. This begins with a note on the term "indigenizing" as used by Paul C. Johnson. A distinction between "Indigenous" and "indigenous" that is of strategic importance, but not universally applied, leads to an introduction to an additional (possibly complementary) use of "indigenizing" that has already been applied to contemporary Pagans in Britain. The "new animism" is introduced next, followed by a contrast between the *conceptual* "individuals" of Modernity and the *conceptual* "dividuals" of Indigenous animist ontologies. After considering these terms, I focus on Bear Feasts themselves, based on my dialogical fieldwork with Bear Feast founders and participants since 2008 (arising from longer-term engagement with Pagans, particularly British Druids). Two sections are devoted to the origins of the British Bear Feasts. The first provides information about the founders and their inspirations (including the influence of my previous and ongoing research among Indigenous animists) and aspirations. The second introduces the sources inspiring the Feasts and, therefore, evidencing one kind of indigenizing as Indigenous practices influence Pagan practice. An outline of the way in which the Feasts have been performed will follow. A concluding section considers how these events might be considered to be indigenizing among people who are not Indigenous, especially as they find themselves resisting the powerful call to try to be more Modern.

Terms

I will argue in relation to the Bear Feast participants that, just as among Candomblé practitioners and the Garifuna of Johnson's work, specific "outsider signs, symbols and practices" are "relied upon" to evolve "a culturally specific form that makes the outsider symbol "ours," even traditional" (Johnson

2002, 312). It is the evolution of a "tradition" which draws on—and, importantly, draws in—ritual and liturgical elements from "outside" that invite this argument.

Importantly, participants in Bear Feasts do not claim to be Indigenous. My capitalization of "Indigenous" requires explanation. In some contexts, "indigenous" and "Indigenous" might be synonymous and equally useful as references to those communities which self-identify in ways that the United Nations Permanent Forum on Indigenous Issues (UNPFII) indicates. Indeed, the *United Nations Declaration on the Rights of Indigenous Peoples* (United Nations General Assembly 2007) does not capitalize "indigenous" even when referring to those who are its principal focus.[1] However, in wider usage the lower-case "indigenous" points to origins (e.g. of persons, oranges or chickens) in particular places at some point in time. If only for strategic purposes, the capitalized "Indigenous" is used here to indicate more specific projects of community or world construction in which colonialization, marginalization and the extinguishing, distancing and other manoeuvres of so-called "Modern Western cultures" are contested. There is more complexity to both uses and considerable debate about them. Two recent works focused on Indigenous religions combining "Indigenous" with a further contested category exemplify important interventions in such debates: Christopher Hartney and Daniel Tower's *Religious Categories and the Construction of the Indigenous* (2017) and Greg Johnson and Siv Ellen Kraft's *Handbook of Indigenous Religions* (2017). This is important in the present context because the possibility being tested is that Bear Feasts might be indicative of an indigenizing movement and an indigenizing of sources by people who might be indigenous to Britain but are not Indigenous in any sense that would justify their inclusion in a book about "Indigenous religions."

There is, however, another emphasis of "indigenizing" that might be generative. While Johnson is particularly interested in processes by which practices and ideas are brought into particular "traditions," "indigenizing" can also point to the importance of locality or localizing. Some Pagans, for instance, most certainly understand their deities (usually plural) to be universal, cosmic, or at least present everywhere around the earth. They invoke such beings in ceremonies regardless of where they happen to be. Similarly, some Pagans celebrate the same set of calendrical festivals regardless of actual seasons in their location. However, others "indigenize" in the sense of fitting in with their locality. They invoke deities from local traditions, seek to develop closer relationships with and within local landscapes, and/or adjust to celebrations

---

1. It is equally true that many Indigenous people, and many scholars interested in indigeneity, do not necessarily capitalize the term.

which honour local seasons. More broadly, some Pagans try to apply the slogan "think globally, act locally" to many areas of their lives. For instance, they seek to source food locally and resist the lure of easy international flights when it is possible to use ground transport. This more geographical localizing sense of "indigenizing" is significant to some regular participants in Bear Feasts and certainly to the founders. It is, perhaps, a resonant theme which underpins (Jenny Blain and Robert Wallis 2007, 10), coining of the phrase "new indigenes" for at least some Pagans.

Another term that has already been used but requires explanation is "animism." To avoid confusion it should be noted that "animism" is used here in line with ongoing scholarly discussions which have been labelled "the new animism." This is a usage inspired by Irving Hallowell's early twentieth century research among the Anishinaabeg in southern central Canada (Hallowell 1960) rather than by Edward Tylor's theorizing about religion (1871). It is not the animism of the Oxford English Dictionary OED and similar works which continue to insist that animism is "the attribution of a living soul to plants, inanimate objects and natural phenomenon" and/or "the belief in a supernatural power that organizes and animates the material universe" (OED 2018). Terms like "inanimate," "natural" and "material" assert that this animism is a false belief. The example sentences provided by the OED insist on the folly of both ancient and contemporary "animists." The spectre of Tylor's "animism" is clear here both in the parallels with his gloss, "belief in spirits," and in his insistence that religion (and all religions to one degree or another) is defined by the animistic mistake that sees souls and human-likeness in unwarranted places and acts.[2]

The "new animism" proposes something different. It re-examines the acts and ideas of Indigenous and other people to better understand their ontologies, epistemologies, lifeways and/or ceremonies and discourses. I have summarized this animism by saying that "Animists are people who recognize that the world is full of persons, only some of whom are human, and that life is always lived in relationship with others" (Harvey 2017, xiii). The pervasive fact of relationship leads to diverse local encouragements to act respectfully towards other-than-human relations. What is new in the "new animism" is not the data (e.g. some people's lifeways or relationships) but the approaches employed by scholars involved (many of whom are contributors to Harvey [Harvey ed. 2013] and Astor-Aguilera and Harvey [2018]). Scholarly "turns" to gender, performance, postcolonialism, materiality and ontology have influenced more relational and more reflexive ways of doing research and of analyzing and presenting arguments. Along with the growth in the

---

2. For more about Tylor and his legacy see Tremlett, Sutherland and Harvey (2017).

multi- and inter-disciplinary field of Indigenous Studies, this is the academic context of the "new animism." Vibrant discussions of what it means to be a person, a relation, a citizen and/or a human have required re-evaluation of the kind of claims expressed in the OED "animism" definition.

Studies of Indigenous ontologies sometimes make good use of yet another contrast that will be employed in arguing that participants in Bear Feasts are indigenizing. Marilyn Strathern (1988) proposed a distinction between Western "individuals" and Melanesian "dividuals." In contrast to Modern projects of individuation, she demonstrated that Melanesians encouraged "dividuation": the effort to improve relations on the assumption that a person is not a solitary, skin-bound (or bark-bound, scale-bound, etc.) being but already necessarily a dynamic interaction of many relations (see Halbmayer 2012). Importantly, Strathern contrasted *concepts* of personhood not descriptive realities. That is, both Moderns and Indigenous people can be either individuals or dividuals (or both at different times or in different relations) in lived reality but their "cultures"—the sedimentation of locally commonplace or widely shared acts, inspirations and aspirations—shape people in particular directions. If we circle back to Tylor and Hallowell we might say that in Tylor's "old animism" people are imagined as individuals whose beliefs are definitive, while in Hallowell's new approach, people are imagined as dividuals whose relations are generative. In the "new animism" which underlies the founding and evolution of the Bear Feast tradition, "What is in question," as Marshall Sahlins says, "is the character of the relationships rather than the nature of the person" (2011, 13). It is the incitement of dividuation and widening of respectful relations that suggests the possibility that Bear Feasts shape an indigenizing movement, albeit among indigenous but not Indigenous people.

Finally in this section, readers will have noticed that "Western" and "Modern" have already been both capitalized and trapped in scare quotes. They, too, are contested and uneasy terms, as Miguel Astor-Aguilera and I argue (2018, 9):

> It is clear to us that "Western" now labels global phenomena and that "Modern" is not an objective synonym of "contemporary" but one way of identifying a project. Or, more carefully (if not more precisely), it is a shorthand for a distillation of a heuristic device which, with varying degrees of success, invites open-ended reflection on and discussion of an ongoing and contested (ongoing-while-contested) project.

If Bear Feast participants are seeking to dividuate rather than individuate and to improve animistic relations with(in) the larger-than-human world, a crucial and integral element of their indigenizing is a contest with the project that is Modernity. We will return to that theme.

Origins of the Bear Feast

The idea for the Bear Feasts originated in conversations between a couple, Corwen Broch and Kate Fletcher, as they made their way from southern England to Santiago de Compostela and Finisterre, on foot apart from the ferry crossings to and from France. Their journey in 2005 could be interestingly considered by those researching the contemporary proliferation and diversification of pilgrims and pilgrimage. For the couple involved, the long walk provided an extended opportunity to further develop not only their personal relationship but also their particular Pagan Druidic understanding and lifeway. This could be summed up as a quest to "live lightly on the land" if not entirely "off grid." As they walked, they discussed ideas about what might really be "the oldest religion" (a common theme among Pagans)—considering arctolatry or "bear veneration" to be a prime candidate—and its relation to "the new animism"—including their reflections on having heard a public presentation about my research among Indigenous animists.

As they talked, an idea grew on them: that of expressing gratitude and apology to food animals and plants in a ritual experimenting with bear ceremonies and narratives. In my talk at a Druid camp, as often in my writing, I had cited Te Pakaka Tawhai's claim that the purpose of Maori religion *could* be expressed as "doing violence with impunity"—i.e. the seeking of permission and the offering of placation to those injured or killed to provide food or shelter to others (Tawhai 1988, 101). I built on this by drawing on Anishinaabe animism partly as presented by Hallowell but also drawing on my short fieldwork visits to reservations within the USA. and on the kinship implications of Darwinian evolution. This led me to emphasize that acts of violence are not only necessary and unavoidable (because all beings need to consume others) but also intimate because they involve our co-evolving relations, some closer than others. For instance, Tawhai's reference to the digging and serving up of kumara, sweet potatoes, as food for guests was not randomly picked but arose from the intimacy of a shared migration of both Maori and kumara to Aotearoa (New Zealand) and of the mutuality of their adaptation to that new land. Since kumara have something of the ancestor about them, their consumption requires careful negotiation. That is just a part of Tawhai's argument as I summarized it in the talk which Corwen and Kate considered and discussed.

In case anyone in the audience imagined that it is possible to avoid acts of violence I had noted an implication of human symbiosis with bacteria. The point here is that one cannot avoid committing the violent act of consuming others by taking one's own life as that would also result in the deaths of millions of bacteria. There is no "elsewhere" or "outside" to the food chain or the "cycle of life." Tawhai's provocative phrase "doing violence with impunity" does not provide an escape from responsibility or an excuse for indulgence but indicates the deep value of ceremonies demonstrative of respect and humility. It does not point to an expectation of automatic impunity but to the pervasive stress on inter-species reciprocity entailed in most Indigenous ceremonies.

The serendipitous trajectory of my research experiences (see Harvey 2015) led me to reflect on how Maori and Anishinaabe perspectives resonate together. Other researchers have brought Anishinaabe and Haudenosaunee knowledges and practices together. For example, the botanist Robin Kimmerer writes compellingly of the pervasive encouragement of respect among Algonkian Nations and of the protocols of the Thanksgiving Address among the Onondaga (Kimmerer 2013, 105–117). What is, perhaps, most challenging about Indigenous ontologies and epistemologies for people of European heritage (especially those of pervasively Protestant north European origin) is the sense that ritual is not best defined as "vain repetition" but as enactments of inter-personal—and often inter-species—relationality. Ritual finds its meaning in the communication (to performers as much as to recipients) of respect and reciprocity. At the heart of the argument arising from my engagement with the Bear Feast community (alongside observation of some other British Pagans) is a recognition that what can be romantic, appropriative and in other ways colonialist, can also be radical and contributory to strategies of resistance to consumer-capitalist Modernity. But that is to get ahead of things.

After their return from northern Spain, Corwen and Kate worked with these and other ideas by researching rituals in which Indigenous animists express gratitude and sought permission from "food persons." Hallowell's (1926) "Bear Ceremonialism in the Northern Hemisphere" resonated with them. This is at least in part because of the invocation of "the great bear of the starry heavens" in the opening and orienting phases of many contemporary Druidic rituals. Perhaps also the association in some Pagan mythologies of Arthur ("the once and future king") with bears played a role in making bears familiar. It was, however, their research among anthropological, folkloric and ethnomusicological sources that strengthened the potential of honouring bears as key players in their emergent ritual complex.

Bear Feast sources

As noted, Kate and Corwen's interests included finding ways of developing their animist practice and localizing lifeway by learning appropriately from others. They were (and remain) explicit that appropriate learning must be distinct from appropriating. They regularly express the importance of acting respectfully towards the owners and conveyers of Indigenous and other knowledges and practices. Simultaneously, but more implicitly, they express a contrast with other people who are at least perceived to take ideas and ceremonies that have not been explicitly offered or shared, and who tend to see such matters as elements of universally available human patrimony.

Hallowell's "Bear Ceremonialism" (1926), introduced Corwen and Kate to similar bear-focused rites which were or are performed around the arctic and subarctic north. This led them to explore scholarly texts about bear rituals "all across the North, from the Finns and Sami of Northern Europe, the Khanty Mansi and other Siberian tribes, to the Ainu of Japan and the Inuit of Hudson's Bay" (Broch and Fletcher 2013, 1). They explored books like Lauri Honko, Senni Timonen and Michael Branch's *Great Bear: A Thematic Anthology of Oral Poetry in the Finno-Ugrian Languages* (1993), and Juha Pentikäinen's *Golden King of the Forest: The Lore of the Northern Bear* (2007). Being determined Finnophiles, they read translations from Finnish of the epic *Kalevala* and the folk poetry collection *Kanteletar*. Anthropologies of animism, particularly those that focus on hunting and foodways, were important (e.g. Rane Willerslev's *Soul Hunters* [2007]). My own contribution to the "turn" to lived religion (Harvey 2013), contributed to further reflection on the value of thinking about food rites when seeking to understand not only "religion" but also human engagements with the larger than human world.

Among the results of drawing on such sources is the following statement of a mythic foundation for the Bear Feasts:

> When we first came to the Northern forests Bear taught us to find food. When we starved in the depths of winter the flesh of the bear sustained us. Teacher and Saviour, his corpse alarmingly man-like when stripped of its warm fur, mystery and taboo surrounded the animal whose name must not be spoken. A child of the Sky God, lowered from on high on a golden chain, he is guest of honour at his own funeral feast. With thanks and messages for his Father, his spirit is sent back to Heaven that he may return and feed us again in our need time. (Broch and Fletcher 2013, 1)

As well as serving to introduce the Feast tradition, the above statement also anticipates its central ceremony. My contention is that it contributes to the possibility of considering the Bear Feast movement to be related to *some* elements of what Johnson calls "indigenizing." Again, it is not the "configuration, at least imaginatively or discursively, of a pure group performing traditional practices on its original homeland" (Johnson 2002, 312) that is the objective of this network. This is a self-consciously hybrid, improvizational and experimental practice. Rather, Bear Feast indigenizing is the appreciation, learning from and adaptation of "outsider signs, symbols and practices" to evolve "a culturally specific form that makes the outsider symbol 'ours,' even traditional" (Johnson 2002, 312). This can now be illustrated.

Bear Feast outline

As consummate performers and teachers, Corwen and Kate knew that ceremonies require communities. Their experiment required extension from their own practice into a shared experience. They inaugurated the first Bear Feast in 2008, attracting nearly sixty participants. The first Feast (and those of the following eight years) was held at the Ancient Technology Centre (ATC) in southern England. This location offered accommodation in reconstructions of ancient buildings such as an Iron Age style roundhouse and a Viking era longhall. The feast itself and some indoor rituals were held within a reconstruction of a vast Earthouse. From the outside this looks like a small hill or large mound with a monumental wooden entrance. It is based on large Iron Age structures from the Isle of Man as well as on henge monuments and roundhouses. The ATC say that the Earthouse

> has an immensely heavy roof of earth and this is supported by 21 oak trees, ash purlins and dozens of pole rafters. The bedrock chalk has been terraced inside to give tiered seating. Earthouse is a 200-seat theatre—lit by lamplight and firelight. (ATC 2017; including photographs)

The wider location, close to Cranborne Chase, enabled the purchase of venison from locally shot red deer along with other local produce. It is at the edge of a rural community and has limited light pollution and occasionally entirely clear dark night skies. These are significant contributions to the success of the first years of the Feast tradition.

In each year of the Feast at the ATC the number of participants remained relatively stable at between fifty and sixty people. These sixty were made up of returners and newcomers, many of the latter becoming returners in turn. For reasons beyond the control of the organizers or Bear Feast group, after eight years of annual midwinter events, it became impossible to host the Feast at the ATC. Subsequently, a number of Feasts were held in different locations in southern England and in Wales. More recently, Feasts have been organized in the Orkneys and elsewhere in the British Isles, usually in private homes, or in woodlands owned by participants. Necessarily they have involved smaller numbers of participants in each location but evidence a growing and spreading movement which is disseminating key ideas and practices among the wider Druid and Pagan movements. The Feasts themselves have a common ethos and similar performative structure. A "manual" with an example programme, invocations, songs and other ideas provide a coherence to the emerging tradition (Broch and Fletcher 2013). This is available to those who join the closed Facebook group, to participants in feasts and in response to enquiries.

Bear Feasts are evolving experiments, changing with venue, participants, weather, experience and other factors. When the Feasts have been held indoors or in smaller venues than the ATC, or over shorter periods, the pattern of the first few annual events has been adapted. The manual was never intended to provide a rigid template, but to enable the kind of tradition that is creatively riffed on and from. However, in the early years, the Feasts happened largely as follows (using the present tense to aid the sense of movement and participation).

People begin to arrive at the venue on Friday afternoon and, after greeting other participants and familiarizing themselves with the place, begin to join in organizing things. They bring contributions of food and drink to the kitchen. They select and organize sleep places in the longhouse or roundhouse. They familiarize themselves with the location. They begin to adjust to the intensified atmosphere of a long-weekend ritual experiment. One vital element of this is a taboo on speaking the word "bear." The taboo is rooted in the widespread avoidance practices performed by hunters: not only not naming their intended prey but also replacing words like "hunt" and "kill" with euphemisms like "walk in the woods" and "seduce." The taboo is frequently broken (as it can be among Indigenous hunters) but becomes more carefully observed as the weekend ritual develops. Failure is met with mild and playful ridicule but the taboo has the serious purpose of intensifying participants' attention and developing their efforts to treat this ritual as more than an enchanting bonding between friends or a colourful romanticism. In addition, a list of alternative names (e.g. Honey paw) introduces participants to various sources drawn on to shape the ritual and familiarizes them with elements of songs they will learn and perform in the central rituals.

In the evening, when everyone has arrived, people gather in a circle, around a fire (this being midwinter and therefore wet or cold, or both). They introduce themselves before sharing a meal. This is less ritualized than the main Feast. Afterwards, some time is spent learning the Feast's songs. Although participants are familiar with the broad aims and focus of the Feast, a brief reminder is offered. All of this

> serves to bond the group together, so people can relax and feel safe and thus more able to appreciate the other parts of the weekend. The setting, firelight etc., also help to add a special mood, though we are not really deeply in "ritual time" yet." (Broch and Fletcher 2013, 25)

While it is still dark on the Saturday morning, a gentle but insistent drumming encourages people to emerge from sleep and, if they are not there already, to gather in the Viking style longhouse. They have been encouraged to speak little and quietly, aiding a growing anticipation of an unusual and potentially profound experience. The following is chanted, usually as a call-and-answer between two people:

Where was Bruin born
the honey-paw turned over?
There Bruin was born
the honey-paw turned over
In the upper air
upon the Great Bear's shoulders
Where was Bruin given birth
the bear's cub brought up?
in a little woollen box
in a little iron box.
On the peg of a small cloud.
How was he let down to earth?
in a sling he was let down
in a silver sling
a golden cradle
On a nameless, quite untouchable string.

(Honko, Timonen and Branch 1993, 184)

Next, the bear hunters are led to the door and offered a blessing based on a Finno-Ugric poem. This includes preparation for the hunt ("Forge a spear of magic metal") and a protective charm ("Hide thy claws within thy mittens, Otso, O thou Forest-apple, That they may not harm the hunter"). The hunters lead the company out to find the bear, hidden in a "den" somewhere nearby. Time is taken over this play-acted hunt but eventually the hunters "find" the den and call to waken the bear from winter hibernation. It is an important feature of the diverse bear ceremonies and of broader hunting traditions that the hunted prey is actually a willing participant. Indeed, they are said to be generous donors of sustenance to weaker and needful humans. Adjusting to thinking differently about those we eat (as gift-givers rather than victims) is one of the potential impacts of learning from Indigenous and other knowledges in this context.

The bear wakes. To state what is hinted at in this article's title—though obvious in reality—as there are no wild bears in Britain the "bear" here is a human in costume. But so are the "hunters" making-believe or making-sense of their relations with those they eat (deer or carrots if not actual bears). The bear frightens the hunters but they boldly approach again—this must not be an entirely casual death even if it is gifted. Finally, the bear runs on to one of the spears wielded by a hunter. The bear dies. In the twilight before dawn, with sunlight just touching surrounding wooded hills, the bear (skin)

41

is removed. Now, at last, this is a real bear skin, originating from Russia over one hundred years ago. Thus, a bear is greeted by the assembled group, honoured with further songs and carried to a place of pride in the Earthouse for the rest of the ceremonies. As the Bear Feast Manual says, "even though everyone knows this is [all] 'pretend' the build up and the imagery is so powerful that you are moved in spite of yourself"(Broch and Fletcher 2013, 25–26).

The Earthouse is made ready for the feast that will take place later that evening, with the bear (skin) in pride of place as most honoured guest. The time between the pre-dawn "hunt" and the evening feast is made good use of. Food is prepared communally and with a heightened sense or awareness of the cost involved to those who gift lives to feed us. There is also time for some playfulness. The hunters for the following year are selected in a series of silly games which also function to keep people warm and, perhaps more seriously, to bond participants together. Laughter breaks down barriers so that people are easier together when it comes to the next round of ritualizing. So does cooking, stacking firewood in the Earthouse and decorating the ritual space together. In some years, talks and meditations reinforce and renew understanding and commitment to these lifelong processes in which the giving and taking of lives will become more deliberately honoured. As the manual says, this phase of talks and meditations is the most transparent part of the ritual with regards to its meaning as it is explicitly stated, but it is woven into the ritual as a whole and serves as part of the preparations for our sacred meal (Broch and Fletcher 2013).

That next round of ritualizing is the meal itself, shared in the Earthouse, and both initiated and accompanied by songs, invocations and expressions of gratitude (e.g. "All praise, to Him We Never Name: Great Uncle Honey Paw"). Various diets are catered for, and all foods are treated as gifts. The animism of the participants is driven "deeply into the bones" (to riff on the title of Ronald Grimes' book [2000] about rites of passage) by the now inescapable knowledge of consuming other-than-human persons—or relations (Bird-David 2018).

Following the meal itself, the bear is sung back into the larger-than-human world. It is easy to describe what happens but hard to convey its power or impact. The manual says, "the bear skin is levitated with the power of our song up (at least that's how we describe it) out of the Earthouse roof" (Broch and Fletcher 2013, 26). Put differently, the bear skin in a basket is pulled up through the Earthouse's smoke-hole. But the songs sung at this point enchant participants to see the bear rising on a golden chain and a silver chain, gladly ascending into the heavens. Processing out of the Earthouse, participants gaze (if the sky is clear enough) at the Great Bear turning around the Pole Star, and either in hushed awe or with loud acclamations address further thanks to the bear who has taken the place of all food-persons in this Feast and now carries the participants' gratitude and requests to the larger world. The rest of the evening is spent sharing songs, stories, jokes and conversation around the fires in the Earthouse or in the other buildings.

On the Sunday, participants exchange gifts (having contributed via a kind of "secret Santa" system). Then the central fire of the Earthouse is extinguished. People begin to pack up, tidy up and leave. In the following days and months, they use email and social media to share memories, impressions, photographs and impacts of the weekend and of the process of reintegration into everyday life that began with the dousing of the fire and the journey home.

How is this indigenizing?

Participants in the Bear Feast are not Indigenous in any sense that would justify their inclusion in UNPFII events or in the growing scholarly project of Indigenous Studies. While contemporary Paganism (the broader context from which most Bear Feast participants come) might be the only religion the English have ever given the world (as Ronald Hutton, professor of history at Bristol University, has often said), that type of indigeneity is hardly definitive or generative. Pagans have, after all, asserted the universality of their deities—venerating the same deities whether they are in Britain or Australia. However, they have also adjusted their festive calendar to local seasonal conditions beyond their origin in northwest Europe. In this it is much like the versions of Christianity that have proclaimed the universality of one deity while adapting to diverse cultural contexts globally. Paganism is not purely "English" in any meaningful sense, being a hybrid formed from many sources and inspirations. In Johnson's terms (2002), it has certainly "extended" not only geographically but also by diversifying and enculturating in new locations.

However, as (capitalized) "Indigenous" can be defined as an explicit and emphasized relation to particular places, ancestries and cultural traditions (see Harvey 2000, 12; Cox 2007, 89; Tafjord 2013, 2017). There are some ways in which Paganism could be said to have indigenized. This is seen in the evolution of Paganism out of an older esoteric tradition. Wouter Hanegraaff has traced the processes by which esotericism was democratized and popularized—and even secularized—in the nineteenth and twentieth centuries. That is, initiatory practices in which people sought self-knowledge and personal improvement became more accessible and less arcane. Ritual complexes were either simplified (so that there were less stages or hierarchies) or more eclectic (so that people were encouraged to draw on a larger array of resources). In one branch of such processes in the early to mid-twentieth century, esotericism was fused with notions of "fertility religion" and emphases on "nature veneration" to create Pagan witchcraft and other traditions as "nature religion." Again, this is not yet indigenizing: celebrations of an imagined pristine "nature" were underpinned by a recognizably Modern distinction between (human) culture and the (nonhuman) "natural" world. However, in the late twentieth century Pagans began to localize and to lay greater stress on ancestral sites, watersheds and ecologies near their homes. In Britain, while large festivals continue to take place at Stonehenge, Avebury and similar places, a proliferation of smaller, more intimate gatherings have developed, including in urban and suburban places, breaking down the romanticism of the nature/culture distinction.

The "turn" to an animism of relationship with other-than-human persons (trees, stones, hedgehogs and horses as much as deities and ancestors) and of relationship within larger-than-human place-communities is a more recent trend within Paganism. Perhaps this is an aspect of the kind of "becoming indigenous to place" that Kimmerer (2013, 205–213) struggles with in writing about how settlers in North America might still learn to live differently in those lands:

> Maybe the task assigned to Second Man [those who have not yet indigenized] is to unlearn the module of kudzu [an invasive colonizing plant] and follow the teachings of White Man's Footstep (*Plantago major*), to strive to become naturalized to place, to throw off the mind-set of the immigrant. Being naturalized to place means to live as if this is the land that feeds you, as if these are the streams from which you will drink, that build your body and fill your spirit. To become naturalized is to know that your ancestors lie in this ground. Here you will give your gifts and meet your responsibilities. (Kimmerer 2013, 214–145)

Certainly there are global themes here (and they are part of the globalized flowering of Indigenous self-representation and self-determination). However, they are rooted deeply in lands, specific places, locations that are communities in which humans are just one species with gifts and goals.

The Bear Feast tradition exemplifies current trajectories within Pagan forms of indigenization in which belonging to places is emphasized. Indeed, it radicalizes these by encouraging experimentation with ways of enacting animist knowledge of what it means to live as humans among our other-than-human relations. While the term "animism" has been used for some time among Pagans, until recently its dominant meaning was a Tylorian "belief in spirits." That is, it was used alongside or in contrast with claims to be theistic, polytheistic, atheistic or to identify with other kinds of theological position. The "new animism" (mediated by books, talks or blogs) has altered the reference of the term. Many Pagans now use it to refer to efforts to renew respectful relationships with the larger-than-human world. It is part of a larger and ongoing evolution of vocabulary in which, for example, the representation of Paganism as a "nature religion" has bumped up against the understanding that humans and their cultures are as much a part of "nature" as other beings and their lifeways. David Abram's terms "more-than-human world" and "larger-than-human world" (Abram 1996) have gained currency. While Pagans seem always to have had a problem with the term "worship," they have laid increasing stress on "respect for" the members of the larger-than-human community. These are elements of indigenizing as Pagan discourses and practices become more like those of Indigenous people. The Bear Feast is attractive to many participants precisely because it enables them to experience a ritual complex that develops this indigenizing animist trajectory.

Johnson's clarity about indigenization as processes by which "our" traditions are enriched by reliance on "outsider signs, symbols and practices" (Johnson 2002, 312). is at the heart of the Bear Feast experiment. Participants indigenize by deliberate and careful learning from Indigenous sources. These may be mediated by scholarly and other texts concerned with understanding animism, hunting rites, ceremonial complexes, and protocols of gratitude. They may be shared directly by Indigenous people at festivals or in social media. They also suggest that Bruno Latour's assertion that "We have never been modern" (1993) needs nuancing. Indeed, Latour has made this provocative assertion more complex by continuing to rail against "Moderns" and their dangerous separatist ambitions—as if humans could really fail to be meshed with all other beings and processes (Latour 2013, 2018). Humans have continued to try to be(come) Modern(s) but sometimes failure spurs people to greater efforts: when we do not fully act on the knowledge that climate catastrophe results from our lifestyle choices we renew our membership of the "Modern" club. However, when we do not fully separate "nature" from "culture" but name our cars, swear at our computers, or insist that we understand our companion animals, then we begin to resist Modernizing. To paraphrase Strathern (1988), we have always been dividuals, relational beings—always coming into being as we relate with diverse others.

The Bear Feast is an element of a challenge to Modernity. It celebrates human belonging among other species, as members of a community but also as links in food-chains—both as consumers and consumed. It honours those who we eat rather than treating them as having only limited rights (e.g. to only limited suffering). It seeks to develop ways of respecting belonging and multi-species kinship by learning protocols and processes of communicating with and about our relations and acts of relating. In particular, it employs ritual in ways that are distinctly against the trend of Modernity. The ferment

of early-Modernity's political and constitutional change that, not acciden-
tally, re-made people into individual citizens owing respect to Nation State
rulers and rules was also entangled with religious reformations that rejected
ritualizing as meaningless. By placing ritual (rather than preaching or writing) at the heart of what Pagans do, something radical had already happened.
Pagans had made a post-Protestant, post-Reformation or, at last, post-Modern move. Nonetheless, an undertow often reclaimed ritualizing as a tech-
nique for increasing or expressing (individual) self-knowledge. However, the
Bear Feast goes further and encourages participants to ritualize not primarily
to gain better self-knowledge but to re-animate their relations with others. In
doing so, these Pagans are becoming more like Indigenous people in encouraging relational dividuation.

As Paul Johnson emphasizes, indigenizing is a process or project. The adoption and/or adaptation of ways of thinking and acting from "outside" can
clash with local, accepted, normative, traditional or "indigenous" ways. This
is exemplified in moments in Bear Feast events in which some participants
evidence nervousness or embarrassment about doing ritual. Five hundred
years of (broadly) Protestant polemics against (perceived) Catholic ritual-
ism make it hard to immerse totally in the playful as-if world of ritual. Ill-
fitting jokes or overly self-conscious or individualistic behaviours indicate
the impact of Modernizing even on these people who have elected to join
an animistic ceremony. That, then, reveals the value of the "silly games" that
intersperse more serious but still playful aspects of the event. Although Bear
Feast participants are resistant to the seriousness of what Roberte Hamayon
calls "God religion", they are not all (yet) completely comfortable with the
playfulness and indeterminacy of 'shaman religion" (Hamayon 2012). Games
at Bear Feast have the effect not only of bonding participants and building a
community (sometimes glossed as "tribe") but also of placing people in the
subjunctive mood, in the "as if" realm in which dressed up actors and an old
bearskin are the bear who feeds people even when there are no wild bears in
Britain. Bear Feasts are ritual as defined by Ronald Grimes:

> Ritual is the predication of identities and differences (metaphors) so profound-
> ly enacted that they suffuse the bone and blood, thereby generating a cosmos
> (an oriented habitat). In rites we enact a momentary cosmos of metaphor.
>
> (Grimes 2006, 156)

Each Bear Feast is a performance that invites the attention of the larger-
than-human community so that thanks can be given for sustenance and other
gifts. At its height, the ceremony exceeds metaphor: in a thoroughly un-
Protestant manner, there *is* a bear in the hunt, the feast, the food and the sky.

In a response to an earlier draft of this article Corwen wrote of the inspiration for the Bear Feast, "It also seemed significant somehow to celebrate the life of an animal rendered extinct through human activity, and the transubstantiation of deer into bear seems to work." In the Bear Feast ritual encounter, participants become the kind of people whose every meal might reinforce and renew animistic relationality. This is the indigenizing of the British Bear Feast: the process of learning to become more respectful dividuals within the larger-than-human world.

References

Abram, D. 1996. *The Spell of the Sensuous: Perception and Language in a More-Than-Human World*, New York: Vintage.

Astor-Aguilera, M. and G. Harvey, eds. 2018. *Rethinking Personhood: Animism and Materiality*. New York: Routledge. https://doi.org/10.4324/9780203709887

ATC 2017. "Public events" https://ancienttechnologycentre.godaddysites.com/

Bird-David, N. 2018. "Persons or relatives? Animistic scales of practice and imagination." In *Rethinking Relations and Animism: Personhood and Materiality*, edited by M. Astor-Aguilera and G. Harvey, 25–34. New York: Routledge.

Blain, Jenny and Robert Wallis. 2007. *Sacred Sites/Contested Rites/Rights: Pagan Engagements with Archaeological Monuments*. Brighton: Sussex Academic

Broch, C. and Fletcher, K. 2013. *The Bear Tribe Manual*, http://www.ancientmusic.co.uk/bear_tribe/files/The_Bear_Feast_Manual_v1.pdf

Cox, J. L. 2007. *From Primitive to Indigenous: The Study of Indigenous Religions*. Aldershot: Ashgate.

Grimes, R. 2006. *Rite out of Place: Ritual, Media, and the Arts*. Oxford: Oxford University Press. https://doi.org/10.1093/acprof:oso/9780195301441.001.0001

———. 2000. *Deeply into the Bone: Re-Inventing Rites of Passage*. Berkeley: University of California Press.

Halbmayer, E. 2012. ""Amerindian Mereology: Animism, Analogy, and the Multiverse." *Indiana* 29: 103–125.

Hallowell, A. I. 1960. "Ojibwa Ontology, Behavior, and World View." In *Culture in History: Essays in Honor of Paul Radin*, edited by S. Diamond, 19–52. New York: Columbia University Press.

———. 1928. "Bear Ceremonialism in the Northern Hemisphere." *American Anthropologist* 281: 1–175.

Hanegraaff, W. 1996. *New Age Religion and Western Culture: Esotericism in the Mirror of Secular Thought*. Leiden: Brill.

Hamayon, R. 2012. *Why We Play: An Anthropological Study*. Chicago, IL: Hau.

Hartney, C. and D. J. Tower, eds. 2017. *Religious Categories and the Construction of the Indigenous*. Leiden: E.J. Brill. https://doi.org/10.1163/9789004328983

Harvey, G. 2017. *Animism: Respecting the Living World.* Second edition. London: Hurst.

———. 2015. "Playing croquet with hedgehogs: (Still) becoming a scholar of Paganism and Animism." Special Section—Paths into Pagan Studies: Autobiographical Reflections. *The Pomegranate: International Journal of Pagan Studies* 17: 99–114. https://doi.org/10.1558/pome.v17i1-2.27747

———. 2013. *Food, Sex and Strangers: Understanding Religion as Everyday Life.* London: Routledge. https://doi.org/10.4324/9781315729572

———. 2000. *Indigenous Religions: A Companion.* London: Cassell.

Harvey, G., ed. 2013. *The Handbook of Contemporary Animism.* New York: Routledge. https://doi.org/10.4324/9781315728964

Honko, L., S. Timonen, and M. Branch. 1993. *Great Bear: A Thematic Anthology of Oral Poetry in the Finno-Ugrian Languages.* Oxford: Oxford University Press.

Kimmerer, R. W. 2013. *Braiding Sweetgrass: Indigenous Wisdom, Scientific Knowledge, and the Teachings Of Plants.* Minneapolis: Milkweed.

Johnson, G. and Kraft, S. E. eds. 2017. *Handbook of Indigenous Religions.* Leiden: E.J. Brill. https://doi.org/10.1163/9789004346710

Johnson, P. C. 2002. "Migrating bodies, circulating signs: Brazilian Candomblé, the Garifuna of the Caribbean, and the category of indigenous religions." *History of Religions,* 41(4): 301–327. https://doi.org/10.1086/463690

Latour, B. 2018. *Down to Earth: Politics in the New Climatic Regime.* Cambridge: Polity.

———. 2013. *An Inquiry Into Modes of Existence: An Anthropology of the Moderns.* Cambridge, MA: Harvard University Press.

———. 1993. *We Have Never Been Modern.* New York: Harvester Wheatsheaf.

Oxford English Dictionary. 2018. "Animism." https://en.oxforddictionaries.com/definition/animism

Pentikäinen, J. 2007. *Golden King of the Forest: The Lore of the Northern Bear.* Helsinki: Etnika Oy.

Sahlins, M. 2011. "What kinship is, Part one." *Journal of the Royal Anthropological Institute* 17(1): 2–19. https://doi.org/10.1111/j.1467-9655.2010.01666.x

Strathern, M. 1988. *The Gender of the Gift: Problems with Women and Problems with Society in Melanesia.* Berkeley: University of California Press. https://doi.org/10.1525/california/9780520064232.001.0001

Tafjord, B. O. 2017. "Towards a typology of academic uses of "indigenous religion(s)", or eight (or nine): Language games that scholars play with this phrase." In *Handbook of Indigenous Religions,* edited by G. Johnson and S. E. Kraft, 25–51. Leiden: E.J. Brill. https://doi.org/10.1163/9789004346710_003

———. 2013. "'Indigenous religions' as an analytical category." *Method and Theory in the Study of Religions* 25(3): 221–243. https://doi.org/10.1163/15700682-12341258

Tawhai, T.P. 1988. "Maori Religion." In *The Study of Religion, Traditional and New Religion,* edited by Stewart Sutherland and Peter Clarke, 96–105. London: Routledge.

Tremlett, P-F., L. Sutherland and G. Harvey, eds. 2017. *Edward Tylor, Religion and Culture.* London: Bloomsbury.

Tylor, E. 1871. *Primitive Culture.* 2 vols. London: John Murray.

United Nations General Assembly. 2007. *United Nations Declaration on the Rights of Indigenous Peoples,* 2 Oct 2007, A/RES/61/295. https://www.un.org/esa/socdev/unpfii/documents/DRIPS_en.pdf

Willerslev, R. 2007. *Soul Hunters: Hunting, Animism, and Personhood among the Siberian Yukaghirs.* Berkeley: University of California Press. https://doi.org/10.1525/california/9780520252165.001.0001

About the author

Graham Harvey is professor of religious studies at The Open University. His recent research largely concerns "the new animism," especially in the rituals and protocols through which Indigenous and other communities engage with the larger-than-human world. He was a member of the international research project, "REDO: Re-assembling democracy" (funded by the Norwegian Research Council). For this, he focused on the Sámi organized Riddu Riđđu festival in Sápmi and the London based ORIGINS Festival of First Nations in which Indigenous performers present their cultures and knowledges to metropolitan and global audiences. Harvey's research interests contribute to his broader, long-term engagement with material- and lived-religion. His recent teaching related work has involved a focus on foodways and associated "purity" practices. His publications include *Food, Sex and Strangers: Understanding Religion as Everyday Life* (2013), and *Animism: Respecting the Living World* (2nd edition 2017). He is editor of the Equinox series "Religion and the Senses," the first volume of which, *Sensual Religion: Religion and the Five Senses* (2018), he co-edited with Jessica Hughes. He is also the founding co-editor of the Routledge series "Vitality of Indigenous Religions," a multi-volume research level monograph series aiming to enhance engagement with the lived realities of Indigenous religions.

Indigenizing the Goddess:
Reclaiming Territory, Myth and Devotion in Glastonbury

AMY WHITEHEAD

The Glastonbury Goddess religion in the South West of England began in the 1990s by a small group of women dedicated to reviving the Goddess of the land surrounding Glastonbury, interpreting and revitalizing myths and legends in relation to her, and reclaiming the Goddess as their own after centuries of male Christian dominated religion. Hugely successful, the group have constructed what they claim to be the first Goddess Temple dedicated to the indigenous goddess of Glastonbury in over 1500 years. The article will argue that territorialization, or "re-territorialization," is one of the main strategies of this indigenizing process, and is carried out through the use and development of Glastonbury Goddess material cultures, ritual creativity and narratives, as well as international Goddess training programmes. Prompting the reclamation of local Goddesses in different parts of the world, the Glastonbury Goddess religion is having local and global reach.

Since the 1990s, the Glastonbury Goddess religious movement based in the south west of England has been growing in popularity. A new religious movement with claims on Britian's ancient past, the Glastonbury Goddess religious movement asserts itself to be the first religious movement appropriately organized and dedicated to an *indigenous Goddess* of the British Isles in over 1500 years. The word "indigenous" is used deliberately by members of the movement for a variety of reasons (explored here); but arguably, its main purpose is strategic. Indigeneity is used as a central identifier from which clear relationships with Glastonbury as a geographical site are claimed, expressed, and stylized, communities are "imagined" (as per Johnson, see below) and built, and the movement's religious material cultures are crafted.

The word "indigenous" is, however, fraught with difficulties. From colonial and post-colonial abuses to political and land rights issues, the construct of the "indigenous" signals ideas about those who occupy particular places and who have been oppressed by more dominant and exploitive powers. A result of these abuses, and combined with the problem of categorization, the "indigenous" has been morphed into a "pure" construct that, according to Paul C. Johnson (2002), has become problematically polarized with the notion of "the global." The term indigenous facilitates the notion that some people in the world are from a particular place "since time immemorial," and their "territory" has clear, identifiable boundaries. In contrast, the "global" has come to signal an "unconstrained circulation of bodies, signs, and capital" (2002, 302) which is not "pure" but messy and convoluted. Johnson explores this perceived polarization of "the global" and "the indigenous" through the examples of Brazilian Candomblé and the Garifuna of the Caribbean and Central America because, in different ways, they challenge the above mentioned "purity" of what it means to be indigenous. Candomblé practitioners consist of "new bodies" and symbols brought about by the fusions of influence from popular/mass media; while the Garifuna have emigrated to the United States, but "who bring new meanings back to the rituals performed in the homeland" (2002, 304). Both of these indigenous communities "imagine themselves in the indigenous form—as, in their own self- understanding and presentation, oriented toward and organically related to a particular place" (2002, 303).

As a useful extension of "indigenous," Johnson suggests that to "indigenize" is to reflect the processes, negotiations and practices through which communities imagine and self-identify as being indigenous, and this chapter will test the theoretical and critical usefulness of the term in relation to the Glastonbury Goddess movement. Placing emphasis on the *–ing* in indigenizing is helpful (as opposed to its more fixed counterpart "indigenous") in that it permits a theoretical fluidity that reflects a) practice, and the nature of the *movement* itself which is cyclical, community oriented, and modern; and b) its strategic self-inscription to the category of "indigenous." This chapter argues that indigenizing is a "style of relating" (Harvey, introduction, this volume) to a territory (Glastonbury) with definite boundaries, and to the community that situates itself in and among that territory. This includes the creativity involved in the design of rituals and performances, newly created religious artefacts, and the re-interpretation of myths and legends to create new Goddess-oriented spiritual and environmental narratives. Last, Johnson's evaluation of "the social and territorial extensions of indigenous communities" (2002, 303–304) will be further tested through the Glastonbury Goddess movement's successful "global mandate" and international priestess training program, raising necessary questions regarding power relations and the socio-economic demographics of Glastonbury Goddess devotees.

Amy Whitehead

Glastonbury: Place, context, landscape

Glastonbury is a small market town in the South West of England with a population of roughly 8,700 inhabitants. Nestled in the green rolling hills of Somerset, Glastonbury is no ordinary British town. Because of surrounding, indeed embedded, myths, legends, and history, Glastonbury and its unique landscape have been written about for centuries. It is, for example, said to be the ancient seat of European Christianity, home to so-called "ancient mystery schools," the burial site of the Holy Grail, the resting place of King Arthur and Guinevere, and more. Such richness in myth and story has played a strong hand in creating a fertile site from which a variety of alternative socio-spiritual experimentations have taken place, particularly in line with the counter-culture movements that have flourished in the post-war British context.

Much of my research (and personal) knowledge about Glastonbury comes from the experience of having lived in and around the town since 1998; and during this time, I have encountered Glastonbury by different names: the "Isle of Glass," the "Isle of Apples," the "Isle of the Dead," and most famously the "Isle of Avalon." The term "Isle" is used due to the prominence of the Glastonbury Tor mound which, along with Chalice Hill, Wearyall Hill, Windmill Hill and Stone Down, stands out amongst an otherwise flat range of levels that were once covered by water. Home to a patchwork quilt of religions, beliefs, alternative spiritualities and mythologies, Glastonbury plays host to different strands of Paganism, Christianity, Buddhism, Hinduism, Islam, Sikhism, Sufism, and those who might self-identify as "New Age" due to the astrological connection more than the label that became popular in the 1970s. Other, individually stylized forms of alternative spiritualities are encouraged and can be found there, too. This variety of beliefs/ideas cross paths with, conflict, complement, or run parallel to each other. Yet despite its current diversity of religiosities, two dominant religions can be identified in Glastonbury: Christian and Pagan (Bowman, 2007, 19).

Christian and Pagan groups alike stake claims on Glastonbury (its stories, myths, legends, land) through annual processions and other events. What they have in common is that, according to Bowman, they both have links with "Celtic Christianity" and stories connected with St. Bride (Bowman, 2007, 19), or St. Brigid/Brigit of Kildare, Ireland, venerated as both Celtic Goddess and one of Ireland's patron saints (alongside St Patrick and St Columba). She is said to have been born into slavery, reared by a Druid, and had the ability to heal. Brigid is also said to have visited Glastonbury in 488 AD. This "Celtic connection" is particularly highlighted and brought to life through the creative endeavours of the Glastonbury Goddess religion (discussed below). The focus on the Glastonbury Goddess religion will comprise the rest of this chapter.

Glastonbury Goddess Religion: Origins, *her*story and landscape

The Glastonbury Goddess religion is a materially vibrant, rich and colourful new religious movement that is dedicated to the idea of rejuvenating, or restoring, an ancient Goddess to the British Isles, particularly to Glastonbury. This movement is of particular interest when thinking about the critical efficaciousness that the term "indigenizing" can have for scholars and practitioners alike. This is because the Glastonbury Goddess religion combines and uses local myth, history, and legend with interpretations of the past, local wells, springs and mounds, newly created narratives, traditions and practices to express indigeneity and in doing so to lay claim to the land.

The movement has its "official roots" in the first "Goddess Conference" held in 1996 (Bowman, 2007, 26). Every year since, a Goddess Conference has taken place in Glastonbury whereby more and more devotees travel nationally and internationally in order to participate in workshops, training, celebrations, and other events. One example of how a Priestess of Avalon and co-organizer of the annual Goddess Conference is working within the movement and with the notion of indigeneity is as follows: "she [Soetens] works internationally, teaching empowerment through Goddess ceremonies, trainings and workshops to honour the spiral of life grounded in the indigenous spirituality of Avalon and the European lands" (Soetens and Brigantia 2018). Through celebration of Her (emphasis on the "H" to indicate discussion about the Goddess), the feminine is honoured, and balance is restored.

Similar to other forms of Paganism, the Goddess movement emphasizes creativity, the cyclical nature of life and time, and events and celebrations revolve around its own Glastonbury/Goddess specific interpretation of the Pagan ritual year (equinoxes, solstices, Imbolc, Beltane, Lammas, Samhain). Some devotees speak about the Glastonbury Goddess in monotheistic terms, while others speak about her more local forms and within a polytheistic framework. Some devotees speak about Her in both forms (universal and local). A notion that will be explored in greater detail further along is that the Glastonbury Goddess religion is not a native faith movement. There is no emphasis on ethnic connections to Glastonbury or Somerset, but instead on devotee's relationships to the land, to the Goddess, and to each other. Devotees mostly distance themselves from Wicca and witchcraft and are concerned with forms of spirituality that are most commonly found within the holistic milieu (Heelas and Woodhead 2005, 1, 31) and that emphasize healing, psychic and personal development, and practices that foster well-being. The difference between the healing practices found within the Glastonbury Goddess movement and those in more "mainstream alternatives" is that emphasis is placed on healing "male-inflicted" wounds. Those wounds will often result from either personally experienced damage inflicted by men on women, or the cultural/social damage that occurs as a result of the wider effects of the Christian oriented "dominator culture" where women have been oppressed. This notion underpins one of the motivating factors involved in "reviving" the Goddess to Glastonbury, much of which is being done through the cultural work whereby new traditions are created and maintained.

Herstory

The significance of the stories about Glastonbury cannot be underestimated in the creation of the Glastonbury Goddess religion. The movement is forged from writings about a perceived pre-Christian ancient Goddess who dominated many parts of the world including the British Isles before Christianity. The Christian version of the story tells us that "st Bridget visited Glastonbury in 488 and spent time at Beckery or Bride's Mound, an area on the edge of Glastonbury where there seems to have been a chapel dedicated to St Mary Magdalene" (Bowman, 2007, 24). And then,

> In the late nineteenth century John Arthur Goodchild claimed that there had been in Glastonbury the survival of an ancient Irish cult venerating the female aspect of the deity which became attached to the figure of St Bride (Benham 1993). (Bowman, 2007, 25)

Kathy Jones (author, writer and resident of Glastonbury) along with small group of other women took this notion of a surviving "cult" dedicated to the feminine divine and used it as the core idea around which the Goddess movement in Glastonbury was conceived. Jones" account of how local factors combined to create a new "Goddess movement" is evidenced in an account given in an interview with the BBC. When asked "What changed to cause this rejuvenation of the Goddess?" Jones replied:

> In my understanding, the awakening came from Her. She calls to us to remember Her. Many people, women in particular, are called to come to Glastonbury, to remember Her, to come and be Her priestesses again. In practical terms, things happened. A sculptor called Philippa Bowers began to create sculptures of the Goddess. We held an art exhibition, in the Glastonbury Assembly Rooms, of Goddess paintings, which was the first time for hundreds of years that this had happened. I, and others, wrote books and plays about the Goddess too. It's like a lot of factors came together all at the same time.
>
> (BBC interview with Kathy Jones, 2005)

Kathy Jones has written several works based on the Glastonbury Goddess, such as *The Ancient British Goddess* (2001). She acknowledges a few of her sources of inspiration such as Robert Graves" *The White Goddess*, Marija Gimbutas" *Language of the Goddess* and *Civilization of the Goddess*, Caitlin and John Matthews" *Ladies of the Lake*, and "Michael Dames for his Goddess inspired views of landscape in *The Avebury Cycle* and *Silbury Treasure*" (Kathy Jones, 2001,ii).

It is important to note that the Goddess figured heavily in the anti-nuclear peace actions/protests at Greenham, Wiltshire, England in the early 1980s (Jones, n.d.); and it was this early movement that fed into the later development of the Glastonbury Goddess religion in the 1990s. The 1980s and 1990s were decades that in many parts of the United Kingdom saw the emergence of environmental movements, the popularity of the "green burial," a growing road protest and counter-culture free party movement, and feminist spiritualities. Within the counter-culture the 1990s in particular were referred to as a second 1960s. Consequently, the 1990s were also a decade that saw a turn of academic interest toward indigenous traditions, most of which, it had previously been predicted, were either extinct or on their way out. Similarly, "all things Irish" or "Celtic" experienced a resurgence in popularity, mainly through music and art. Arguably, this decade was rife with attempts at the restoration and/or revitalization of cultures that had previously been either dislocated or marginalized. Further, the idea of marginalization can also be carried over to Glastonbury's landscape. The land, nature, and all things earthy, bodily, and material (matter, mother) have also been suppressed, abused, and exploited as a result of perceived Christian and modern discourses that prize the transcendent mind over earthly matter (or that which is valued significantly in Pagan, animist, and nature-venerating religions).

Landscape: wells, springs, mounds

In addition to historical accounts and popular literature, Glastonbury's land and landscape play an equally if not more significant role in its prominence as both axis and access points for the creation and sustainability of contemporary Goddess devotion. Bowman says

> Some regard [Glastonbury] as a significant prehistoric centre of Goddess worship, confirmed for present day devotees by figures of the Goddess they discern in the landscape and by the existence in the Christian era of strong devotion to Our Lady St Mary of Glastonbury and to St Bridget, both widely regarded as Christianized forms of the Goddess. (Bowman, 2004, 273)

This discernment of the body of the Goddess in the land that makes up Glastonbury's township and surrounding countryside is central to the origins of the movement, as well as its claim that a Goddess is, indeed, indigenous to Glastonbury. When asked in an interview with the BBC: "How does the Goddess relate to Glastonbury in particular?" Kathy Jones reported that the Goddess is found through the shapes of the hills and valleys. Glastonbury is a town situated on a small group of hills, composed of Glastonbury Tor, the Chalice Hill, Wearyall Hill, Windmill Hill, and Stone Down. These hills rise out of the flat lands surrounding Glastonbury, and when you look at the shape of them, you can see different outlines from the contours of the hills. One of the forms that we see is the shape of a giant woman lying on her back on the land. She is the mother Goddess in the landscape. (interview with Kathy Jones, BBC, 2005)

By this account, the personhood of the Goddess as it is discerned in the landscape offers an idea about that which constitutes the Goddess" territory. A further indication is revealed by a priestess of Avalon who states: "Our Lady of Avalon, keeper of the mysteries, and Lady of the Mists of Avalon presides over the lands from which the Tor is visible to the naked eye." Since Glastonbury's iconic Tor mound can be seen from South Wales on a clear day, this account provides a vast, loose and subjective parameter around that which is the Goddess" domain, as well as accounts of the Goddess as being identifiable in the features of the land "herself." Further, different deities who have been identified by Jones (2001) are also "the Goddess." These are the Lady of Avalon (who is Morgen la Fey), the Nine Morgens, Brigit or Bridie of the Sacred Flame, Modron who is Great Mother of the lineage of Avallach, Our Lady Mary of Glastonbury, the Crone of Avalon, the Tor Goddess, Lady of the Hollow Hills, Lady of the Lake and the Lady of the Holy Springs and Wells. The Goddess of Glastonbury is monotheistic, polytheistic, and She *is* also the land.

Significantly, and not dissimilar to Johnson's Garifuna and Candomblé examples, the Glastonbury Goddess people not only imagine and present their community as organically related to a particular place, but understand the Goddess as being in and of the land. Significantly, members of the Goddess movement do not claim to be "indigenous" to Glastonbury. This indicates that "indigenous" is not being used as tool to express indigeneity within the imaginary "pure" form romantic construct whereby a people are believed to be from a particular locale from "time immemorial" (2002, 302); but that by extension of the term, indigeneity is a negotiated and fluid status that is acted out in varying degrees through the types of performances, created narratives, and individualized relationships that devotees have with the Goddess who is in Glastonbury or who *is* Glastonbury.

Belonging, relating, indigenizing

The Glastonbury Goddess movement is not a native faith movement. Devotees do not have to be blood related or ethnically connected to Glastonbury's ancient residents. Unlike native faith movements, the Glastonbury Goddess religion is not ethnically oriented, but spiritually oriented. Spiritual homes are found in and through Goddess devotion, and devotees belong to the Goddess and to each other. Emphasis and significance is not placed on a necessity to be from Glastonbury, or from other European countries. It does, however, claim to be an "indigenous spirituality" and some devotees have claimed a kind of belonging or "spiritual homecoming" to Glastonbury, to the religion, and to themselves. This section explores the dynamics of that belonging and the role that indigenizing plays therein.

Because of its reputation (which is spun from a combination of its history, its status as pilgrimage site, and its role in providing a place for spiritual and other seekers), Glastonbury is a transient town. That is not to say that there are not "real locals" in Glastonbury. On the contrary, there are families who have been in Glastonbury for generations and who can document their family's historical place there. But in addition to this small core of real locals, a significant proportion of Glastonbury's population are outsiders who come from other parts of the United Kingdom, and from other parts of the world. Glastonbury, a small market town in Somerset, is pluralistic, and it is full of "migrating bodies" (Johnson 2002). People come and people go, including Goddess devotees.

From this the question of indigeneity must be further addressed. Johnson tells us that typically, "A religion that is indigenous is the religion of indigenous peoples, those etymologically characterized as "born of" or "born into" (indi-, in; gegnere, born) a specific place" (2002, 308), but that we need "categories that help us describe not just indigenous versus other kinds of people and religions, but the sense in which, and processes by which, peoples "indigenize" new territories and historical conditions to make them their own" (2002, 311). In a modern world that facilitates global travel and knowledge/information exchange so readily, what does it mean "to belong" to a place? And further, what happens when that which is normally considered "to belong," gets flung into the throws of "process"?

This gets to the heart of the usefulness of "indigenizing" as a critical term. Due to increasingly recognized relationships between "the local" and "the global," the process of indigenizing reflects a contemporary, modern position of that which actually takes place in the Glastonbury Goddess context due to the emphasis that the movement places on individual experience and individual choice. But modern in what way? People from different parts of the world come to Glastonbury in order to join the Goddess community there; but they also bring their own personal visions to this site. This is encouraged. Empowerment in the movement is found in finding oneself, but in individualistically stylized and inspired ways. So when Johnson says "Defining indigenous religions a the religions of those communities that imagine them-selves in indigenous style—as organically bound to a land site—brackets the impasse between so-called romantic or essentialist and deconstructivist views of indigenous socieites" (2002, 306), progress is made that takes us out of misconceived static categories and into that which moves. Modernity has, after all, according to Abramson and Holbraad, "somehow entered into a distinctive new phase that is post, late, or liquid" (2012, 43). Indeniz-ing, then, reflects this fluidity and non-fixedness.

Building on this, it can be argued that indigenizing is generative, and belonging is generated through indigenizing attempts that take place between a variety of entanglements. These entanglements are not dualistic, but evenly and relationally distributed between individual experiences, ideas, place, space, time of day, people, and things. The connection to Glastonbury and the Goddess in the land is not only co-inspired between individual devo-tees and place; but conglomerate. So although romanticized inspirations are drawn from Arthurian myths and writings about Bridget's coming to Glas-tonbury centuries ago, central to the Glastonbury Goddess religion are the multi-faceted relationships that take place between a variety of elements in the contemporary here and the now. From this it is difficult to quantify to what degrees the Goddess is indigenized. As discussed before, some devotees consider the Goddess as a transcendent being who hovers above Glaston-bury; while others will focus more on the land aspects and particular sites. In some relationships with the Goddess, the process or act of "indigenizing" is clearer than in others. Therefore, it can be argued that in European contexts such as the Glastonbury Goddess movement, the fluid interplays take place between modernity, monotheism, polytheism, tradition, myth, legend, land, feminism, bodies, specific sites, ritual interactions (public and personal); and depending on who or what is taking part in relationships, indigenzing can be happening to greater or lesser degrees at any one time.

Whatever the degree of indigenizing, one thing remains certain. Glaston-bury Goddess devotees have what Kathryn Rountree refers to as "a lived rela-tionship with the same land [which] is enough to confer authenticity on their contemporary Paganism" (2015, 6). Central to the movement is the act of relating. And laying claim to, indeed practicing, indigeneity provides new ways of understanding this relating. But both indigenizing and belonging require action and effort. One can be born in any place on the planet, but does that being born of or into mean that one belongs to/with that place? Johnson states in what might have been more significant than a footnote, that "The material and cultural relation to any landsite is not natural or given, but rather made, even in contexts of long historical occupation of a specific place. This seems obvious but is often occluded" (2002, 306 footnote 13). From this it can be gathered that belonging is constructed. It is, after all, created from the processes and cultural work involved in the configuration of culture and indigenous religious identities. In these ways, the landscape, indeed the Goddess, are indigenized. The historical fact of indigenousness, or of a Goddess who was indigenous to the land around Glastonbury, would be, for Johnson of less importance than what the current Goddess religionists make of their connection to the land and to their perceived past, and how they "present themselves to make community in the present" (2002, 306). This making of community, belonging (to the Goddess, to each other), and indigenizing can be considered "cultural work." The next sections examine how this is being done at local and global levels.

Indigenizing the local: Procession, territorialization, material culture

Indigenizing signals action, and it is carried out in Glastonbury in a variety of ways, shapes, and forms, and to varying degrees, e.g. through performing, through ritualizing, through creating materiality, imagining community, and through (re-) territorializing. This section will begin to test the usefulness of the term "indigenizing" and explore the word "indigenous" as strategic in marking territory and developing the practices, rituals, material cultures, and newly created traditions. It begins, significantly, with the Goddess" annual procession.

Procession

In order to gain ground and prominence ("once again"), the Glastonbury Goddess religion has established itself as a visible and active force in Glastonbury. This is most visibly performed in the Goddess processions that take place once a year, around Lammas (August 1st), and during the time of the annual Goddess conference, the first of which (as discussed before) set both the Goddess and the movement in motion in Glastonbury in 1996. This first procession is significant because it ritually marked off territory and re-staked a claim on the land that is Glastonbury, publically signalling that the Glastonbury Goddess movement was back in the running.

To this day, the procession continues to be a beautifully colourful, loud, and joyful event, involving the use of flags, banners, candles, costumes, drumming, singing, and shouting to express devotion. The Goddess is processed up Glastonbury's High Street to the Chalice Well, through the Victorian Well House that houses the White Spring, then up the hill to Glastonbury Tor, and then back down again. Bowman suggests that the procession mirrors Christian Pilgrimage processions that begin from the Tor and proceed to the

Abbey (2004, 283). The Goddess procession is, however, far more colourful, loud and vibrant than that of the Anglican and Catholic processions. Arguably, Goddess material culture and performances are bright, colourful, and eye-catching for this very reason. As noted previously by Bowman (2004), the more material and performance cultures are created in relation to the Goddess movement, the more visible the Goddess religiosity becomes in Glastonbury.

The Goddess procession is a public ritual performance that facilitates what Gilles Deleuze and Pierre-Felix Guattari (1972) refer to as "reterritorialization" in that Glastonbury Goddess devotees are creating and making elements of culture their own. This is seen in how they loudly, boisterously, and ritually mark off the Goddess" terrain counter to the Christian processions. In relation to the reclaiming initiatives carried out by the Goddess movement, Kellie Jones refers to reterritorialization as "recapturing one's (combined and various [and imagined]) history, much of which has been dismissed as an insignificant footnote to the dominant culture" (Kellie Jones, 2011, 339). This "recapturing" is done both through the interpretation and re-creation of local narratives, as well as through physical and visible action. In relation to the Garifuna and Candomblé practitioners, indigenizing is a "response to a perceived breach of boundaries and an attempt to redraw them" (2002, 32). Goddess devotees imagine/know that the Goddess has suffered dislocation at the hands of Christian invasion and conversion. The Goddess has been banished from being acknowledged in Her rightful place in Glastonbury. The dislocation is one of marginalization or of being hidden or nearly forgotten. The fight then, so to speak, is with a perceived replacement culture that forcibly took power, rights, and importance away from women and "the feminine." Thus the re-territorialization of Glastonbury by those who recognize and celebrate the Goddess in Her rightful place is essential to the movement. Here, boundaries were certainly felt to have been breached, and they are fighting back in a plethora of creative ways. In some respects, "to indigenize" is similar "to reterritorialize." It can mean "to make something one's own," but in way that indicates differences to dominator discourses. In support of this, Johnson writes: "When outsider signs, symbols and practices are relied upon, they are quickly indigenized—given a culturally specific form that makes the outsider symbol "ours," even traditional" (2002, 312).

Temple, statues, and Goddess materiality

The Glastonbury Goddess Temple is claimed to be the first indigenous temple dedicated to the Goddess in perhaps 1500 years. This claim is stated widely in the movement's literature and by word of mouth. Group members are deliberately bringing the word "indigenous" into their common parlance through the books they produce and through talks, and secondly, through their use of materials that come from Glastonbury to craft Goddess statues and to create protocols for temple offerings.

The Goddess Temple itself was established in 2002, and is a large studio-type room that has been bought, dressed and decorated and ritually made into the temple. The Temple sits at the heart of the religion and provides a place where the people can go in, sit, pray, meditate, make offerings, or ask to be "smudged" (have their auras cleared through the burning of sage or sweet grass) by the temple care takers. Reflecting both the movement's creative eclecticism and Johnson's example of how media and popular culture have inspired Candomblé practitioners, the act of "smudging" is "borrowed" (or appropriated) from "other" indigenous (principally non-descript Native North American) groups along with a vague notion that that is what they do. Following Johnson's idea again that "given a culturally specific form that makes the outsider symbol "ours," even traditional" (2002, 312), the question is begged as to whether or not a distinction can be made between indigenizing and appropriating? This question will be explored further in relation to materials, stories, and value as the rest of the chapter unfolds.

The Temple aesthetic and material cultures found within are direct, visible and practical expressions of the narratives, ideas/beliefs, stories, and creative found in the movement. Reflecting the reverence for natures cyclical/seasonal changes, the Temple aesthetic changes every six weeks; but Goddess paintings and/or statues are usual residents (even if dressed up in different ways). Altars sit at eight points in the Temple and correlate directly with the movement's ritual year, as well as with the deities/goddesses that occupy Glastonbury's local wells, springs, groves and mounds. These deities take the forms of willow wickerwork statues who are venerated, spoken with, petitioned, and said to "embody" the Goddess. Made by a local artist and devotee, skill, craft and devotion go into the work. Significantly, the material is sourced from willow trees found on Glastonbury's levels, and it is essential that the material be indigenous to Avalon and that it comes from the body of the Goddess Herself. Myth and story are woven into the narrative of the indigeneity of the willow statues. This is particularly exemplified in Jones" writing in relation to the willow figures of the Nine Morgens. The Nine Morgens are said to be a ninefold Sisterhood who "rule over the Isle of Avalon surrounded by the Lake of Mysts" (Jones, 2001, 213). Their names were recorded by Geoffrey of Monmouth in the *Vita Merlini* in the twelfth century, the most well-known of which is Morgen La Fey. There were also nine legendary ladies of the lake named by John and Caitlin Matthews, four of the more widely known of which include "Igraine, Guinevere, Morgan, Nimue or Vivienne, who derive their powers from the Otherworld" (Jones, 2001, 213). The statues are permanent residents in the Goddess Temple, and their roles within the movement can be best described as healing Goddesses. In the Temple the Nine Morgens form of a "protective circle" around a small space that is dedicated to those who want or need healing. Visibly, this is one of the Goddess Temple's unique and creative features that has not been "borrowed" or appropriated from another culture; yet it can be argued that certain parts of history, along with writings of Geoffrey of Monmouth, John and Caitlin Matthews, and the before mentioned Arthur Goodchild have been appropriated, "made one's own" (Johnson, 2002, 212) and indigenized.

Along with the willow used to weave and create the Goddess statues, Temple offerings are a significant medium through which to test the role of value within the movement, and how the placing value on things found local to the land in Glastonbury is evidence of their indigenizing practice. First, however, it should be noted that the main altar further houses many different types of offerings brought into the temple by devotees. I have observed such objects such as bones, feathers, acorns, wild flowers, berries, hazelnuts, stones, photos, jewellery, and more. An overall rubric appears to have been set in the aesthetics and arrangement of objects found in the temple. This rubric is directed by an appreciation for the fact that the Goddess *prefers* things that are indigenous to Glastonbury's landscape. The valuing of indigenous materials is, however, a further strategic move that not only reflects the Goddess" indigenous identity; it is also a deliberate critique of mainstream society where animal bones, feathers, and acorns are not particularly valuable.

Naturally, it must be noted that the Glastonbury Goddess movement are not the only counter-culture alternative spirituality that appreciate and value "things of nature" (although what is gold if not a thing of nature?). On the contrary, many individuals and groups value specific places and do this. But by claiming and valuing indigenous local land materials that are not economically viable in the mainstream but specific to Glastonbury, the group further carve out their indigenous niche in the counter culture whereby a different type of fluid, spiritual economy exists that is unique to them. Of course offerings of money are welcome in the Temple; and although this might sit at odds with the valuing of so called natural objects from the land, it does reflect the contemporary nature of the movement and its connection to a wider global economy (discussed further along). Thus here it can be strongly suggested that Goddess materiality is a physical and visual connecting constructor of indigenous religious identity. When devotees collect natural things from the land around, they are enacting generative indigenizing processes, creating belonging, and reimagining relationships with specific territory.

Indigenizing the global: Extending

It has been established that the Glastonbury Goddess religion retains its local character in a variety of ways, e.g. the ritual marking of territory and boundaries, the preference for indigenous materials that originate in the land that is Glastonbury, and the association with and adoption of the myths, stories, and history of Glastonbury. Such as in the cases of the Garifuna and Candomblé, who respond "...to crises of dislocation, such that the more actual transformation and mobility encountered, the more valued the ideology of unchanging permanence and territorial stability becomes" (Johnson, 2002, 304), the Glastonbury Goddess movement have a clear sense of their territory and its stability. On the other hand, however, the Goddess movement is continually expanding, or doing the cultural work that is "extending" (Johnson, 2002). Much like Candomblé and Garifuna, they have gone global.

The Glastonbury Goddess religion's global reach is mainly facilitated by the internet. Here, they are able to advertise programmes of study, events, and training; and this attracts people from all over the world. The Glastonbury Goddess Temple website is an expansive hub of information; and like the Temple, its aesthetics change every six weeks to reflect the current season. The information highway has provided endless amounts of inspiring information for religions all over the world, as exemplified by Johnson's discussion of how the so called "secret" Candomblé tradition has been influenced by popular culture (Johnson 2002, 303). In comparison, while native faith groups attempt to "counter such processes, downplay them, or adapt imported global traditions to give them a local character and relevance," some Pagan groups "choose to participate in global and globalizing religious processes" (Rountree, 2015, 7). The Glastonbury Goddess movement does both. It is locally focussed, while being globally influencing, and globally influenced. As Rountree says: "In many instances the two [the local and the global] are bound up with each other" (2015, 7). This is certainly the case, not only for the Glastonbury Goddess movement, but for Glastonbury generally. In support of Kathy Jones" notion that Glastonbury is the "special place" that draws people there, Bowman writes:

> Glastonbury has consistently localized the global and globalized the local, locating itself in a prominent position, pulling in and projecting out significance. Of course that has happened elsewhere, but this "hyperlocalization" seems particularly marked in Glastonbury at present. For while at one level the world may be a single place, currently Glastonbury is the centre of a num-

ber of worlds, because of the way Glastonbury functions as a multiple choice or multivalent location. (Bowman, 2005, 164)

This "hyperlocalization" could play a definitive role in the global success of the Glastonbury Goddess movement (one of Glastonbury's religious ontologies). In its eclecticism, the movement pushes out and pulls in. It breathes, so to speak, and with each breath it expands further. As the nature of the movement is one that celebrates rejuvenation and flux, it continually incorporates that which presents itself and emerges at a local level, in Glastonbury, and then flings what it finds out to the rest of the world via the internet. Members of the Goddess community often express that they were "called" to Glastonbury and the Goddess while living in other places in the British Isles, as well as in other countries. According to Jones, in Glastonbury, the Goddess is literally visible in the landscape and there is something special and powerful about Glastonbury that draws people there (interview with Kathy Jones, BBC, 2005). When asked if the Goddess is… "…only found in Glastonbury, or is She elsewhere?" Jones said that the Goddess is everywhere, and that although beautiful landscapes can be found in most places in the world, some are more significant and beautiful than others. The Goddess is also elsewhere and connected with other landscapes whereby she will have her own vernacular, unique to place form, and the Glastonbury Goddess movement is deliberately setting a model from which other Goddess movements in other countries/landscapes can occur. As with the quote from Soetens, the Goddess is being revived in European lands, too.

The Glastonbury Goddess Temple can be considered the "parent temple" to the ones affiliated in the Netherlands, Argentina, Portugal, Chile, Belgium, Austria, Italy, Germany, Argentina and South America, the United States and Australia as it has "trained" many of the founding members of these temples. It does this through a three year Glastonbury Goddess Priestess of Avalon training programme that is offered both face to face and through a distance training email correspondence course for people who are unable to attend the Temple in Glastonbury in person. Priestess of Avalon training is distinct in that strong similarities can be found in terms of the materiality, ritual-making, terminology, ethos, and social class among its members. Significantly, through the Glastonbury Goddess movement, shape is being given and protocols are being set as to how the Goddess religion should form in specific locales. On the 18th of October, 2018, the Glastonbury Temple website read:

> Thankfully Goddess is returning to our awareness. She is once again being recognized as Divine Source and Great Mother of All. Many women and some men are beginning to re-member and re-claim an ancient path of devotion and service to Goddess. Communities and Temples of Goddess are being

built anew in Her world, allowing people to come together to learn who Goddess is, to celebrate Her, to recreate Her Sacred Sanctuaries and to experience Her wonderful loving nature.

The training of priestesses internationally is akin to toiling land and planting seeds and reflects further the attempts being made by the Goddess movement to indigenize at a variety of local levels. It also reflects the beginnings of a new form of cultural heritage where Temple members are embedding the Goddess and its values not only into the local psyche, but into a vision with global reach that speaks to current political and environmental movements, as well as to women's spirituality and to healing past abuses.

The Priestess training programme is not, however, without its territorial limits and boundaries. As of the 18th of October, 2018, the stipulations of the programme are as follows:

> The Priestess of Avalon Training is only open to people living in the Northern hemisphere as we follow the cycle of the Seasons of Her nature here, and you need to be able to visit and experience the land here eight times in the Glastonbury Training, and at least 3 times a year in the Correspondence Training (Goddess Temple website, n.d.)

By refining its reach and territory, the movement is asserting its indigenousness to/of lands that relate cyclically to the seasons as they are experienced in the Northern Hemisphere; and this move deepens its relationship to its locale. This movement toward defining boundaries is exactly what one can expect from the process of "indigenizing." Once again, religion has done what religion does, e.g. it moves the goal posts; and we, as scholars, must be prepared to roll with the changes. As Johnson writes:

> We should take care that the category [of indigenous religions] not be used as our own crisis response, a fetish in a quixotian quest for stable, located meanings, for at least a wobbling pivot to steady shaking hands in a world where nothing rests. We should honour indigenous religions" claims to a unique relation to the land not by simply reproducing or essentializing them, but rather by critically investigating them—as we do all religious traditions—as they are mediated by language and history and as a magnificent part of the human repertoire of making place, not merely being "of" the land. (2002, 327)

Concluding thoughts

When I began conducting research among the Glastonbury Goddess religion in 2007, I was initially both troubled and intrigued by their claim of being an indigenous religion. Too many injustices have been done; cultures and languages have been obliterated, and the ensuing horrors are too many to mention.

In many ways, I initially considered the use of "indigenous" as demonstrating a recklessness or lack of awareness of so called "indigenous issues," especially because the majority of the members of this group also form part of the dominant culture. Demographically and in terms of socio-economic statuses, Goddess devotees are often white, university educated, privileged (compared with some second and third world cultures) and middle class. As many aspects of Goddess spirituality form part of the holistic milieu, neither the factor of choices nor power relations should be ignored when considering how Western European traditions are constructing or imagining the identity of "indigenous." Critically, it could be understood as a form of colonizing a perceived historicity, or past. However, on balance, movements such as these can be seen in the more positive light of cultural and religious creativity, especially since much of the aim is to redress a cultural imbalance of injustice and marginalization of both nature and the feminine. Rountree writes (citing Barnard) "while anthropologists hotly debate "the indigenous" as an anthropological concept, the concept is "defined intuitively by ordinary people—indigenous and non-indigenous alike—around the world, it does have meaning" (Barnard in Rountree, 2015, 8). This is certainly the case for the Glastonbury Goddess movement. In essence, the strategic function of this community's use of the term "indigenous" lies in its ability to conjure a different style of relationship to the land that is different to that of the predominantly mainstream and Christian-oriented culture. Significantly, then, the term "indigenous" as an identifying tool should only be considered in context. Goddess devotees are not claiming that they are indigenous to the land that is Glastonbury, but claiming that the Goddess is indigenous to the land. This is not, however, to say that some devotees do not claim indigeneity to the British Isles; many do. This is where the extension of the term "indigenous" into indigenizing as per Johnson could be more useful and accurate for both devotees and scholars alike. It emphasizes the fluidity of movement needed to avert the critical gaze of anthropologist and others who would take issue with use of the term. Yet still, solid critical foregrounding is needed to highlight that indigenizing can be used in European contexts as a verb that points toward creative processes and relationships that the non-indigenous, but spiritual, have with the land and its stories.

In conclusion, the concept of "indigenizing," when understand as processual, volatile and fluid, is readily applicable to that which is taking place in the Glastonbury Goddess religion because first, with its emphasis on movement it reflects the cyclical, generative and creative nature of the religion. Under the umbrella term "Glastonbury Goddess religion" there is room for personal interpretations, within which related constructs are continually in the process of being broken down and rebuilt. Second, indigenizing is a style of relating that reflects attempts to refocus attention on the land in and around the defined parameters of Glastonbury specifically. Goddess devotees are often transient, and belonging to the Glastonbury Goddess movement is in answer to an individual calling that links devotees into the religion as a social group with a variety of shared and individualized social identities. Within this, indigenizing takes the form of cultural work—and this work is carried out through newly creating material and performances cultures, interpreting and re-interpreting myths and stories, creating reclaiming, environmental and feminist narratives, as well as new forms of heritage and tradition. Indigenizing indicates, in this case, new found forms of relating to the land, to the mother, and to each other; and indigeniz-*ing* is a style and a strategy that is helping this new religious movement to have both local and global reach.

References

Abramson, A. and M. Holbraad. 2012. "Contemporary cosmologies, critical reimaginings." *Religion and Society: Advances in Research* 3: 35–50. https://doi.org/10.3167/arrs.2012.030103

Bowman, M. I. 2007. "Arthur and Bridget in Avalon: Celtic myth, vernacular religion and contemporary spirituality in Glastonbury." *Fabula* 48: 16–32. https://doi.org/10.1515/FABL.2007.003

———. 2005. "Ancient Avalon, New Jerusalem, heart chakra of planet earth: The local and the global in Glastonbury." *Numen*, 52: 157–190. https://doi.org/10.1163/1568527054024722

———. 2004. "Procession and possession in Glastonbury: Continuity, change and the manipulation of tradition." *Folklore* 115: 273–285. https://doi.org/10.1080/0015587042000284266

Deleuze, G. and F. Guattari.1972. *Anti-Œdipus*. Translated by Robert Hurley, Mark Seem and Helen R. Lane. London and New York: Continuum, 2004. Vol. 1 of *Capitalism and Schizophrenia*. 2 vols. 1972–1980. Translation of *L'Anti-Oedipe*. Paris: Les Editions de Minuit.

Glastonbury Goddess Temple. nd. "Priestess of Avalon with Glastonbury Goddess Temple." Last updated: "Autumn Equinox" 2018. https://goddesstempleteachings.co.uk/wordpress/priestessofavalon/.

Heelas, P. and L. Woodhead. 2005. *The Spiritual Revolution: Why Religion is Giving Way to Spirituality*. Oxford: Blackwell.

Johnson, P. C. 2002. "Migrating bodies, circulating signs: Brazilian Candomblé, the Garifuna of the Caribbean, and the Category of Indigenous Religions." *History of Religions* 41(4): 301-327. Essays on the Occasion of Frank Reynolds's Retirement. https://doi.org/10.1086/463690

Jones, Kathy. 2005. "The Goddess in Glastonbury." Interview by Helen Otter. *Where I Live, Somerset, Faith*, BBC, Last updated: December 11, 2008. http://www. bbc.co.uk/somerset/content/articles/2005/09/13/goddess_in_glastonbury_ feature.shtml.

———. 2001. *The Ancient British Goddess*. Riverside, CA: Ariadne Publications.

———. n.d. *In the Heart of the Goddess: the website of Kathy Jones*. https://www. kathyjones.co.uk/on-finding-treasure-mystery-plays-of-the-goddess/2/

Jones, Kellie. 2011. *Eye Minded: Living and Writing Contemporary Art*. Durham, NC: Duke University Press. https://doi.org/10.1215/9780822393498

Soetens, K. and Brigantia M. 2018. "Site content for Glastonbury Goddess Conference." https://goddessconference.com/speakers/katinka-soetens/

Rountree, K., ed. 2015. *Contemporary Pagan and Native Faith Movements in Europe: Colonialist and Nationalist Impulses*. Oxford: Berghahn. https://doi. org/10.2307/j.ctt9qctm0

About the author

Amy Whitehead is an anthropologist of religion and Senior Lecturer in Social Anthropology at Massey University in Aotearoa, New Zealand. Born in the USA, she moved to the UK after finishing her BA in English Literature at the University of Tennessee, Knoxville in 1996. In 2002 she began her MA in Contemporary Religions and Spiritualities at Bath Spa University, UK. From there she went on to do a PhD in Religious Studies which was awarded by the Open University in the UK in 2011. She has since published widely in books and journals on the material and performance cultures of Goddess Pagans in England and Marian devotees in Andalusia, Spain. Amy has also contributed to the development of new critical approaches to indigenous religions, the fetish (in animism), and to the recent "ontological turn to (religious) things" in anthropology. She is the currently the managing series editor of Bloomsbury Studies in Material Religion, which enhances her continued interest and research into material religions where she currently resides in Auckland, NZ. Amy is committed to the development of a "bottom up" approach to religions, as well as to the development of "thing" based methodologies. These are concerned with broadening debates about the objects and places that sit at the heart of religious/traditional communities and that matter most to people.

— 5 —

Is Druidry Indigenous?
The Politics of Pagan Indigeneity Discourse

SUZANNE OWEN

This chapter asks if "indigenous," associated as it is with "colonized peoples," is being employed strategically by Druids in Britain to support cultural or political aims. Prominent Druids make various claims to indigeneity, presenting Druidry as the pre-Christian religion of the British Isles and emphasizing that it originated there. By "religion" it also assumes Druidry was a culture equal to if not superior to Christianity—similar to views of antiquarians in earlier centuries who idealized a pre-Christian British culture as equal to that of ancient Greece. Although British Druids refute the nationalist tag, and make efforts to root out those tendencies, it can be argued that it is a love of the land rather than the country per se that drives indigeneity discourses in British Druidry.

Introduction

In a previous publication, "Druidry as an Indigenous Religion" (Owen 2013, 86), I proposed an inclusive definition of "indigenous religion" as a religion that relates to the land, the people (including other-than-human persons) and that which has gone before. While this avoids an ethnic criterion for "indigenous religion" derived from colonialist classifications, as it applies to practices rooted in or honouring local places and people whoever the practitioner, it is ambiguous about the need for community recognition favoured by indigenous people themselves. Therefore, this chapter investigates to what extent contemporary Druidry may be considered rather an "indigenizing movement," following Johnson (2002), with the view that it is primarily the love of the land that drives indigeneity discourse in contemporary British Druidry.

A significant development was when the Druid Network, one of many Druid organizations in Britain, gained charity registration as a "religion" in England and Wales on the 21st September 2010. In one response, BBC News (2010) quoted Arthur Pendragon, a renowned Druid activist, as saying "We are looking at the indigenous religion of these isles—it's not a new religion but one of the oldest." Pendragon implies there was an unbroken tradition from pre-Roman Druids to today, though most contemporary Druids acknowledge that they are reinventing Druidry, drawing inspiration from sources such as the Welsh Mabinogion, and cultivating a relationship with nature and ancient sites. In the late 1980s and early 1990s the British Druid Order (BDO), founded by Philip Shallcrass, distributed a booklet entitled *Druidry: Native Spirituality in Britain*. Since then, Druids have often represented Druidry as the "native spirituality" of Britain, which informs their engagements with the land and heritage.

It is difficult to determine a common element between the various groups of Druids today, though many contemporary Druids are familiar with *awen*, the "inspiration" (from Welsh) of bards and Druids and have an interest in trees and tree lore. With the emphasis on inspiration, Druidry has many musicians, artists and storytellers, such as Robin Williamson, founder of the Incredible String Band and honorary bard of both the British Druid Order and the Order of Bards, Ovates and Druids. I have not heard better renditions than his of tales from the Mabinogion (Welsh) and the Battle of Moytura (Irish, which features the Dagda, a god-Druid with a cauldron, staff and harp). *The Tale of Taliesin* (Welsh) is perhaps the most popular Druidic story and the one the Order of Bards, Ovates and Druids have used for their training course. As for ritual practice, like other Pagan groups in Britain, many Druids celebrate the eight seasonal festivals (winter and summer solstice, spring and autumn equinox and the four "fire" festivals: Beltane, Lammas, Samhain and Imbolc.)[1]

Ancient British Druidry

Many Druids assert that Druidry originated in Britain. For example, Shallcrass and Restall Orr (2001) wrote: "What most modern Druids do believe is that Druidry originated in what we now call the British Isles" (2001, 5). This view is mainly based on a comment by Julius Caesar (100–44 BCE) about Druids in Gaul (covering an area that includes modern-day France): "It is believed that the training for Druids was discovered in Britain and from there it was transferred to Gaul. And now those who wish to learn the matter carefully depart for Britain for the sake of learning" (Caesar, *De Bello Gallico* [Of the Gaulish Wars], trans. Lea, in Koch 2003, 21–22).

The notion that there are three grades or specialisms associated with Druidry has its roots in antiquity, too. Strabo (Greek geographer, ca. 63 BCE–

---

1. Some of these festivals are known by other names, e.g. Lughnasadh for Lammas.

ca. 24 CE) wrote: "As a rule, among all the Gallic peoples three sets of men are honoured above all others: the Bards, the *Vates* and the Druids. The bards are singers and poets, the Vates overseers of sacred rites and philosophers of nature, and the Druids, besides being natural philosophers, practice moral philosophy as well" (*Geography* 4.4.4, trans. Fortson, in Koch 2003, 18). He placed the Druids in Gaul, while Pliny the Elder (Roman naturalist, 23–79 CE) located them in both Gaul and Britain:

> Gaul also possessed [magic] down to the time of our memory. Thus it was during the reign of the Emperor Tiberius that a decree was issued by the Senate against the [Gauls'] entire class of Druids, *Vates*, and physicians. Why do I comment on this craft that has spread beyond the ocean to the far reaches of the earth? Nowadays, Britain continues to be held spellbound by magic and conducts so much ritual that it would seem that it was Britain that had given magic to the Persians. (*Natural History* 30.13, trans. Freeman and Koch, in Koch 2003, 33)

Pliny the Elder also gave us the image of white robed Druids cutting mistletoe: "A priest in white clothing climbs the tree and cuts the mistletoe with a golden sickle, and it is caught in a white cloak" (*Natural History* 16.24, trans. Freeman and Koch, in Koch 2003, 32).

While the Greek and Roman sources provide much of what we think of as Druidic—oak trees, mistletoe and the three divisions—stone monuments were not mentioned. It was later in the seventeenth and eighteenth centuries that a nationalistic interest in Britain's ancient monuments led to speculation about the possibility that Britain once had a culture to rival the Greeks. Early antiquarians, including John Aubrey (1626–1697) and William Stukeley (1687–1765), suggested that it was Druids who built stone circles such as Avebury and Stonehenge, and this idea persisted until later archaeologists dated these monuments to the late Neolithic (ca 3000 to 2300 BCE) and thought it unlikely Druids existed that far back. However, many Druids speculate, as Kris Hughes does, that they "have always existed here in the British Isle from the Neolithic era through to today… The Druids of the Iron Age were simply an extension of an older priesthood" (2007, 17–18).

The Druid fraternities that emerged in the seventeenth and eighteenth centuries, detailed in Ronald Hutton's *Blood and Mistletoe* (2009), considered themselves "revivals" of ancient Druid groups. Hutton attributes to Stukeley the idea that Aubrey revived the fourteenth century Mount Haemus Grove, itself said to have been reformed from remnants of earlier Druids (Hutton 2006, 6–7). A plaque on the King's Arms pub in London says the Ancient Order of Druids were "revived" in 1781, also making a direct link to earlier Druids. Another figure, Edward Williams (1747–1826), who took the bardic name Iolo Morganwg, claimed to have found ancient Druid manuscripts.

He also founded the Gorsedd (gathering of bards), which still exists today. His "Druid's Prayer" is still chanted at the Gorsedd and other Druid gatherings, though Pagan Druids replace references to God with Spirit or Goddess.[2] Williams also depicted the symbol for *awen* (inspiration of bards) as three rays: /|\, widely used to symbolize Druidry today.

Despite the unreliability of the Greek and Roman sources (with most based on second-hand reports), and the speculative and dubious nature of the antiquarian sources, the figure of the white-robed Druid emerged, blended with Arthurian romance tales of Merlin, and portrayed as a bearded wizard meddling in politics and urging on armies of Britons against invaders. As Ronald Hutton observed: "The process of selection made to compose the result is more or less an arbitrary one, determined by the instincts, attitudes, context and loyalties of the person engaged in it" (2009, 48), in this case Celtic revivalism with nationalistic overtones.

While contemporary Druids accept Hutton's historical analysis that Druidry is, for the most part, a modern invention, it doesn't prevent them from voicing opinions about how to manage ancient sites and care for any human remains found therein. It is interesting that some site managers appear to have accepted Druids and Pagans as representing the ancient Britons in some way. Blain and Wallis have noted that heritage managers, in England at least, have co-opted the term 'sacred site" from Pagans, who in turn co-opted it from indigenous archaeology discourse (Blain and Wallis 2007, 1). The authors provide several examples of this, such as one from The English Heritage World Heritage Site Management Plan for Avebury: "Paganism may well be the fastest growing religion in Britain and this is linked with the increasing interest in the mystical significance of Avebury as a 'sacred' place" (quoting Pomeroy, 1998); and, on the *Time Team* (TV programme), archaeologist Francis Prior said: "I think what I have learnt, largely due to our pagan friends, is that as an archaeologist I'm too analytical and I'm too removed from [Seahenge]… I've learnt to get back to treating it as a religious site, as a religious thing."

Indigenous or indigenizing?

The question remains, though, on whether Druidry can be considered an indigenous religion, even if it had originated in Britain (whether 2500 years ago or 50). This is because Druidry does not fit usual definitions of "indigenous religion." Its practitioners are not indigenous people, at least not accord-

---

2. The most common form of the "Druid's Prayer" by Iolo Morganwg begins with "Grant, O God, Thy protection" (Williams, ed. 2004, 363, from *The Barddas*, originally published in 1862), rephrased as "Grant, O Spirit [or Goddess], Thy protection."

ing to definitions accepted by the United Nations or most anthropologists (see Owen 2013, 82–83). Despite animist rhetoric in more recent forms of Druidry, neither are they kinship-based, meaning based on maintaining relations among extended family groups, accepted as a criterion for "indigenous religion" by scholars such as James Cox (2007, 69), who gives his "minimum definition" of indigenous religions as "bound to a location," sharing a "kinship-based worldview in which attention is directed towards ancestor spirits as the central figures in religious life and practice." That these elements exist in all recognized indigenous religions is debatable, but Druidry is neither bound to a specific location nor practised only among closely related individuals, and only vaguely refers to ancestors, which may be connected to a place, Druids who have passed on, or times in a ritual when each individual contemplates their own ancestry rather than that of the group's.

Nor is Druidry in Britain strictly an "indigenizing movement" in the sense outlined by Paul Johnson (2002), although it does reconstruct pre- and early-Christian practices and borrows from or is inspired by the practices of indigenous peoples. Since it is possible that Druidry originated in Britain, or at least was part of a pre-Roman culture in Europe, can it be said to be indigenizing? However, what they are indigenizing is the rhetoric derived from Native American campaigns, including the practice of acknowledging the local often unnamed "spirits of place."

Johnson (2002, 302) views indigenizing as the opposite of globalizing, yet modern Druidry does both—one could say it is globalizing what it is indigenizing. Johnson does recognize that this is a spectrum and not either/or, but more of an emphasis, but this is difficult to generalize one way or the other with British Druidry, which includes the whole spectrum, with some close-knit localized independent Druid groups to global enterprises such as the Order of Bards, Ovates and Druids (OBOD). In this sense, Druidry is also extending: described by Johnson (2002, 312) as "the lowering of social boundaries, the circulation of religious knowledge and symbols into wider availability, and the overt assimilation of new forms acknowledged to be from outside." That is, practitioners in other parts of the world are encouraged to adapt Druidry to their own local seasons and flora and fauna.

Indigeneity discourse

Whilst indigenous discourses are in part a product of displacement either in territory or culture, modern Druids might develop a grudge against Romans or Christians in the romantic sense of an imagined loss of ethnic British culture, identity or religion, but cannot claim to be "colonized," which fuels much indigeneity discourse (e.g. as described by Linda Tuhiwai Smith, 1999,

7). There are cases among indigenous groups where the boundaries between colonized and colonizer, a binary which may have had historical relevance, has been blurred. This is so in cases where indigenous people claim mixed heritage, such as the Metis, or where boundaries were always ambiguous, such as in India and in some areas of Africa.

While Dakota scholar Vine Deloria (1973; also see Owen 2013) urged Europeans in North America to look to Druidry rather than Native American traditions to engage in their own native spirituality, it is not clear how much he understood Druidry. If, following common Pagan Druid practice, they would learn the seasons, plants and animals of their region, it would then be difficult to avoid overlapping with Native American cultural practices and accusations of appropriation. As far as I can determine, they only fall foul of this if they misrepresent themselves or practices as "Native American" or employ virtually identical practices and profiteering from them. They also create conflict when conducting ceremonies on sites associated with Native American groups (e.g., Mount Shasta in California; see Albanese 1990).

Harvey (2007, 232) alludes to these tensions, saying: "Even if some Pagans romanticize native peoples as "close to nature," and may even appropriate indigenous practices, few are actively engaged, or even concerned, with what activates and constrains indigenous well-being today." Likewise, Armin Geertz (2004, 62) argues that the generally positive primitivism which romanticizes indigenous cultures tends to "keeps real indigenous peoples out of the picture just as effectively as the scientific racism of the nineteenth century" as it does not address the varied situations indigenous people are in today. However, there are a few Druids who do engage with indigenous communities, such Philip Shallcrass of the British Druid Order (more on this below).

Native versus indigenous

The difference between "native" and "indigenous" is more in how the terms are employed. The most common application of "indigenous" is to a group of people based on an ethno-political category identifying only those who have experienced colonization. Indigeneity, as an identity formation, is prominent in discourses distinguishing between the culturally or genetically threatened "us" (the indigenous) from the polluting, controlling or otherwise threatening foreign "them" (the colonizer), contrasting themselves with those they construct as their alterity.

In British Druid publicity, including websites, "native" is the more common term over "indigenous" (with some exceptions), possibly because it has a wider application and can mean "coming from" or "belonging to" a place in non-ethnic terms, such as being a "native of New York," and, in Druidry, includes making physical and imaginative connections to a place, which is regarded as the more appropriate use of the term for many of those identifying Druidry with "native spirituality."

Rarely do British Druids refer to themselves as native or indigenous as a personal identity. However, they do cite connections between Druidry and Native American ways, as seen in this example from the Order of Bards, Ovates and Druids:

> Yes, they have much in common: sacred circles, the honouring of the directions, a deep reverence for the natural world, a belief in animal guides, and an abiding sense that the land itself is sacred. There is even evidence that the Druids worked in sweat-lodges and we know that birds' feathers were used in ceremonial clothing and headdress...[3]

This is followed by a statement exempting Druidry from accusations of "appropriation" by implying that Druids are not taking from Native American traditions but have commonality.

However, several prominent Druids have had direct contact with Native American groups—Of those personally known to me, Philip Shallcrass (BDO) has visited the Quileute in Washington State and the late David Morgan Brown (Druids of Albion) spent time with the Dakota in Midwest USA. Philip Shallcrass, known as Greywolf, published a blog post recently about Druidry as an indigenous tradition (Shallcrass 2019).[4] In this piece, Shallcrass addresses criticisms about the claim first by quoting Julius Caesar on Druid learning coming from Britain (see above). Although they may have been indigenous to Britain two thousand years ago, Shallcrass states that "endeavouring to reconstruct it as a spirituality indigenous to those regions seems perfectly valid" and that this is further justifiable because "Native Americans encourage people of European descent to find their own ancestral tradition, rather than steal theirs." As elsewhere, he follows this by rejecting nationalism and racism and ends his post by saying the British Druid Order is open to all.

Some Druids have also been inspired by Saami people, Australian aborigines and other indigenous peoples. For example, the drum most used is less like an Irish bodhran and more like one played by a sub-Arctic shaman or Plains Indian, perhaps, though other Druids have reconstructed old north European folk instruments out of deer antler, animal hide, etc. Philip Shall-

---

3. Order of Bards, Ovates and Druids (OBOD), "About us," date unknown. http://www.druidry.org/about-us/frequently-asked-questions [accessed 04.04.2015].

4. Shallcrass, Philip, "Indigeneity and Celtic Druidry," British Druid Order Blog, 31 January 2019. https://britishdruidorder.wordpress.com/2019/01/31/indigeneity-and-celtic-druidry/?fbclid=IwAR0cKaYaQLR72zWe40-Oq6MjefSk9cfU2QhpdnM-1h9EreZvQZr0zIznDytM [accessed 20.02.19]

crass and friends have re-created an iron-age roundhouse, with others trying their hand at iron-age jewellery, wool-craft, brewing mead—all more or less engaging in their own experimental archaeology. Modern Druids, if put together, could constitute a reasonably productive late iron-age village. In this way, these contemporary Druids might observe what other indigenous peoples are doing, in supporting native crafts and produce, and then look for something similar within their own cultures and histories.

Native faith?

How does Druidry compare to Native Faith traditions and their nationalistic tones? Some forms of Druidry may be characterized in this way but the majority of Orders in Britain largely avoid this through openness to non-British participants and encouragement to those in other cultures to adapt Druidry to their own landscape, mythology and heritage, just as many British Druids have substituted Native American flora and animal symbols with British ones.

Some of the rituals I've attended in England in particular have striven to be apolitical in terms of national identities. They have tended to articulate "native spirituality" as inclusive of all the British Isles and removing distinctly Irish, Welsh and Scots political identities, perceiving that the land, or rather group of islands, has no borders. In Scotland, I have come across both pan-British and Scottish nationalist (including Gaelic) identifications, depending on the group, though none that I know of have excluded participants based on ethnicity or nationality. The only incident I have witnessed was in 1989 when Kaledon Naddair, a Scottish Druid, charged up Arthur's Seat in Edinburgh to criticize a Mexican Indian conducting a non-native (to Scotland) ceremony. This ended peacefully when it was admitted he had a point and that the ceremony was conducted with respect to the land. Naddair himself has made the claim that "Pictish and Keltic shamanism is the native initiatory system practised by the ancient Druids" (Naddair 1990, 94, quoted in Wallis 2003, 84).

The Druidry that regards itself as "native spirituality" also tends to refer to Spirit or spirits in their rituals, as mentioned before, rather than specific deities from Irish, Welsh or other sources. And they are certainly not "reviving" ancient Druidry, whatever it was, though some have made that claim in the past (e.g. the Ancient Order of Druids). According to Graham Harvey (2007, 231): "The claim that Pagans are reviving ancient pre-Christian religious practices and cultures is less common than it once was, but can still be encountered…." In any case, more recently, Harvey (2007, 231) says, "To be indigenous is to know where one is in relation to a place and an ancestry that are both conceived of in ways distinguishable from racially centred, individu-alistically consumed modernity."

It is this that brings me to argue that British Druidry is more concerned about respectful relations to the land and heritage than to nationalistic inter-ests. When the Druid Network applied for charitable status in England and Wales, its application stated that "Druidry is based on the reverential, sacred and honourable relationship between people and the land" (Charity Com-mission for England and Wales 2010, Annex 1). Ancestral dimensions do play a part for some—especially those with strong connections to Irish, Welsh or Scottish ancestry. Few people claim to be hereditary Druids, and more likely those who live outside of Britain (perhaps to bolster their legitimacy). It is unlikely a Welsh Druid within Wales would make such a claim. Kris Hughes spoke about this at a Druid Camp I attended. He said that, although he was taught by an older relative, he would not claim hereditary status.

Does Druidry escape nationalism? Most Druid group leaders and individu-als root out these tendencies, calling out those who post anything discrimi-natory on group forums and promoting respectful, internationalist, liberal and inclusive attitudes. The British Druid Order "pinned post" on Facebook by Adam Sargant says: "Our membership is international and we welcome friends from all cultures" (dated 26 August 2016).

Romantic Druidry

Indigeneity is an act of the imagination combining ideas of emplacement, the past and personal identity. Johnson (2002, 327) recognizes this, too:

> When understood as an imagined community, as a processual term, and as an ideal type never fully manifested in history, the indigenous can yet prove an important category for the comparative study of religion, both to understand those "on the land" as well as those for whom the homeland is an idea, an image, and a memory.

Blain and Wallis (2007, 10) "proposed the term 'new-indigenes' to describe those Pagans whose re-enchantment practices involve perceiving nature as animate—alive with spirits [etc.] and who identify with pagan Iron Age and Early Mediaeval ancestors from ancient Europe, finding resonance with ear-lier prehistoric cultures and indigenous 'tribal' societies elsewhere, particu-larly those whose 'religion' is animist and/or 'shamanistic.'" Yet, they also say "lineage and authenticity *vis-à-vis* the ancient pagan past…is less of an issue" than making pagan practices relevant in the contemporary world.

It is this romantic quality, not too far from that of the nineteenth century romantics, that imbues Druidry with a special emphasis on nature that is shared with many earlier romantics from Goethe to Morris. Blain and Wallis

(2007, xiv) also recognized this, saying Pagan interest in heritage is not new, referring to romanticism. They describe Paganism as having a "focus on direct engagements with 'nature' as deified, sacred or otherwise animated by 'spirit' or forming a living community of 'spirits'" (Blain and Wallis 2007, xiv).

Likewise, Harvey (2007, 232) says: "That Paganisms offer re-enchantment of the world is a common theme among academic discussions... Pagans can evidence a romantic (and, thus, still modernist) view of their relation to 'nature.'" Thus, Druid interest in nature and heritage is more akin to the romanticism of the Arts and Craft Movement of William Morris.

Druidry as nature spirituality

Examples from contemporary Druid authors that illustrate this engagement with nature and heritage are numerous. Taking a selection of books by well-known British Druids, all the covers show trees. The association of Druids with trees stems from ancient sources associating them with carrying out rituals in groves, cutting mistletoe, and the word itself is understood by many Druids to come from a Welsh word for oak, *derw*, combined with *wid*, Indo-European root for knowledge. The path these Druid authors describe is based on a personal experience of nature.

The blurb on the back of *Living Druidry* (2004) by Emma Restall Orr (once of the British Druid Order and founder of the Druid Network) says: this "book guides you to find your own vision, and your own deep, ecstatic relationship with nature.... so that each moment is enriched with nature's power and beauty." In the first chapter, Restall Orr likens her message to that of an indigenous woman, while also addressing romantic notions of such:

> many might well find it easier to accept what I have to say if I were writing from the context of a rainforest in Central America, southern Africa or south-east Asia, where the women trancing to the drumbeat she hears in her soul is dark skinned, barefoot, dressed in nothing but a strip of cloth, beads and feathers, with wild black eyes—or even if she were some European apprentice to a "native shaman" in the American desert. (Restall Orr 2004, 4–5)

In other words, someone in Britain need not search for a native spirituality in another continent under the tutelage of an indigenous teacher but can find it on their doorstep: "the spiritual tradition that offers me the language with which I understand the world I see... is the tradition of our own ancestral heritage, the native nature religion of the British Isles: Druidry" (Restall Orr 2004, 5). And it can be found in "the themes and visions of children's tales, in folklore, ale songs, superstitions and mythologies" and, where there are gaps, we can "study the archaeology" (2004, 22). In the same year her book was published, Restall Orr set up Honouring the Ancient Dead (HAD) to dialogue with archaeologists and museums over the treatment of ancient human remains. Druids therefore claim a similar role as indigenous people acting as cultural representatives when calling for the repatriation of indigenous remains held in museums where there are no known direct descendants.

A Druid who is actually Welsh and speaks the language is Kristoffer Hughes of the Anglesey Druid Order. The back-page to his *Natural Druidry* (2007), after quoting Taliesen "The Awen I sing, from the deep I bring it," says that the book "is a deeply personal account of one man's journey through the dappled groves of culture and tradition." At the end of the blurb it says: "Journey with Kris into the magic of the past and the present, deep into the vast cauldron of spiritual enlightenment that sings from the land, that whispers to us upon the breeze as the breath of our ancestors." Although Hughes draws heavily on his Welsh heritage and landscape, he claims "I am no one particularly special; I have no direct lineage to the ancient Druids, no secret or ancient manuscript that only I will ever see" (2007, 8)—he is reaching out to everyone to say his Druidry is for all. Like Restall Orr, his book tells a personal story to encourage others to be inspired by the land.

In the final example, the blurb on the back of *The Path of Druidry* (2011) by Penny Billington of the Order of Bards, Ovates and Druids reads: "Listen to the call of spirit and seek truth in wild groves, the shifting seasons, and the beauty of the Old Ways." The "exercises will help you internalize these truths, develop a spiritual awareness rooted in nature…." This leaves the reader in no doubt that this is a "nature spirituality" that is accessible to all who follow the path laid out by Billington based on her years of experience of running workshops and rituals. It is not an imaginary nature she refers to but urges the reader to walk in a green space (2011, 28), even if a city park. The content is structured around the Four Branches of the Mabinogion, lending contemporary Druidry an air of authenticity as a continuation and adaptation of an older tradition.

Druidry by these accounts is thus a nature-based native spirituality lived within Northern European landscapes, seasons and myths. All three emphasize Druidry's contemporary relevance and universality, quite far removed from the Druids encountered by Romans two thousand years ago, though for any tradition to be a living one it must be as thus.

Conclusion

The stumbling block for Druids, still, is that indigenous religions are usually defined as the religions of indigenous people (as does Johnson 2002, 308), which has always struck me as odd, considering many indigenous people are Christian, Muslim, Buddhist or whatever.

Johnson adds that indigenous religion, like the French term *les autochtones*, "connotes the religion of peoples that is the natural growth of a particular land, an organic, biological relation between a group and a place" (2002, 309). But nothing actually springs from the land in terms of human culture—it is what humans make of the land and imagine it to be. Yet, being born in a place where your ancestors have been buried is a special quality that has been threatened by modernity let alone colonization. People in Britain have had to move for education and work, or because they can and want to explore somewhere else. It is this response to modernity that leads Druids to yearn for a connection to place they believe is possessed by indigenous people; but they too have experienced its loss. Thus "indigeneity" becomes conscious when threatened.

References

Albanese, Catherine L. 1990. *Nature Religion in America: From the Algonkian Indians to the New Age.* Chicago, IL: University of Chicago Press.

Billington, Penny. 2011. *The Path of Druidry: Walking the Ancient Green Way.* Woodbury: Llewellyn.

Blain, Jenny and Robert Wallis. 2007. *Sacred Sites/Contested Rites/Rights: Pagan Engagements with Archaeological Monuments.* Brighton: Sussex Academic.

Cox, James. 2007. *From Primitive to Indigenous.* Farnham: Ashgate.

Deloria, Vine. 1973. *God is Red.* New York: Grosset and Dunlap.

Harvey, Graham. 2007. *Listening People, Speaking Earth: Contemporary Paganism.* 2nd edition. London: Hurst and Co.

Hughes, Kristoffer. 2007. *Natural Druidry.* Loughborough: Thoth Publications.

Hutton, Ronald. 2009. *Blood and Mistletoe: The History of the Druids in Britain.* New Haven, CT, Yale University Press.

Johnson, P. C. 2002. "Migrating bodies, circulating signs: Brazilian Candomblé, the Garifuna of the Caribbean, and the category of indigenous religions." *History of Religions* 41(4): 301–327. https://doi.org/10.1086/463690

Koch, John T. 2003. *The Celtic Heroic Age: Literary Sources for Ancient Celtic Europe and Early Ireland and Wales.* 4th Revised edition. Aberystwyth: Celtic Studies Publications.

Naddair, Kaledon. 1990. "Pictish and Celtic shamanism." In *Voices from the Circle: The Heritage of Western Paganism.* edited by P. Jones and C. Matthews, 93–108. Northampton: Aquarian.

Owen, Suzanne (2013) "Druidry as an indigenous religion." In *Critical Reflections on Indigenous Religions*, edited by J. Cox, 81–92. Farnham: Ashgate.

Restall Orr, Emma. 2004. *Living Druidry: Magical Spirituality of the Wild Soul.* London: Piatkus.

Shallcrass, Philip and Emma Restall Orr. 2001. *A Druidry Directory: A Guide to Druidry and Druid Orders*. Devizes: British Druid Order.

Smith, Linda Tuhiwai. 1999. *Decolonizing Methodologies: Research and Indigenous Peoples*. London: Zen Books / Dunedin: University of Otago Press.

Wallis, Robert. 2003. *Shamans/Neo-Shamans: Contested Ecstasies, Alternative Archaeologies, and Contemporary Pagans*. London: Routledge. https://doi.org/10.4324/9780203417577

Williams ab Ithal, John, ed. 2004. *The Barddas of Iolo Morgawg: A collection of original documents, illustrative of the theology, wisdom, and usages of the Bardo-Druidic system of the Isle of Britain*. Boston, MA: Weiser Books.

About the author

Suzanne Owen obtained her PhD from the University of Edinburgh in 2007 and is currently Reader in Religious Studies at Leeds Trinity University researching indigeneity in Newfoundland, including representations of the Beothuk, contemporary British Druidry and public classifications of "religion." She was Co-Chair of the Indigenous Religious Traditions Group at the American Academy of Religion from 2009–2015 and has been the Coordinating Editor of the Journal of the *British Association for the Study of Religions* (formerly *Diskus*) since 2012. Her first monograph, *The Appropriation of Native American Spirituality*, was published by Continuum (now Bloomsbury Academic) in 2008. Her next monograph with Bloomsbury will be on Contemporary Druidry as a "native tradition".

— 6 —

Powwowing My Way: Exploring Johnson's Concepts of Indigenizing and Extending through the Lived Expressions of American Indian-ness by European Powwow Enthusiasts

CHRISTINA WELCH

This chapter explores Johnson's concepts of indigenizing and extending through the lens of European pow-wow. Drawing on his argument that "identifying practices of indigenousness…are imagined through global media and often expressed in their forms" it begins with an overview of historical European representations of American Indians: representations that were virtually global at the time, and have led to the ubiquitous image of the Indian (or possibly *indian* using the hyperreal simulation argument put forward by Vizenor). Such representations dominate the European pow-wow scene, where individuals don Indian garb and dance at social events, many of which are open to the public. The chapter then focuses on the English pow-wow scene, contrasting it with parade Hobbyism. Here individuals dress up as *indians* for public commemorations on Bonfire Night (November 5th annually). Both groups can be understood as conforming to Johnson's extending narrative: the "circulation of religious knowledge and symbols into wider availability…[allowing] what was once a local truth [to be] presented as a more broadly applicable, even a universal one." However, the far more complex matter of indigenizing requires discussion of contentious issues of appropriation.

Paul Johnson suggests in his article "Migrating Bodies, Circulating Signs," that the "identifying practices of indigenousness…are imagined through global media and often expressed in their forms" (2005, 65). Nowhere is this more the case than with a specific group of Europeans who find a form of indigeneity through interactions with American Indian-ness, typically mediated via influences from the global media: European powwow enthusiasts —individuals who, put simply, dress up and dance as American Indians in public pow-wow-style events. In this chapter I explore European pow-wowing in general, and English pow-wowing in particular (alongside an allied phenomenon of parade hobbyism), and do so through Johnson's concepts of indigenizing and extending.

Indigenizing, for Johnson, is a process of bringing the outside world into the boundaries of a Weberian ideal-typical construct of the "Indigenous." He defines this as an abstract and imagined discrete fusion of "a people, a place, and a set of beliefs and practices" that never was, nor ever has been (2002a, 312). He contrasts indigenizing with what he terms an extending discourse (2005, 70–71) where the ideal-typical passes out into the wider world. He argues that these two processes can occur together although "extensions and indigenizations will entail changes in tradition [which] purists…will not approve [of]" (2005, 80). Although tradition in Indigenous lifeways is dynamic and evolving (Dayton and Ragoff 2013, 109), including pow-wow activity (Johnson 2013), there is often a sense in European culture of what Indigenous tradition is, or should be (Welch 2007). Thus, whilst Johnson may argue that the ideal-typical does not in reality exist, for many Europeans the ideal-typical American Indian is a reality. Their sense of the ideal-typical American Indian is based around visual and literary representations that romanticized the pre-reservation largely Plains and Woodlands Indian lifeway of the nineteenth century. This is particularly the case with European pow-wow activity.

Pow-wows are essentially highly symbolic American Indian ceremonial social gatherings with spiritual elements. Although their roots lie with the Plains and Prairie peoples of North America, pow-wows have become a pan-Indian phenomenon, a vibrant and developing tradition that features singing and dance. Pow-wows act as an opportunity for American Indian peoples to honour their cultures and heritages, and pow-wowing today stands as a major signifier of American Indian-ness for both American Indian peoples, and the wider populace.

The predominantly White-Western pursuit of dressing, dancing and ritualizing as American Indians through pow-wow, although not a mass activity, is one to be found in the U.S.A., Canada, Australia, Japan, and across large stretches of Europe, with regular gatherings in England[1] (Welch 2007), Germany[2] (Colloway, Germünden and Zantop 2002), Denmark,[3] Poland,[4] France[5]

---

1. See: https://www.bisonfarm.co.uk/Events.html and http://northamptonpowwow.co.uk (last accessed 19/8/2018)

2. See: http://www.naaog.de/about-us-1.html (last accessed 19/8/2018)

3. See: http://www.powwows.dk/eng/en/eng_why.html (last accessed 19/8/2018)

4. See: http://www.huuskaluta.com.pl/powwow.php (last accessed 19/8/2018)

5. See: https://www.festivalpowwow.com and http://www.courrier-picard.fr/105896/article/2018-04-25/les-savignons-de-lassociation-savy-western-partagent-leur-rencontre-avec-les (last accessed 19/8/2018)

(Jacqueman 2018), Bulgaria,[6] the Czech Republic[7] (Holley 2007), Sweden, and Switzerland (Browner 2011, 74). Although not all pow-wow enthusiasts seek to identify as American Indians, most do experiment with indigeneity based around their notion of the ideal-typical American Indian.

In order to understand the construct of the ideal-typical American Indian as it relates to European pow-wow enthusiasts, and explore how the concept of indigenizing relates to this construct, this chapter briefly (and somewhat simply) explores the long history of global media representations of American Indians. It was these representations that allowed, and continue to allow, Europeans to take on aspects of an ideal-typical American Indian-ness, and locate themselves within a form of indigeneity.

Very early European representations of American Indians include illustrations in the 1590 book *America*, by Theodore de Bry; a work that was almost global (or at least almost global for the era) in its reach. Reprinted fifty times in four languages, *America* was used as the authoritative text on American Indians well into the nineteenth century and as such has to be seen as a form of early global media informing Europeans about peoples in the New World (Pratt 2005). Interestingly in terms of Johnson's concepts of indigenizing and extending, *America* visually associated American Indians with Ancient Britons. John White, an artist on Sir Walter Raleigh's expedition to the New World in 1585 illustrated tattooed Virginians on Roanoke island (c. 1585–1586) and these formed the basis of representations of Ancient Picts: a pre-Christian Scots-Celtic tribe associated with nakedness and savagery (Smiles 2009). The illustrations, modified by de Bry, also appeared in *A Briefe and True Report of the New Found Land of Virginia* by Thomas Hariot (1588), a scientist, scholar and explorer. Hariot's use of the term "True" in the book title added weight to veracity of the visual claim that there was a link between Ancient Britons and American Indians, particularly in terms of their opposition to colonizing forces—the Pictish people were popularly believed to have held the Romans at bay, although in reality took on some aspects of Roman culture (Foster 2014, iv). As such, these early images set-the-tone for the use of visual representations of American Indians as uncivilized yet somewhat-noble savages; arguably the over-riding understanding for much of the colonial period. This statement gains in significance when it is recognized that the rhetoric behind the images in Hariot's work was highly political as they had an anti-Catholic bias at a time when Protestant countries were competing with Catholic ones to colonize the New World (see Canny 2012), and

---

6. See: http://www.eaglecircle.org (last accessed 19/8/2018)

7. See: http://powwow.cz and https://www.woodcraft.cz/index.php?right=history_czechin-dian&lan=en (last accessed 19/8/2018)

sought to Other the New World's original inhabitants and thereby demonstrate the need for a civilizing Protestant guiding influence (see Moran 2017).

From the mid-nineteenth century onwards the predominant global media representations of American Indians were found in the phenomena of the so-called World's Fairs. These international expositions started in London in 1851 with the "Great Exhibition of the Works of Industry of All Nations"; commonly known as the "Crystal Palace Exhibition" or "Great Exhibition" (Allwood 1977). Although the 1851 Crystal Palace Exhibition did not feature actual American Indians, a large marble statue entitled *The Wounded Indian* (Stephenson 1850) depicted a romanticized dying Eastern Woodland Indian in Greco-Roman style. This normalized the body image of the represented man making him look less of an "outsider" to the largely White-Western viewing public. Praised for its 'anatomical and ethnographic accuracy' this piece was considered a central exhibit for the Fair and featured both in the official souvenir handbook and in a prominent descriptive publication of the event: *Tallis' History and Criticism of the Crystal Palace* ([1852] in Clark 1997, 186). Perceived as immensely symbolic, the sculpted figure of the "wounded and fallen [Indian was understood as]…typifying the race" (Tallis [1852] in Clark 1997, 187): a once proud people vanishing into history, much like the Picts.

The effect of this life-size marble statue on the sensibilities of the Victorian public was furthered by an exhibition of the paintings, writings, and collected artefacts of the traveller and painter George Catlin (d. 1987). Catlin, who had already toured much of Europe with his exhibits (American Indian garb and artefacts, his own paintings of American Indian people and their lifeways, and also on occasions live American Indians), was well known for his romanticized representations of the American Indian peoples, and particularly their buffalo hunts (Moore 1997). However, although glorifying their alleged undomesticated freedom, Catlin's writings emphasized the imminent downfall of traditional American Indian lifeways as Christian civilization advanced ever more westwards (Catlin 1840, 1848). The situating of the "Wounded Indian" statue and Catlin's artefacts in such close proximity at "Crystal Palace" ensured that the overall perception of American Indian-ness to the visiting public was that of a homogenized race in terminal decline. This was reinforced by notions of Manifest Destiny (effectively the God-given right of territorial expansionism) and the overarching power of the White Protestant Northern European civilized world (Bass and Cherwitz 1978).

Interestingly, the romanticized Victorian perception of the American Indian found its way into the bohemian literary society founded in 1857 called the Savage Club, where authors, journalists and artists would meet in "wigwams" (a meeting room often in taverns) to "pow-wow" (chat). The name of the society reflected the members' perceived status as "outside the pale of civilization" (Watson 1907, 19), a perception that, as I will show later, resonates particularly with English pow-wow enthusiasts.

The reach of the World's Fairs (also known as Expositions or Exhibitions), and thus the reach of the Western constructed image of the American Indian, took shape in the U.S.A. Here American Indian peoples and aspects of their lifeways were displayed in anthropological exhibitions, and the Midway area of the Fairs; the pleasure rather than the education section, and one which typically featured real-life American Indians in constructed village situations. The Philadelphia Exposition of 1876 is particularly notable for its homogenizing of American Indians into a primitive, static, and undifferentiated mass of people. Coming barely a month after the defeat of General Custer by the Sioux and the Cheyenne at the Battle of Little Big Horn (1876), newspapers of the time reinforced public perceptions of American Indian brutality, and although the Exposition sought to educate visitors about the diversity of American Indians and their customs, the seemingly savage undifferentiated artefacts on display emphasized the barbaric nature of this uncivilized race, whilst their religious paraphernalia emphasized them as un-Christian (Greenhalgh 1988; Rydell 1987; Maxwell 1999). By the time of the Louisiana Purchase Exposition (1904) however, with so-called troublesome leaders such as Sitting Bull, Red Shirt, and Geronimo either killed, captured and capitulated, there were opportunities at the Fairs to show the assimilation of American Indians peoples into the dominant culture. Such displays included the alleged benefits of a Christian mission-school style education where American Indian children could be "educated, civilized and enlightened:" effectively de-Indianized (Troutman and Parezo 1998).

Attended by millions of people from all over the Western and Westernized (colonized) world, the World's Fairs of the late-nineteenth and early-twentieth century were truly global (for their time) with people travelling from as far away as New Zealand to witness the spectacles on show in Europe or North America. Although there is no record of American Indians appearing in the Australian or New Zealand expositions, in 1927 a group of so-called "Red Indians" visited a number of locations in Australia and New Zealand to publicize a film called "The Vanishing Race." This was influenced by the photographs and salvage ethnography of Edward Curtis' *The North American Indian* which was published between 1907–1930 with the title image captioned "The Vanishing Race (1904)."[8] Although the visiting delegation to the Antipodes consisted of

---

8. See "Red Indians 'United' en route to Rotorua" 1927, NGĀ TAONGA Sound and Vision Wellington, Ref: F20904 https://www.ngataonga.org.nz/collections/catalogue/catalogue-item?record_id=71825 (last accessed 19/8/2018)

members of the Navajo and Hopi tribes, the men dressed as Plains warriors in elaborate feather headdresses. Not only was the perception of the American Indian as a dying or vanishing race now normative, but so too was the ubiquitous image of the befeathered Indian or, to draw on the terminology of Gerald Vizenor, "*indian*" the "hyperreal" simulation of what is not, nor ever has been (Vizenor 1998, 28). This notion resonates with Johnson's use of the Weberian ideal-typical, and as such the *indian* as a concept has relevance to this chapter.

The overall ethos of visual representations of American Indians developed during the era of Victorian colonialism was arguably one that defined the image of the American Indian (or more probably *indian*) that Hollywood would later depict. Interestingly, the American Fairs and Expositions were often accompanied by Wild West Shows such as Buffalo Bill's. These toured their 'Indian versus Cowboy' theatricals around much of Europe as well as North America and helped to ensure that popular culture of the day depicted the American Indian as brutal, savage, homogenous, and ultimately destined to vanish in the wake of Christian colonialism (Welch 2011). However, American Indians were also the ultimate romantic anti-hero for those opposed to the Imperial West and its ideologies, such as those who founded the Savage Club; and the paintings of Catlin and especially the photographs of Curtis did much to add to this image. Noble chiefs, brave warriors, and often un-named but pretty young American Indian girls and women peppered the paintings and photographs, capturing a growing nostalgia for a country inhabited by people who were spiritually in touch with the land, and were prepared to defend their way of life with their life (Davis 1985). Writers such as James Fenimore Cooper (d. 1851), Henry Longfellow Wadsworth (d. 1882), and Karl May (d. 1912), wrote romanticized fiction about *indian* characters (*Last of the Mohicans* and the *Longstocking Tales, Hiawatha*, and *Winnetou; Chief of the Apache* respectively) and thus provided a literary addition to the noble savage genre (Smith 2000).

Further to this, over the twentieth century the John-Wayne-style Hollywood cowboy figure that was based on the Wild West shows noted above, shifted to the John Dunbar *Dances with Wolves* (1990) style protagonist (Rollins and O'Connor 1998), and thus the movie and novel *indian* became increasing the good-guy and the typical settler/cowboy, the bad-guy. Disney's animated film *Pocahontas* (1995) summed up the shift in the lyrics of the song "Savages"[9]: whilst in the movie the English may have been hurling the term at the American Indians, it was clearly a label they themselves fully inhabited.[10]

---

9. See "The Disney Wiki" http://disney.wikia.com/wiki/Savages (last accessed 19/8/2019)

10. For an exploration of the term savage see Jahoda (1999).

Although this seems a somewhat unsophisticated articulation of how those who came to take-on an indigenous identity through European pow-wowing, got to where they are, it is one that has been repeated to me time and again in my own research with English pow-wow enthusiasts,[11] and has resonance with interviews conducted with pow-wowers from wider Europe, especially Germany and countries in the former Soviet Union.

Beyond the German pow-wow scene, little has been written about Europeans who take on aspects of an American Indian identity. However, because there are very few American Indians living in Europe and, as Goetzen and Greer have noted, "few non-Indians at Indian pow-wows" (2012, 272), it is not always simple to assume whether the activities of those who take on aspects of American Indian-ness are approved of, vilified, or largely ignored by American Indians themselves. In England, pow-wowing was largely initiated by American Indian military personnel stationed in the U.K., and there are clear examples of continued Native involvement in the English pow-wow scene (Welch 2007). The same appears to be the case for German pow-wowing, where there is a long history of German-Indian contact (Sieg 2002, 217). Leaving aside the Prussian exploration of the American West (1832–1834) under Prince Maximillian (Moore 1997), it is notable that American Indians serving in the U.S. military were stationed in Germany from 1917, and due to the Cold War (1947–1991) remained post-WWII (Calloway 2002, 73, 76).

Despite the German popular cultural interest in all things American Indian being somewhat complicated by the 1939 German Government declaring "the Sioux to be 'Aryans'," and Hitler extolling the virtues of May's Apache chief Winnetou (Feest 2002, 25–26), "Indianthusiasm" is part of German subculture (Zantop 2002, 3). A number of re-enactment clubs and societies exist where members dedicate themselves to the "study and simulation of Oglala Sioux culture of the nineteenth century, crafting clothes and weapons with devotion to historical accuracy" (Goertzen and Greer 2012, 286). Seig argues that this has led to German re-enactors perceiving themselves as the "gatekeep of the Indian past," even if this is a somewhat idealized past (2002, 230–231). The historical re-enactment aspect of Indianthusiasm however, often rubs up against the German pow-wow scene. In 2002, during a research fieldtrip exploring Indianthusiasm, Watchman overheard an argument between these divergent groups of Indianthusiasts over what they each perceived as authentically traditional (2005, 244). However, in general both groups tend toward traditional garb, hence Seig's comment on Indianthusiasm tending towards salvage ethnography.

---

11. Research carried out at English pow-wow's between 1998–2004, and again between 2016–2017.

However, not all Indianthusiasts in wider Europe wear traditional clothing, and for some there is an element of dress-up. Seig interviewed a man who wore only a loin cloth and a feather in his hair whilst pow-wow dancing with a stone axe. His outfit, he stated, made his feel like a proper 'red man' (Asten in Seig 2002, 233). Whilst it is easy to scoff at this sort of play acting (Churchill 1998; Feest 2002), for some individuals such dressing-up was a form of a political protest. In the German Democratic Republic (GDR), hobbyism was often the only alternative to 'the prevailing drab and conformist lifestyle' and one that the authorities found 'hard to crack down on' given American Indians were being oppressed by the American Imperialism; and the GDR believed it too was being similarly oppressed by the same foreign force (Feest 2002, 32). Since German re-unification, Indianthusiasm has continued unabated. Two further examples offer (in part) contrasting trajectories. In 1999 the "Indian Village Europe" in Schloss Schönav was opened and regularly features American Indians who sell native goods (Calloway 2002, 76)—reinforcing the argument that Indigenous agency must be acknowledged in regard to those who take on American Indian-ness. In July 2004, "Silverlake City," a Wild West theme park inspired by May's books, opened at Templin, near Berlin (Hall 2004). It has been rebranded "El Dorado" and is a popular American West themepark with a more retrograde "Cowboys vs Indians" premise.[12]

But as noted earlier, pow-wowing in Europe is not confined to Germany, and there have been two anthropological/ethnographic films made concerning pow-wowing in Eastern Europe. Medicine and Baskauskas made a short film about Russian pow-wows called *Seeking the Spirit: Plains Indians in Russia* (1999) which included interviews with pow-wowers from across parts of the former Soviet Union including Russia and Lithuania, together with responses to their filmed activities from members of the Wakpala community of Standing Rock, South Dakota. The Russian pow-wow included aspects of vernacular folk dance, and incorporated aspects of American Indian-ness based on the adventure novels by May about the romantic noble savage, the Apache chief Winnetou, and his German blood-brother Old Shatterhand; given the fictional nature of the source for the Russian pow-wow participants, Vizenor's *indian*-ness might well be a more appropriate term here than American Indian-ness. However, the recorded activities clearly stemmed from a genuine interest in learning about American Indian culture and spirituality, and with popular culture severely limited under the Soviet regime, May's writings provided hope to oppressed peoples about the possibility of a better life, whilst providing an outlet for romantic yearnings of a time before their own colonization. As such, whilst from an academic standpoint these pow-wowers were

---

12. See https://www.eldorado-templin.de (last accessed 19/8/2019)

appropriating aspects of *indian*-ness *a la* May, from their own perspective they were sincerely attempting to indigenize as an American Indian; expressing a set of beliefs and practices that they identified with, and which echoed their own once-prohibited and now largely-lost vernacular culture.

Noticeably, one of the Wakpala stated on watching the recorded pow-wow that, 'if they're going to do that, they should have someone to teach them to do it right' (in Medicine and Baskauskas 1999). This is an interesting comment and speaks to the complexities around appropriation, as the Wakpala community members largely did not see those at the Russian pow-wow as appropriators. Although there has been much written on the appropriation of American Indian-ness (specifically the commercialization of spiritual practices, and the misuse and misrepresentation of American Indian signifiers), much tends to belittle those who are heartfelt in their allegedly appropriative actions (Hladki 1994; Ziff and Rao 1997; Deloria 1998; Aldred 200), and little acknowledges indigenous agency in cultural exchange (Welch 2007). With those at the Russian pow-wow, as the Walpaka noted, there was no commercialization of spirituality but there was misrepresentation, as the homespun event was ridden with inaccuracies; in part through the peppering of aspects of their own traditional culture, but largely due the work of fiction on which their perception of American Indian-ness was based. This latter issue resonates with Watchman's concern that European pow-wowers "have no familial connections to pass on pow-wow knowledge, [and thus] rely on a memorized embracing of a distinct, abstract form" of pow-wow, often taking ideas from popular cultural sources, including the ubiquitous novels about *indians* by May (2005, 248).

The influence of May in non-Native pow-wowing was also evident from the second film; Paskievich's *If Only I were an Indian* (1995). This documentary records the experiences of three American Indians (a Cree couple and an Ojibway woman), who were brought over from the U.S. to witness a Czech pow-wow. As with the Russian pow-wow, there were major issues with the dancing and singing, and the garb was largely inaccurate, and in conversation with the Czech pow-wowers, it was clear that May's writings provided the impetus for their activities. But again, as with the Russian pow-wowers, the Czech pow-wowers were sincere in their intentions which also provided a much-needed form of escapism from the after-effects of Soviet occupation. Once more, not understood by their American Indian audience as appropriators, a quote from one of Watchman's Wakpala interviewees resonated with their perceptions of the three native people; the Czech pow-wowers were "Indian in [their] heart" identifying more with "part of the culture, not of the people" (2005, 250).

This cardiac-American Indian phenomena was also evident from my contact in the Bulgarian pow-wow scene, which is similar to those in Russia and the Czech Republic in combining pow-wowing with weekend rural retreats. However, rather than May being the main influence, *Black Elk Speaks* by John Neihardt (1961) was virtually the only publication about American Indians available in Bulgaria at the inception of *Eagle Circle Indian Society* in 1990. A book with widespread influence (Powers 1990), it was the base for almost all their ceremonials. However, rather than vernacular traditions being included in the Bulgarian pow-wows, I was told that several members of the *Eagle Circle Indian Society* were also attracted to Celtic lifeways and had taken on aspects of an imagined Celticity alongside their American Indian one.[13] This once more raises issues of appropriation. In Bulgaria, another previously Soviet occupied country, there was the same romantic resonance of pre-occupied life that was evident in the pow-wowing activities at the Russian and Czech events. Yet whilst both of those incorporated dances from their own folk traditions, in Bulgaria this was not evident, and none of those at the Russian and Czech events incorporated an imagined Celticity. No work to date has been done on why there are such differences between pow-wowing influences in former Soviet states, but the colonization/occupation of these countries does upset the traditional rhetoric of the standard appropriation argument, which is heavily informed by perceptions of cultural theft by Westerners, and unbalanced power relations between native communities and the consumerist West. As such pow-wowers in England and Germany are potentially more open to accusations of being appropriative "culture vultures" (Rose 1992, 414) than those whose history did not shape the contemporary popular cultural representation of American Indians.

In England, with far more access to a wide variety of sources of information about American Indians, as well as long-standing contact with native people themselves, May and Black Elk are not so prevalent as pow-wow influences. Yet, in a similar vein to dancers at the Russian, Czech, and Bulgarian pow-wows, many of the English pow-wowers I interviewed perceived traditional Plains Indians to be the counterpoint to the contemporary industrialized Western culture. One man told me how beading his own regalia was his secret hobby. He claimed that his work mates would not understand how it allowed him to express an inner creativity as sewing was seen more as a female pursuit in England than one suitable for a burly working-class guy. He told me how on the Plains, "real men sewed, it wasn't only woman's work" (in Welch 2007). Another dancer spoke of the importance of Plains-style

---

13. Lymbo, personal correspondence 2003 regarding Bulgarian pow-wowing. See also Bowman (1995) for issues around Celticity as an imagined identity.

spirituality, and how he had completed several Sun Dances, as well as numerous sweat lodges and vision-quests (all under American Indian teachers); these he stated helped him to come to terms with emotional issues in his life. Further, female pow-wowers also found potent meaning in taking on aspects of an ideal-typical American Indian identity, and many I interviewed felt their femininity was more valued within American Indian culture (and thus the English pow-wow movement), than in their everyday Western life (Welch 2007). Some of the activities of these English pow-wowers can be understood as appropriative; Aldred for instance asserts that the impersonation of American Indian spirituality as a panacea to consumer capitalism is nothing more than "imperialistically nostalgic fetishization" (2000, 346), while Cuthbert and Grossman censure the de-historicization and de-politicization of American Indian culture by European pow-wow enthusiasts and others (1996). However, the issue of appropriation is far from clear with indigenous agency playing a role in the establishment and continuation of English pow-wow (and allied) events, and activities engaged in by English pow-wowers done so with a sense of respecting, rather than misrepresenting, the originating culture (Welch 2007).

I would argue therefore that despite potential issues of appropriation, in the examples of European (including English) pow-wowing noted above, there is a form of indigenizing, although in a way that adapts Johnson's concept. The European pow-wowers do not claim to be American Indians, although many believe they have a native soul/spirit, or some sort of spiritual connection with typically Plains people, although it is evident that this is an ideal-typical form American Indian-ness. In terms of the English pow-wow scene, regalia designs for example are taken from the historic portraits of Catlin, and the ethnographic photographs of Curtis, rather than from Youtube videos of contemporary native pow-wows. Indeed, the English pow-wow scene has a real sense of the traditional: I have not seen any Christian symbolism incorporated into regalia, yet this is not uncommon in American and Canadian pow-wow garb. Similarly, no English pow-wow I have attended has fancy dancers incorporating brightly coloured plastic tape into their regalia, although this is a regular feature in Stateside competition pow-wow garb (Welch 2007).

One young woman who was visiting England from Scandinavia however, danced in garb that incorporated a Nordic knotwork design into her Jingle Dress. Interestingly, she received a dressing down from the organizers and there were mutterings about the inappropriateness of her bricolage (Welch 2007). This is of note as essentially the English pow-wowers see themselves as representing how things were, not how things are, and as such there is much overlap with the observations of German pow-wow activity.

With an emphasis on the past over the present, English pow-wowers frequently told me that they gained wider information about American Indian culture from films. Indeed, some informants realized they had an affinity with American Indians through movies: from Hollywood "Cowboy and Indian" films, where they always took the side of the native characters, to *Dances with Wolves* which was almost universally understood by them as the most authentic portrayal of Plains culture on celluloid. However, the English pow-wow circuit also has regular visiting American Indians and these often teach about native spirituality, passing on what they claim to be long-held traditional knowledge. One informant spoke of how she learnt from Wa-Na-Nee-Che (Dennis Renault), an Ojibway medicine man who regularly taught in the U.K. and who co-published a DIY book on *Native American Spirituality* (1996). She found his sweat lodges helped her to grow spiritually and become more connected with nature; her own and the natural world. Other informants told me they had learnt from Tony Dreamwalker of Thunderwarriers, who claimed lineage from the Creek and Cherokee Nations, as well as from the Scottish (Celtic) Cameron and Davidson clans; notably his pow-wow garb physically embodied both genealogies utilizing tartan as the main material for his regalia. Dreamwalker's ancestry has echoes of White's late-sixteenth century Celtic/Pictish images, and speaks to the Bulgarian cardiac-Celts who also pow-wow. Dreamwalker ran weekend camps where he passed on his allegedly sacred knowledge to fee-paying Westerners eager to learn about spiritual lifeways, and unsurprisingly his connecting American Indian and Celticity resonated with his customers.

But how European, including English, pow-wowers express aspects of Johnson's indigenizing and extending discourses needs to be unpacked. In terms of extending, the existence of European pow-wowing bears witness to the "circulation of religious knowledge and symbols into wider availability… [allowing] what was once a local truth [to be] presented as a more broadly applicable, even a universal one" (Johnson 2002a, 313). As Johnson notes in the Brazilian and Garifuna context, "anyone, regardless of African descent, can practice the religion of the African gods" (2002a, 313). European pow-wow enthusiasts similarly see no issue in taking-on aspects of an American Indian spiritual lifeway, especially when their source material claims to be authentic; neither May's novels, nor Neihardt's *Black Elk Speaks*, suggest they are anything but based on facts, the imagery of Catlin and Curtis is undeniably historical, movies echo the Wild West shows and often include actors who claim to be, or are American Indian, and native teachers come with claims of passing on their traditions. So, just as Johnson's Brazilian Candomblé priests on TV encourage viewers to work with the African deities, European pow-wowers have found inspiration from a number of popular cultural sources; although as Johnson notes with his extending discourse, they have lowered or expanded traditional indigenous "boundaries to encompass a wider domain of peoples" (Johnson 2002b, 189).

As regards Johnson's indigenizing discourse however, this is far more problematic as in no way can it be claimed that European pow-wow enthusiasts are "performing traditional practices on [their] original homeland" (2002a, 312). Thus, I have looked to the work of Wallis and his exploration of neo-shamanic appropriation (2003), and Moran's (2002) critique of Australian settler narratives, to expand this aspect of Johnson's concept.

Wallis notes that few Western neo-shamans aim to fully inhabit being native, nor do they do what they do simply for fun, but find deep meaning in practices which help them "radically reorientate their worldviews" (2002, 233). This has in general been my experience of English pow-wow enthusiasts who typically seek to indigenize themselves to become less stereotypically-English, and more stereotypically-native. This notion resonates with Moran who notes that for contemporary Australian settlers coming to terms with their history of enforced indigenous dispossession, increasingly they understand native people as being able to "add depth...[to an Anglo-Australian] culture that has...shallowness" (2002, 1033). English pow-wowers typically see Englishness as lacking depth and spiritual connections to oneself, one's community, and the land; indigenizing proves meaningful as helps them integrate "understandings of what it is to be..." (Blain and Wallis 2000, 405).

Clearly there are issues with the taking-on of aspects of indigenous culture and spiritual lifeways, although it must be noted that many pow-wowers do it, or try to do it, with a good deal of respect, taking pride in their research to learn more about those they seek to emulate. However, the fixation that European pow-wow enthusiasts have for their "ideal typical" American Indian is one that keeps them fixed in the past. It would be easy to suggest that because of where the source material for this past is from, this past is an imagined one but Archie Lame Deer, a Lakota Sioux medicine man from Pine Ridge Reservation, has noted that "if you want to find authentic Indian dances, customs, artifacts, don't look to the reservations in South Dakota or Nebraska. Go spend a weekend at an Indian club in Belgium or Germany" (Hollick 1992). With the meaningfulness of Europeans pow-wowers taking-on of traditional American Indian-ness, Johnson's notion of indigenizing has resonance. Further, it proves useful in critiquing the historiography that this group of people use to construct their indigenized identities; identities which are constructed and fortified with "strictly bounded traditions" (Johnson 2002b, 189).

However, pow-wow enthusiasts are not the only people in England who take on aspects of an American Indian identity, and it is with these people that Johnson's twin terms become less useful and thus here they act as a contrast to pow-wowers. This other group are individuals who annually display an American Indian (or more possibly *indian*) identity to the general public: I have termed them parade-hobbyists.

In England, on November 5th, there are annual celebrations of Guy Fawkes Night (also known as Bonfire Night). The event commemorates the uncovering of the Gunpowder Plot of 1605, an attempt by Roman Catholics to destroy King James I and his Protestant parliament who had continued to ban their religion. Although Bonfire Night celebrations pepper the country, a few towns hold a particular type of Bonfire celebrations; ones with a decidedly anti-Catholic undertone. The most well-known location for these Bonfire Night celebrations is Lewes, although there are a number of towns on the Sussex coast that hold this particular type of Bonfire event. Lewes has a particular political interest in the anti-Catholic rhetoric of their Bonfire Celebrations as seventeen Protestants from Lewes were martyred between 1555 and 1557 during the Marion-era persecution of Protestants during her brief Roman Catholic reign (1553–1558). Seventeen burning crosses, one for each of the martyred men and women of the town,[14] are carried through Lewes to commemoration these individuals each Bonfire Celebrations, while effigies of Guy Fawkes, leader of the Gunpowder Plot, and Pope Paul V, who became head of the Roman Catholic Church in 1605, are burnt (Thomas 2008, 46).

The commemoration of Bonfire Night dates to 1606, and Lewes has continued to remember and celebrate on and off ever since. However, the current iteration of the town's celebrations has only been going for 164 years (Jay 2005, 136; Pugh 2011). The event is popular and in 2017 over 60,000 people flocked to the town to witness the spectacle put on by the seven Bonfire Societies that each organize displays in the town (Anon 2017b).

One of the Societies, "The Commercial Square Society" (CSS) founded in 1855, has long had a theme of "Pioneers and Indian Braves and Squaws." The Society's webpage states:

> Commercial Square's pioneer front and society emblem were born out of protest, rather like the Bonfire tradition itself. During the late 1800s a handful of society members went to America to find their fortune helping to construct the ever-expanding railways. During their time there, they observed the dreadful treatment of the Native American population. Upset by what they

---

14. See 'Lewes Bonfire Celebrations' website for the names of the martyred individuals https://www.lewesbonfirecelebrations.com/lewes-sussex-protestant-martyrs-reformation-6/ (last accessed 19/8/2018)

saw, upon their return to Lewes, they decided to wear North American Indian costumes to raise the profile of the Native Americans' plight. This costume was so popular that it did not take long before the Indian motif became the society's leading costume and our emblem.[15]

And the popularity of the CSS costumes has remained. A 1958 report notes that, "the CSS has built up a collection of Red Indian [sic] dresses which never fail to win enthusiastic applause wherever they are displayed" (in Pugh 2011, 51). Moran's study of Australian settler attitudes towards their own indigenous peoples resonates with the statement above, pointing to an "attitude of mourning and sorrow in relation to past…forms of oppression." However, it is notable that whereas for the Australian settlers indigenizing involves "a desire to make reparation" (Moran 2002, 1014), this notion is absent from the CSS activity. A 2004 write-up of CSS preparations notes how the Bonfire activity seemed more geared up around looking good than reflecting the original aims of the costume choice. It states, "Indian braves wear authentic costume including magnificent sun dancers, medicine men, devil dancers and Apaches in full tribal regalia. Meanwhile 'squaws' [… put] finishing touches to their intricate, hand worked beaded head-dresses…."[16]

The language used in the 2004 CSS report is highly problematic and does not reflect the initial empathy redolent in their 1855 aims, especially in regard to gender and gender-roles (Bird 2001). Yet sadly a lack of respect for American Indian culture is not unusual in England. An American Diner called "Route 303" on a southern English road has labelled its toilets "Chiefs" and "Squaws,"[17] whilst the Exeter Rugby Club, known as Exeter Chiefs, has used the head of an *indian* chief as its logo since 1999, side-on and befeathered.[18] There have been calls for the rugby team to rethink their mascot (Hermann 2016)—a rugby player in a feather-headdress with axe[19]—but fans have urged this not to happen (Oldfield 2018). Indeed, the use of *indian* logos and mascots is a European phenomenon (Keh 2018), doubtless allied the historic and contemporary popularity of American Indian-ness across Europe (Welch 2013).

---

15. See the "Commercial Square Bonfire Society" page on the *Lewes Bonfire Council's* website http://www.lewesbonfirecouncil.org.uk/societies/commercial/index.html (last accessed 19/8/2019).

16. See Sussex Express Supplement—Lewes Bonfire Night Supplement, on the Lewes Bonfire Celebrations website https://www.lewesbonfirecelebrations.com/article/lewes-bonfire-sussex-express-supplement-2004/ (last accessed 19/8/2019).

17. Author visit in August 2016.

18. See https://www.exeterchiefs.co.uk (last accessed 19/8/2019)

19. See https://www.exeterchiefs.co.uk/gifts-accessories/key-rings-pin-badges/big-chief-key-ring for mascot image (last accessed 19/8/2019).

This lack of respect is now very evident in the activities of contemporary parade-hobbyists, and in recent years photographs have shown women as well as men wearing feather head-dresses.[20] Interestingly, although the Lewes Borough Bonfire Society, founded in 1853, costumes as Zulus, this choice of outfit (for which no reason is given on their website) has caused controversy with their garb branded as "disrespectful and racist" (Anon 2017a). However, to date there is no indication that this allegation has been levelled against CSS or any other Bonfire Society that uses *indian* garb (Lewes is one of three towns with annual Bonfire celebrations where *indian* costumes are worn by men, women and children).[21] I therefore contend that the dressing-up activities of English Bonfire Society parade-hobbyism is appropriative, and contrasts with the activities of European pow-wowers.

In conclusion, European pow-wowers I suggest conform to Johnson's indigenizing discourse when amended to include the theory of Wallis, and Blain and Wallis. Although allegations of appropriation have been, and continue to be, levelled at European pow-wow enthusiasts, their activities must be explored in a more nuanced light as they are far more complex than traditionally presented. Indeed, many of the usual arguments concerning neo-colonialist commercial exploitation are nullified in relation to pow-wowing in the former Soviet occupied states due to their own experience of colonization/occupation. The German and English pow-wow scenes meanwhile, have long experienced indigenous agency, and across the European pow-wow genre *per se*, there is little in the way of disrespectful commercial exploitation of American Indian spiritual practices or cultural lifeways. And whilst it could be argued that many of the influences on European pow-wowing are somewhat *indian* in tone due to their Euro-centric baggage, it appears in terms of their garb at least, they are keeping to traditions. Overall then, Johnson's concept of indigenizing is useful in exploring alleged appropriated indigenous identities such as European pow-wowing.

---

20. To see photographs of the 2009 parade see https://www.slideshare.net/gmarlowe/gary-marlowe-images-of-lewes-bonfire-2009; slide 21 shows a woman wearing a feather head-dress (last accessed 19/8/2019).

21. It should be noted that the Sussex town of Rye also holds an annual Bonfire Society event. Photographs taken between 1978-1983 by the secretary of one of the societies shows that plains-style Native American garb was worn by both men and women including full headdresses. For the webpage see http://www.virtualrye.org.uk/Rye%20Bonfire%20Society.htm and for a photograph of head-dressed and costumed society members which includes children see http://www.virtualrye.org.uk/rbs005.jpg (last accessed 19/8/2019). The Sussex town of Littlehampton are a further example of a Bonfire Society utilizing Native American garb. See https://www.nothhelm.com/blog/2017/10/30/littlehampton-bonfire-night for a 2017 write-up on activities (last accessed 19/8/2019).

References

Aldred, Lisa. 2000. "Plastic shamans and Astroturf Sun Dances: New Age commercialization of Native American spirituality." *American Indian Quarterly* 24(3): 329–352. https://doi.org/10.1353/aiq.2000.0001

Allwood, John. 1977. *The Great Exhibitions*. London: Studio Vista.

Anonymous. 2017a. "Lewis bonfire night's parade 'racist' costumes to be axed." *BBC News*. 3 November 2017 https://www.bbc.co.uk/news/uk-england-sussex-41835690

———. 2017b. "Lewes bonfire festivities attended by thousands." *BBC News*. 5 November 2017 https://www.bbc.co.uk/news/uk-england-sussex-41873512

Bass, Jeff D. and Cherwitz, Richard. 1978. "Imperial mission and manifest destiny: A case study of political myth in rhetorical discourse." *Southern Speech Communication Journal* 43(3): 213–232. https://doi.org/10.1080/10417947809372382

Bird, S. Elizabeth. 2001. "Savage desires: The gendered construction of the American Indian in popular media." In *Selling the Indian: Commercializing and Appropriating American Indian Cultures*, edited by , Carter Jones Meyer and Diana Royer, 62–98. Tucson: University of Arizona Press.

Blain, Jenny and Robert Wallis. 2000. "The Ergi Seidman contestations of gender, shamanism, and sexuality in northern religion past and present." *Journal of Contemporary* Religion 15(3): 395–411. https://doi.org/10.1080/713676039

Bowman, Marion. 1995. "Cardiac Celts: Images of the Celt in Paganism." In *Paganism Today: Wiccans, Druids, the Goddess and Ancient Earth Traditions for the Twenty-first Century*, edited by Graham Harvey and Charlotte Hardman, 242–251. London: Thorsons.

Browner, Tara. 2011. "Tradition, and mimesis: American Indian style Pow-wow singing and dancing in Denmark." *American Studies in Scandinavia* 43(2): 71–84.

Catlin, George. 1848. *Catlin's Notes of Eight Years' Travel and Residence in Europe, with His Native American Indian Collection*. Vol. II. London: G. Catlin.

———. 1840. *Descriptive Catalogue of Catlin's Indian Gallery containing Portraits, Landscapes, Costumes etc. and Representatives of the Memories and Customs of the Native American Indians*. Bartholomew Close: C. Adland.

Calloway, Colin G. 2002. "Historical encounters across five centuries." In *Germans and Indian: Fantasies, Encounter, Projections,* edited by Colin G. Colloway, Gerd Germünden and Suzanne Zantop, 47–81. Lincoln: University of Nebraska Press.

Calloway, Colin G., Gerd Germünden and Suzanne Zantop, eds. 2002. *Germans and Indian: Fantasies, Encounter, Projections*. Lincoln: University of Nebraska Press.

Canny, Nicholas. 2012. "A Protestant or Catholic Atlantic world? Confessional divisions and the writing of natural history." *Proceedings of the British Academy* 181: 83–121. https://doi.org/10.5871/bacad/9780197265277.003.0004

Churchill, Ward. 1998. *Fantasies of the Master Race: Literature, Cinema and the Colonisation of American Indians*. San Francisco, CA: City Lights Books.

Curtis, Edward. 1907–1930. *The North American Indian*. http://curtis.library.northwestern.edu

Cuthbert, Denise and Michelle Grossman. 1996. "Trading places: Locating the indigenous in the New Age." *Thamyris* 3(1): 18–36.

Clark, Henry Nicols Blake. 1997. *A Marble Quarry: The James H. Ricau Collection of Sculpture at the Crysler Museum of Art*. New York: Hudson Hills Press.

Davis, Barbara. 1985. *Edward S. Curtis: The Life and Times of a Shadow Catcher*. San Francisco, CA: Chronicle Books.

Dayton, Andrew and Barbara Ragoff. 2013. "'On being indigenous' as a process." *Human Development* 56: 106–122. https://doi.org/10.1159/000346771

Deloria, Philip J. 1998. *Playing Indian*. New Haven, CT: Yale University Press.

Feest, Christian F. 2002. "Germany's Indians in a European perspective." In *Germans and Indian: Fantasies, Encounter, Projections,* edited by Colin G. Colloway, Gerd Germünden and Suzanne Zantop, 25–43. Lincoln: University of Nebraska Press.

Foster, Sally, M. 2014. *Picts, Gaels and Scots*. Edinburgh: Birlinn.

Goertzen, Chris and Tammy Greer. 2012. "Powwows." In *American Indians and Popular Culture: Media, Sport and Politics,* vol II, edited by Elizabeth DeLancey Hoffman, 271–287. Santa Barbara, CA.: Praeger.

Greenhalgh, Paul. 1988. *Ephemeral Vistas: The Expositions Universalles, Great Exhibitions and World's Fairs, 1851–1939*. Manchester: Manchester University Press.

Hall, Allan. 2004. "Germans infatuated with cowboys and indians." *The Times*. 30 July 2004. http://hnn.us/roundup/entries/6569.html

Hariot, Thomas. 1588. *A Briefe and True Report of the New Found Land of Virginia*. University of Nebraska-Lincoln. https://digitalcommons.unl.edu/cgi/viewcontent.cgi?article=1020andcontext=etas

Herrman, Rachel. 2016. "'Playing Indian': Exeter rugby in a postcolonial age." *Imperial and Global Forum*, 9 June 2016. https://imperialglobalexeter.com/2016/06/09/playing-indian-exeter-rugby-in-a-postcolonial-age/

Hladki, Janice. 1994. 'Problematizing the issue of cultural appropriation'. *Alternative Routes* 11: 95–119.

Holley, Linda A. 2007. *Tipi, Tepees, Teepees: History and Design of the Cloth Tipi*. Layton, UT: Gibbs Smith.

Hollick, Julian C. 1992. "Karl May's imaginary America" http://sites.fas.harvard.edu/~gerdb/Handouts/Texthandouts/Karl_May/MayText.pdf

Jacqueman, Sylvie. 2018. "*Indians Like Us; A Documentary Film*" http://www.indianslikeus.com/index.php/en/

Jahoda, Gustav. 1999. *Images of Savages: Ancient Roots of Modern Prejudice in Western Culture*. London: Routledge.

Jay, Mike. 2005. "Bonfire Night in Lewes." In *Gunpowder Plots: A Celebration of 400 years of Bonfire Night*, edited by Brenda Buchanan, David Cannadine, Justin Champion, David Cressy, Pauline Croft, Antonia Fraser, Mike Jay, 118–144. London: Allen Lane.

Johnson, Jay. T. 2013. "Dancing into place: The role of Powwow within urban indigenous communities." In *Indigenous in the City: Contemporary Identities and Cultural Innovation*, edited by Evelyn Peters and Chris Anderson, 216–230. Vancouver: University of British Columbia Press.

Johnson, Paul C. 2005. "Migrating bodies, circulating signs: Brazilian Candomblé, the Garifuna of the Caribbean, and the category of indigenous religions." In *Indigenous Diasporas and Dislocation,* edited by Graham Harvey and Charles D. Thompson, 63–81. London: Routledge.

———.2002a. "Migrating bodies, circulating signs: Brazilian Candomblé, the Garifuna of the Caribbean, and the category of indigenous religions." *History of Religions* 41(4): 301–327. https://doi.org/10.1086/463690

———. 2002b. *Secrets, Gossip and the Gods: The Transformation of Brazilian Candomblé*. Oxford: Oxford University Press. https://doi.org/10.1093/0195150589.003.0008

Keh, Andrew. 2018. "Tomahawk chops and Native American mascots: In Europe, teams don't see a problem." *New York Times*, 7 May 2018. https://www.nytimes.com/2018/05/07/sports/native-american-mascots-europe.html

Maxwell, Anne. 1999. *Colonial Photography and Exhibitions: Representations of the 'Native' and the Making of European Identities*. London: Leicester University Press.

Medicine, Beatrice and Liucija Baskauskas. 1999. *Seeking the Spirit: Plains Indians in Russia*. Watertown: Documentary Educational Resources.

Moore, Robert John Jr. 1997. *Native Americans: A Portrait: The Art and Travels of Charles Bird King, George Catlin, and Karl Bodmer*. New York: Stewart, Tabori and Chang.

Moran, Anthony. 2002. "As Australia decolonizes: Indigenous settler nationalism and the challenges of indigenous/settler relations." *Ethnic and Racal Studies*, 25(6): 1013–1042. https://doi.org/10.1080/0141987022000009412

Moran, Michael G. 2007. *Inventing Virginia: Sir Walter Raleigh and the Rhetoric of Colonization, 1584–1590*. New York: Peter Lang.

Oldfield, Edward. 2018. "Fans on social media mostly reject new call for Exeter chiefs to rethink their use of American Indian branding," Devon Live, 1

February 2018. https://www.devonlive.com/news/devon-news/fans-social-media-mostly-reject-1150307

Paskievich, John (with David Z. Scheffel). 1995. *If Only I Were an Indian*. Zema Pictures.

Powers, William K. 1990. "When Black Elk speaks, everybody listens." *Social Text* 24: 43–56. https://doi.org/10.2307/827826

Pratt, Stephanie. 2005. *American Indians in British Art, 1700–1840*. Norman: University of Oklahoma Press.

Pugh, Brian, W. 2011. *Bonfire Night in Lewes*. London: MX Publishing.

Rollins, Peter C. and John E. O'Connor, eds. *Hollywood's Indians: The Portrayal of the Native American in Film*. Louisville: The University of Kentucky Press.

Rose, Wendy, 1992. "The great pretenders: Further reflections on Whiteshamanism." In *The State of Native America; Genocide, Colonization and Resistance*, edited by M. Annette Jaimes. 403–421. Boston, MA: South End Press.

Rydell, Robert W. 1987. *All the World's a Fair: Visions of Empire at American International Expositions, 1876–1916*. Chicago, IL: University of Chicago Press.

Seig, Katrin. 2002. "Indian impersonation as historical surrogation." In *Germans and Indian: Fantasies, Encounter, Projections*, edited by Colin G. Colloway, Gerd Germünden and Suzanne Zantop, 217–242. Lincoln: University of Nebraska Press.

Smiles, Sam. 2009. "John White and British antiquity; Savage origins and the context of Tudor historiography." In *European Visions; American Voices*, edited by Kim Sloan, 106–112. British Museum Research Publication 172. London: British Museum. https://www.britishmuseum.org/pdf/4-Smiles-JW%20 and%20British%20Antiquity.pdf

Smith, Sherry L. 2000. *Reimaging Indians: Native Americans through Anglo Eyes, 1180–1940*. Oxford: Oxford University Press.

Thomas, Andy. 2008. *Lewes on the Fifth*. Seaford, East Sussex: SB Publications.

Troutman, John W. and Nancy J. Parezo. 1998. "'The overlord of the savage world:' Anthropology and the press at the 1904 Louisiana Purchase exposition." *Museum Anthropology* 22(2): 17–34. https://doi.org/10.1525/mua.1998.22.2.17

Vizenor, Gerald. 1998. *Fugitive Poses: Native American Indian Scenes of Absence and Presence*. Lincoln: University of Nebraska Press.

Wallis, Robert. 2003. *Shamans/Neo-Shamans: Ecstasy, Alternative Archaeologies, and Contemporary Paganism*. Oxford: Routledge. https://doi.org/10.4324/9780203417577

Watchman, Renae, 2005. "Powwow overseas: The German experience." In *Powwow*, edited by Clyde Ellis, Luke Eric Lassier and Gary H. Dunham, 241–256. Lincoln: University of Nebraska.

Watson, Aaron. 1907. *The Savage Club: A Medley of History, Anecdote and Reminisce*. London: T. Fisher Unwin. https://archive.org/stream/savageclubmedley00watsuoft/savageclubmedley00watsuoft_djvu.txt

Welch, Christina. 2013. "Teepees and totem poles: Imaginings of North American Indians in European popular culture for children." In *Tribal Fantasies: Native Americans in the European Imaginary, 1900–2010*, edited by David Stirrup and James McKay, 101–116. New York: Palgrave. https://doi.org/10.1057/9781137318817_6

———. 2011. "Savagery on show: The Popular visual representation of Native American peoples and their lifeways at the World's fairs (1851–1904) and Buffalo Bill's Wild West (1884–1904)." *Early Popular Visual Culture* 9(4): 337–352. https://doi.org/10.1080/17460654.2011.621314

———. 2007. "Complicating spiritual appropriation; North American Indian agency in Western alternative spiritual practice." *Journal of Alternative Spirituality and New Age Studies* 3: 97–117.

Zantop, Suzanne. 2002. "Close encounters: *Deutsche* and *Indianer*." In *Germans and Indian: Fantasies, Encounter, Projections*, edited by Colin G. Colloway, Gerd Germünden and Suzanne Zantop, 3–14. Lincoln: University of Nebraska Press.

Ziff, Bruce and Pratima V. Rao, eds. 1997. *Borrowed Power: Essays on Cultural Appropriation*. New Brunswick, NJ: Rutgers University Press.

About the author

Christina Welch is an inter- and multi-disciplinary Religious Studies scholar who gained her PhD in 2005 through the University of Southampton. Her thesis (funded by the Arts and Humanities Research Board) explored the role of popular visual representation in the construction of North American Indian and Western Alternative Spiritual identities. She has maintained her research interest in the intersections between religion and visual/material culture, although in recent years, has focused on death as a central theme exploring late-medieval and early-modern *transi* sculpture, and the erotic death art produced during the Reformation and at the turn of the 20th century. She is also involved in a number of collaborative projects: examining pre-Vesalian anatomical knowledge in England with a forensic anatomist, Winchester's West Hill Cemetery with a Modern historian, and planter memorials in Barbados and St Vincent with an historical archaeologist. Christina has also collaborated with members of Winchester's Jewish community, and Winchester City Council, on a public engagement project to highlight Winchester's medieval Jewish heritage. Together with Dr Niall Finneran, she is currently working with the Garifuna Heritage Foundation in St. Vincent, and Greiggs village heritage group, to explore and celebrate the Vincentian Garifuna identity. A latecomer to academia, Christina had a career in finance before having a family and then going to University. She is dyslexic with short-term memory issues and has an impressive collection of heels.

7

"Witch" and "Shaman":
Discourse Analysis of the Use of Indigenizing Terms in Italy

ANGELA PUCA

From the very birth of the term, *Strega* ("Witch") has been used with a negative connotation to describe women with powers aimed at harming people.
Strega has its etymological origin in the Latin *Strix*, the owl believed to feed
on human blood. Pop culture, books and media alike, also portrayed the
witch as an evil character to the point where it became common parlance
to address a person deemed evil as a witch. In the last three decades, with
the popularization of Paganism and Wicca, the term has been reclaimed and
somehow sanitized by Pagans who neutrally describe this figure as someone
who has the ability to change reality in accordance with the will. In more
recent years, with the spread of shamanism, more practitioners start to either
renounce the term "witch" in favour of *Sciamano/sciamana* ("Shaman") or use
them both to define themselves. By analyzing the discourses that practitioners create around the terms "witch" and "shaman" by means of Paul Johnson's
categories, I will illustrate how both terms manifest a form of indigenization
and extending. In conclusion, I will argue that indigenizing and extending
may be seen as two aspects of the same phenomenon entailing the opening
of cultural borders to the outside, reshaping both the imported and exported
cultural elements.

Introduction

In studying Brazilian Candomblé and the Garifuna of the Caribbean, Paul
C. Johnson (2002) highlights two aspects emerging from the contemporary
development of their religious practices, "indigenizing" and "extending."
By indigenizing, Johnson refers to the inclusion of outsider elements to a
local tradition in a way that the outer inclusion is reshaped and ingrained as
part of the local tradition. On the other hand, there is an openness on the
part of the locals to export their local traditions and make them available to

outsiders,

> When priests of Candomblé (*pais*, or *maes de santo*) appear on Brazilian na-
> tional television advising how anyone regardless of African descent, can prac-
> tise the religion of the African gods (*orixas*) in the privacy of their own home,
> with or without initiation and a community of practice, this is an example of
> an extending move. (Johnson 2002, 313)

Drawing on Johnson's categories, I will argue that discourses surrounding
the terms Witch (*Strega*) and Shaman (*Sciamano, Sciamana*) in the Italian
context show two examples of how indigenization and extension manifest
and can be seen as aspects of the same process. Also, alongside some degree
of universalization, the two show a significant contribution to the cultural
integration of these identities within paganism and shamanism. Witchcraft
and shamanism are two somewhat different movements that can entail overlaps since often those who describe themselves as witches are also shamanic
practitioners. The terms "witch" and "shaman" appear the most significant to
understand how the mechanism of indigenizing and extending can manifest
through language and the discursive understanding of certain categories. The
adoption of a new term (shaman) or a revised term (witch) seems able to
reconsider and shed a positive light on practices once considered malicious,
unacceptable and hence kept hidden. This may suggest that a change in the
discursive understanding of religiously related identifiers can lead to a change
in the development of the tradition itself.

The corpus investigated is comprised of data collected during fieldwork
conducted between September 2016 and September 2018, attending gatherings of Pagans and Shamans across the Italian territory through the lens of the
participant observer. I also conducted several interviews, used questionnaires
and created a Facebook group called "Practitioners of shamanism in Italy"[1]
with the declared purpose of studying the content and dynamics arising from
social interactions and discussions among members. Other significant material derived from casual conversations, texts, books, articles used as reference
within the community will be included.

I will interpret my data through Discourse Analysis, a methodology which
is becoming increasingly popular in Religious Studies and represents a suitable approach to the academic inquiry of Paganism and shamanism (Taira
2013). Traditions devoid of a centralized dogma or leadership, such as paganism and shamanism, make it challenging to discern the theoretical and epistemological components upon which their practices are based. For this reason,
analyzing the discourses (verbal and non-verbal) and the narratives created by

---

1. *Praticanti di Sciamanesimo in Italia.*

practitioners can be a meaningful light shed on the background assumptions and underlying beliefs that are socially constructed within the community (Blain and Wallis 2007, 11–17).

The evolution of the "Witch"

For the majority of its history, the term *Strega* ("Witch") has been used with a negative connotation to describe women with powers aimed at harming people. *Strega* has still a debated etymological origin, though the most agreed root comes from the Latin *Strix-Strigis*, the owl believed to feed on human blood and associated with the Autumn Equinox which heralds the death of the year (Fusco di Ravello 2009, 98). Around the sixth century CE, the term probably began to be applied to certain individuals who lived in the country-side and refused to embrace the Christian religion (Malossini 2011).

The view of the witch as a malicious worker dealing with dark forces survived throughout the Middle Ages and the Inquisition, which lasted in Italy until the eighteenth century (Romeo 2011). During the Renaissance, magic was re-evaluated as the practical fulfilment of Natural Philosophy (*naturalis philosophiae consummatio*), which at the time referred to natural science (Della Porta 1677). Nonetheless, a distinction was still made between the witches, who were communing with demons and other spirits, and the Mages who were interested in practices of Natural Magic, such as herbalism, healing and alchemy.

Throughout the Enlightenment and the establishment of a Positivist paradigm, the witch slowly moved from being an evil worker of dark forces to a delusional charlatan who either believed in non-existent powers or deceives others for a personal gain. Despite the negative connotation that the Strega has always had in Italian history, the practices kept existing in a hidden way. The only major consequence was that the term *Strega* became unused, devoid of identifiers and yet existent in practice. Those who practised magic became label-less, for there was no term to adopt which implied a positive connotation and hence they renounced any label to identify themselves. This still appears to be true in current times for older generations of vernacular witches. Michela explained to me, "According to the women with whom I grew up, the term *Strega* was heavily offensive, even worse than 'whore.' It was an unimaginable offence, the worst you can imagine."[2] For this reason, none of them would dare to call themselves witches and would certainly be offended if somebody were to address them as such.

---

2. "Secondo le donne con cui sono cresciuta, l'appellativo Strega era fortemente offensivo, peggio di puttana. Era un'offesa incredibile, la peggiore tu possa immaginare." (All English translations are mine.)

As multiple interviews and encounters with Celeste B. highlighted, there is a silent unspoken agreement according to which you are allowed to talk about the performed rituals, such as the Evil eye removal or healings, but not identify them as forms of witchcraft. The "witch" was therefore obliterated from the lives of individuals and set aside as a character in tales and folklore stories. Yet the use of *Strega* saw a new beginning and a reclamation thanks to the younger generations of folk witches.

When talking about vernacular magic in Italy, it is important to distinguish between the older and younger generation of practitioners. By older generation I refer to practitioners usually over the age of 60 who are not prone to share their practice with people other than family or community members. They are very secretive and avoid talking about their rituals to outsiders. On the other hand, younger generations are those who are generally under the age of 60 and keen on sharing their practices and syncretizing them with other, usually Neo-pagan, methodologies that have slowly permeated the Italian scene.

In the last three decades, in fact, with the popularization of Paganism and Wicca, *Strega* has been reclaimed and somehow sanitized by Pagans who neutrally describe this figure as someone who has the ability to change reality in accordance with will thanks to her or his connection to Nature. Also, the way witches were portrayed by media started to change: books like the "Harry Potter" series and TV shows like "Charmed" depicted witches with a positive outlook, portraying them as persons who use their rituals to help other people and the community (Dimitri 2005).

When Wicca began to take root in the country in the early 2000s, Pagans were using "Witch" and "Wiccan" almost interchangeably and often described what being a witch meant by employing the etymology of the English "Witch" or "Wicca," as explained by Gerald Gardner, the father of the Wiccan tradition, and consequently adopted by other Wiccan-derived traditions around the world (Husain 1999, 154). As Gardner explains in his famous *Witchcraft for Today*,

> They are the people who call themselves the Wica, the "wise people," who practise the age-old rites and who have, along with much superstition and herbal knowledge, preserved an occult teaching and working processes which they themselves think to be magic or witchcraft. (Gardner 1982, 102)

This process of assimilation of the two terms, Witch and *Strega*, was facilitated by the limited sources found in the late 1990s and early 2000s. At the time, the only books regarding magic that a potential practitioner could have accessed were those written by Wiccans, especially from America.

Scott Cunningham, Silver RavenWolf, Phyllis Currot and other authors from the United States became increasingly popular within the Italian Pagan community. As a consequence, it was frequent in the early 2000s to have practitioners during Pagan gatherings explaining what *Strega* meant by referencing its English translation and hence the Gardnerian etymological explanation.

As more sources on different forms of witchcraft and Pagan traditions became available to the readers, a starker difference between witch and Wiccan developed. Nonetheless, the more positive connotation that Wicca brought to the practice of Witchcraft kept on influencing the understanding of magical practices within the Pagan community and helped them to be reclaimed as non-malicious. This act of importing a new term from the outside and integrating it by merging the new label with an existing one, can be seen as a form of indigenizing. This specific act of indigenizing deals with the identity formation of a community and how the contours of that identity are able to fit into the wider context of what is deemed acceptable to the social framework.

As a result of indigenizing Neo-pagan terminology, the younger generation of vernacular healers and witches are coming out and more openly defining themselves as *Streghe*. This openness is also reflected onto the new syncretism they are operating. Whilst the older generation employed rituals with an inner syncretism with Catholicism, the younger generation is syncretizing their rituals with Neo-paganism and contemporary shamanism. For instance, Francesca C. who practises Core Shamanism and was initiated into the Tradition of *Segnatori*[3] explained to me that according to the tradition, only family members should be initiated on Christmas Eve's night. However, not being a Catholic, she deemed more appropriate to perform the Initiations on the Winter Solstice's night and to open the transmission of the *Segnature* to people outside the circle of blood relatives. Francesca's viewpoint appeared to be shared by the majority of interviewees. There are also online communities on Facebook that gather folk magic practitioners in Italy, the most popular of which counts more than five thousand members, people with various forms of physical or mental health issues who seek help from the *Segnatori* in the group. Liliana is one of these healers who help people at a distance as well as in person. She is mostly a healer but also performs other forms of rituals for prosperity or love and, during an interview, she defined herself as a witch,

---

3. I adopt the definition "Tradition of *Segnatori*" to systemitize the various forms of folk magic found throughout Italy, since they all employ in their rituals the *Segnature*, magical gestures accompanied by words of power believed to have the ability to manifest an intended change.

alongside being a *Segnatrice*.[4] Thus, a new indigenized understanding of the meaning of "witch" helped old folk traditions to re-surface. The shift in the understanding of what *Strega* means and what being a witch entails contributed to a significant change in the spreading and openness of the vernacular tradition as well as its practitioners' self-perception.

The extending of "Strega"

While the Italian Pagan scene has been massively affected by the Wiccan tradition, the United States saw the birth of a tradition called "Stregheria" or "La vecchia religione" (Grimassi 1995). The term Stregheria has its roots in the works of the folklorist and author of the nineteenth century, Charles Godfrey Leland, who claimed he had discovered an ancient unbroken witch cult in the north of Italy that survived the advent of Christianity. Leland's most popular books are *Aradia: the Gospel of the Witches* (Leland 2017) and *Etruscan Roman Remains* (Leland 2007), both first published in 1899 and drawing on to the alleged Italian "old religion," whose magical practices are claimed to have survived without syncretism with Catholicism.

As Sabina Magliocco points out, for Italian American Neopagans the location of an ancient goddess worshipping religion in Italy drawn from Italian folkloric traditions was the most relevant contribution of Leland's Aradia. All the rituals Leland described allowed Italian Americans to reclaim a Pagan tradition they could feel as part of their heritage, which was also a way to disassociate themselves from perceived Church or State oppression (Magliocco 2006, 58–60).

Claims on the "purity" of this tradition and its lack of involvement with the Catholic Church is particularly evident when followers highlight the difference between *Stregheria* and *Stregoneria*. Paolo Giordano explains,

> Stregoneria contrasts sharply with the tradition of Stregheria. The former is now a quasi-Catholic oriented sorcery found in common Italian folk traditions, and the latter is a pagan oriented religious system with a magical structure for rituals and spells. The word "stregheria" is an archaic word for witchcraft that is now applied in place of the word "stregoneria." Those wishing to differentiate themselves from Christian stregoneria, (which usurped and distorted the pre-existing tradition of witchcraft) now use the term stregheria. The use of the word stregheria is now reclaimed by those who are not ashamed or fearful of their Italian pagan roots. (Giordano 2006)

Raven Grimassi is the creator of what is now defined as Stregheria (Magliocco 2006, 61–62). He leads a website, a Facebook group where practitioners share their experiences and doubts, and has published two main books on the

---

4. Female singular of *Segnatori*, a female practitioner of the Tradition of *Segnatori*.

topic: *Italian Witchcraft: the Old Religion of southern Europe* (2000), previously entitled *The Ways of the Strega* (1995), and *Hereditary Witchcraft* (1971).

Stregheria appears therefore to its practitioners as inspired by and a reinterpretation of Italian folk magic traditions and intends to make them available to people outside of Italy and outside the usual community-family context whereby these traditions are traditionally taught and practised. The very existence of this tradition appears to be an example of an extending move. Thanks to *Stregheria*, alleged Italian rituals can be now performed in a different country, widening the field of action to include people from a geographically and culturally distant country.

This example shows once again that extending and indigenizing are two sides of the same coin, for the practice of *Stregheria* represents an extension from the Italian point of view and an indigenization for those living in the United States. Interestingly, American followers of *Stregheria* claim to follow the most authentic and untainted form of Italian witchcraft, more genuine even of what is found it Italy itself. Instances of this attitude are shown in conversations which occurred within the online community and on Grimassi's website page, where it is explained that,

> Unfortunately, at this time, we have not found websites in Italy that we feel portray authentic Italian Witchcraft traditions as they appear to lack accurate historical or cultural material related to the Old Religion of Italy. Instead they appear to contain reconstructions of Egyptian and Hermetic traditions reworked into a newly constructed system that is passed off as Witchcraft. Other sites feature a modified form of *Stregoneria* that is Catholic-rooted in nature and conflated with folk magic traditions having little if anything to do with authentic forms of Italian Witchcraft. (Grimassi 2011)

The term "Shaman" and the understanding of shamanism

The process of indigenizing-extending in the Italian use of the word "Shaman" has a particular relevance to the process of identity formation initiated by a new imported label. The birth and development of shamanism in Italy will only be addressed here in regards to the use of the label among practitioners as evidenced by the data collected in two years of fieldwork.

Within Pagan communities and other New Age movements, the term "Shaman" began to have a shared and loosely understood meaning thanks to Mircea Eliade and Carlos Castaneda. It is hard to trace back to when exactly this process started but I can cautiously assume that, since Mircea Eliade was first published in Italian in 1974 (Eliade 1974) and Carlos Castaneda in 1999 (Castaneda 1999), the spreading of shamanism began no more than four decades ago. Its diffusion escalated in the early 2000s thanks to the internet and the popularization of Michael Harner's Core Shamanism (Harner 1995).

The most common understanding that practitioners have is that shamanism is something that comes from elsewhere, Siberia, the Andean regions, the Amazonian forest or from the Native communities in North America. Even the most popular form of trans-cultural shamanism comes from the United States. Consequently, more and more people use the term to define their practice but avoid it as a self-identifier. A survey conducted in August 2018 showed that none of the hundred respondents call themselves a Shaman, preferring to self-identify as practitioners of shamanism. This happens mostly due to the respect towards the indigenous shamanisms and the related acknowledgement of their differences compared to the Western manifestations. Furthermore, as Vanth[5] pointed out, being a Shaman is like being beautiful, something that is yours only when acknowledged by others.

Many scholars have highlighted that a form of romanticizing of the indigenous non-Western traditions occurs in Neo shamanism (Johnson 1995; Wallis 2003) and Italy is no exception to that. On an average, practitioners seem to understand the role of the shaman as solely beneficial towards other people and the community. Data collected from approximately 200 informants confirm this view. Definitions emerged of what the Shaman's role entails all gravitate around some key concepts. The Shaman accesses non-ordinary realities and communes with Spirits, being "A man or a woman who cooperates with the Spirits of the Otherworld with the aim of healing, divining and helping their own group or those who seek help."[6] The purpose of the Shamanic journey is therefore to help the community and people in need.

I have addressed how Neo-pagan traditions, especially Wicca, have contributed to cast the label "witch" in a more positive light. As a consequence, a witch is not exclusively a harmful individual but also someone who uses the Craft to create beneficial changes to the life of others. This shift in perception appears predominantly limited to the Pagan community or those who are acquainted with Neo-pagan traditions. Similarly, both for Pagans and non-Pagans, the Shaman appears to be almost exclusively a benefactor and a healer. Commonly described as "A person who is elected by the Spirits to be the link between the physical and the spiritual worlds to alleviate the suffering of human beings,"[7] the Shaman is believed by many to have power only

---

5. Practitioner of Core Shamanism and president of Pagan Pride Italy.

6. "Uomo/donna che collabora con gli Spiriti dell'Altromondo con lo scopo di guarire, divinare e aiutare il proprio gruppo di appartenenza o chi si rivolge a lui/lei." Anonymous answer to the Survey "Lo Sciamanesimo in Italia" created in August 2018.

7. "Una persona che viene designata dagli Spiriti a essere il tramite tra mondo fisico e mondi spirituali per alleviare le sofferenze degli esseri umani." Anonymous answer to the

as long as it is used to help and heal others. Differently, a witch might do harm or give help depending on the moral code of the individual. As a result, practitioners have often introduced themselves saying "I practise shamanism, I'm a good witch" or described someone they know as "She is a Shaman. Or rather a witch, one of the good ones" (Lioni 2016) utilizing the term Shaman as a sign marking the goodwill of the witch, a way to guarantee his or her goodness.

In addition, "Shaman" is perceived as more neutral and versatile than "Witch" to the wider audience because it is not considered a religion and therefore has no contrast with the dominant religious system nor with any other religion. Rather, it is mostly deemed to be a set of techniques (Arcari and Saggioro 2015). Witchcraft has, instead, a long history of antagonism with the Catholic Church and tends to be related more to a religious system, which makes it more intimidating to those who have a religious affiliation (Malizia 1992; Romanazzi 2014).

During the last two decades, with the increasing interest towards shamanism, there has been a related change in the way practitioners perceived themselves. Although during the first diffusion of Neo-paganism practitioners were claiming back the renewed term "witch," now more members of the community appear to favour or add the term "shaman" to describe their practices. Consequently, the indigenization of the term shaman has resulted in two main outcomes. It birthed a new definition for the regional forms of folk magic on the territory, which might now be considered indigenous manifestations of Italian shamanism, and enriched the use of the term "witch" by reshaping its meaning to include connotations attributed to Shamanic practices. Thus, "witch" encompasses now the new positive associations provided by Wicca and inherits traits of the shaman, as explained by Michela in a representative account:

> The witches are the daughters and the shamans are their mothers and grandmothers, for it is an evolution of the same technique. Considering that Gardner came to Italy and took from the women in Tuscany the basis for modern Wicca, there is basically no difference (between witch and shaman). There are differences on the practical level (in the types of rituals), but they have the same spirit, they come from the same tradition.[8]

Survey "Lo Sciamanesimo in Italia."

8. "Le streghe sono le figlie e le sciamane sono le mamme e le nonne, è un'evoluzione della stessa tecnica. Considerato che Gardner è venuto in Italia e ha preso dale donne toscane le basi con le quali ha costruito la moderna Wicca, tendenzialmente non c'è differenza (tra Strega e sciamana). Delle differenze a livello pratico ci sono, ma hanno lo stesso spirito, vengono dalla stessa tradizione."

Another distinctive way whereby the term shaman manifests a form of indigenizing is when it is used in reference to autochthonous folk magic traditions. Folk magic in Italy is widespread and concealed at the same time, discursively marginalized for it has no shared recognized label. Every region has a different name to refer to their healers and they also tend to use different prayers chanted in the local dialect (Bartolucci 2016). Such practices have existed, especially in the countryside, for centuries but there was no concept nor a word to make sense of and systematize them (Ginzburg 2013; Turchi 2017). For ages, the closest category has been witchcraft, which has a history of antagonism with Catholicism and a negative connotation to many people. The label "Shaman," with its—albeit romanticized—positive connotation and a-religious status, is potentially the perfect label to make folk healers visible again.

Michela Chiarelli and the way she portrays her tradition are good examples of that. Michela is originally from the South, specifically from Calabria, and her family has been practising shamanism for six generations. In every generation, a female Shaman is born, and she fears to be the last one of the lineage because she has two sons. Michela defines herself as an 'Italian shaman' coming from a hereditary tradition, her grandmother was a local healer and passed knowledge and power on to her through an initiation process. Despite the fact that her grandmother didn't use the word shaman because there was no knowledge at the time of such a label, she acknowledged that what is deemed to be shamanism was in fact not different from what her grandmother taught her. Consequently, she started to adopt the term and gave an understandable identity to her tradition (Chiarelli 2017).

During an interview in May 2017, I asked her to elucidate the major traits of her tradition and Michela openly discussed a few interesting features. She explained that the main aim is to heal and help those in need as well as the community and the Earth and that the main deity is Uni, an Etruscan mother goddess, which represents everything that lives. Also, there seems to be a significant importance given to the "worms" (*vermi*), which are parasitic spirits that bring illnesses, and to the magical gestures to remove them, that she referred to as *Segnature*. Following her explanations and my acknowledgement of striking similarities, I asked whether her tradition was yet another manifestation of Italian folk magic. At the time, Michela replied that the main difference was that her tradition was not syncretized with Catholicism whereas all the other forms of folk magic are. A year later, during a second interview, Michela declared she had thought a lot about that specific question and over time she had become increasingly more convinced that her Italian shamanism was in fact related to the folk magic practices found throughout

Italy. The fact that Michela had never thought about the relation between the two shows how the process of indigenizing can be unintentional and manifests as an evolution in the understanding of a local tradition that was there before a new concept was introduced to foster a new perspective and hence a further development.

Michela also tends to use "witch" and "shaman" interchangeably in conversations and books, though showing a preference towards the label "shaman." Since I stayed at her house during my fieldtrip in May 2017, I found myself browsing through her published books, fourteen at the time, and noticed that she described the eight festivals of the year similarly to the Wiccan representation (Chiarelli 2018). The book also listed both the Wiccan names (for instance, Yule) and the Italian-Etruscan ones (for example, Saturnalia or brumaia for the winter solstice). Thus, I asked Michela why was she using Wiccan terminologies and structure and she explained that it is mostly to make her tradition more comprehensible to a wider audience.

Another area of Michela's Italian Shamanism that shows an extending attempt is manifested through her choice to break the tradition, or rather create a new one, by not keeping these practices reserved to blood relatives but extending their teaching to selected people in Italy and abroad. From October 2018, Michela will also offer a three-year programme of study, articulated in modules, to become a "Holistic operator"[9] in the tradition of Italian Shamanism.

In Michela's Italian Shamanism, we can see an example of how the term shaman was indigenized, reinterpreted to fit the local context and existing practices formerly labelled in a different way. At the same time, she extended its practices, once prerogative of family members, and now available to people outside the family and the country of origin.

Conclusion

According to my analysis, indigenizing and extending appear as two processes that mutually influence each other. They might also be seen as entailing certain preconditions, like the idea that there are borders dividing one place from another or that these borders can be surpassed. Once this crossing occurs, it is likely that something might immigrate into the new territory concurrently as some other aspect is emigrating from it.

In order to have a process of indigenizing, it is necessary to open the gates to the outside, introduce a foreign element and reshape it to become somewhat Neo-native. The dynamic created by indigenizing and extending moves may be figuratively associated with a bridge that connects two interlocked

---

9. "Operatore Olistico" is a recognized professional figure regulated by Italian law.

ends or to a communication between two people, where you can have no speaking without hearing. This may suggest that the cultural boundaries between different countries and local traditions are increasingly blurring in the development of certain new religious movements. It seems to be the case with Pagan and Shamanistic traditions, whose fluidity and eclectic nature favour indigenizing/extending dynamics that help these movements to find their own identity and reclaim their roots.

The introduction in Italy of an outsider concept such as shamanism appears able to help people claim back their own indigenous practices, whose previous label was keeping them in the shadows of unacceptance. The same happened with the new positive connotation that Wicca gave to the term "witch" (*Strega*). Thus, the discourses created and used around the terms that identify practitioners of certain traditions appear to have a significant weight to determine to what extent the tradition itself will be accepted and understood by the surrounding framework of thought. Discourse analysis of the terms "witch" and "shaman"showed in what way two different words applied to the same manifestation can impact on how successful a re-appropriation or re-integration of a local tradition can be.

References

Arcari, L. and A. Saggioro. 2015. *Sciamanesimo e sciamanesimi. Un problema storiografico.* Rome: Nuova Cultura.

Bartolucci, A. 2016. *Le streghe buone. I simboli, i gesti, le parole. Come muta la medicina tradizionale nell'era di Internet.* Reggio Emilia: Compagnia Editoriale Aliberti.

Blain, J. and R. J. Wallis. 2007. *Sacred Sites, Contested Rites/Rights: Pagan Engagements with Archaeological Monuments.* Brighton: Sussex Academic Press.

Castaneda, C. 1999. *Gli insegnamenti di Don Juan.* Milan: Bur.

Chiarelli, M. 2018. *A scuola dalla sciamana. Un'estate di iniziazione allo sciamanesimo di tradizione italiana.* Verona: Cerchio della Luna.

———. 2017. "La custode dell'arte Sciamanica Italiana di Tradizione Ereditaria familiare." *michelachiarelli.com.* [Online]. Accessed 22 September 2018. https://www.michelachiarelli.com/chi-sono-2/.

Della Porta, G. B. 1677. *Della magia naturale del signor Gio. Battista Della Porta Napolitano libri XX.* Napoli: Antonio Bulifon.

Dimitri, F. 2005. *Neopaganesimo: perché gli dèi sono tornati.* Rome: Castelvecchi.

Eliade, M. 1974. *Lo sciamanismo e le tecniche dell'estasi.* Rome: Edizioni Mediterranee.

Fusco di Ravello, A. 2009. "Il male come limite e confine." In *Sociologia: Rivista Quadrimestrale di Scienze Storiche e Sociali,* edited by A. Bixio, 97–110. Rome: Gangemi Editore.

Gardner, G. B. 1982. *Witchcraft Today*. New York: Magickal Childe.

Ginzburg, C. 2013. *The Night Battles: Witchcraft and Agrarian Cults in the Sixteenth and Seventeenth Centuries*. Baltimore, MD: Johns Hopkins University Press. https://doi.org/10.4324/9780203819005

Giordano, P. 2006. "What is Stregoneria vs Stregheria." *Stregheria.com*. [Online]. Accessed 10 September 2018. http://www.stregheria.com/

Grimassi, R. 2011. "The home of authentic Italian witchcraft." Accessed 10 September 2018. http://www.stregheria.com/

———. 2000. *Italian Witchcraft: The Old Religion of Southern Europe*. Revised edition. St. Paul, MN: Llewellyn Publications.

———. 1995. *Ways of the Strega: Italian Witchcraft: Its Lore, Magick, and Spells*. St. Paul, MN: Llewellyn Publications.

———. 1971. *Hereditary Witchcraft: Secrets of the Old Religion by Raven Grimassi*. St. Paul, MN: Llewellyn Publications.

Harner, M. 1995. *La Via Dello Sciamano*. Rome: Edizioni Mediterranee.

Husain, S. 1999. *La dea. Creazione. Fertilità e abbondanza. La sovranità della donna. Miti e archetipi*. Turin: EDT srl.

Johnson, P. C. 2002. "Migrating bodies, circulating signs: Brazilian Candomblé, the Garifuna of the Caribbean, and the category of indigenous religions." *History of Religions* 41(4): 301–327. https://doi.org/10.1086/463690

———. 1995. "Shamanism from Ecuador to Chicago: A case study in New Age ritual appropriation." *Religion* 25(2): 163–178. https://doi.org/10.1006/reli.1995.0015

Leland, C. G. 2017. *Aradia: The Gospel of the Witches*. CreateSpace Independent Publishing Platform.

———. 2007. *Etruscan Roman Remains*. New York: Cosimo Classics.

Lioni, S. 2016. Incontro con una strega tenera. *Sulla Via degli Sciamani*. [Online]. Accessed 21 September 2018. http://sullaviadeglisciamani.it/index.php/2016/03/12/incontro-con-una-strega-tenera/

Magliocco, S. 2006. "Italian American Stregheria and Wicca: Ethnic ambivalence in American Neopaganism." In *Modern Paganism in World Cultures: Comparative Perspectives*, edited by M. Strmiska, 55–86. Santa Barbara, CA: ABC-CLIO.

Malizia, E. 1992. *Ricettario delle streghe: incantesimi, prodigi sessuali e veleni*. Rome: Edizioni Mediterranee.

Malossini, A. 2011. *Breve storia delle streghe*. San Lazzaro di Savena: Area51 Publishing.

Romanazzi, A. 2014. *Guida alle streghe in Italia*. Rome: Venexia Editrice.

Romeo, G. 2011. *L'Inquisizione nell'Italia moderna*. Rome: Edizioni Laterza.

Taira, T. 2013. "Making space for discursive study in religious studies." *Religion* 43(1): 26–45. https://doi.org/10.1080/0048721X.2013.742744

Turchi, D. 2017. *Lo sciamanesimo in Sardegna*. Rome: Newton Compton.

Wallis, R. J. 2003. *Shamans/Neo-Shamans: Ecstasies, Alternative Archaeologies and Contemporary Pagans* 1 edition. London: Routledge. https://doi. org/10.4324/9780203417577

About the author

Angela Puca is a doctoral researcher and graduate teaching assistant at Leeds Trinity University. Her research is in the field of the anthropology of religion and focusses on subjects such as shamanism, witchcraft, Paganism and Western Esotericism mainly in reference to the Italian manifestations of such phenomena. Her publications cover topics such as the Italian "Strega" tradition—which she systematized as the Tradition of Segnature—indigenous and trans-cultural shamanism in Italy and the philosophical underpinning underlying various magical practices and Pagan rituals.

8

Negotiation of the Prehistoric Past for the Creation of the Global Future: "Back to Nature" Worldview and *Golden Age* Myth among Lithuanian Anastasians

Rasa Pranskevičiūtė-Amoson

The chapter presents a study into the implementation of environmental and spiritual ideas of alternative communitarian movements during the establishing of quickly spreading nature-based spirituality communities and their settlements in the East-Central European region. It focuses on the Anastasia "spiritual" movement, classifiable as New Age, which emerged in Russia in the aftermath of the collapse of the Soviet Union, and since has spread to East-Central Europe and beyond. It considers the process of indigenization via assembled nature-based spiritualities and traditionalistic ideas in the movement. It will discuss how the Anastasian process of sacralization of natural space, together with the romantic mode of a narrativization of the archaic past, serve as a source for the formation of images of "indigenousness" in the movement. During the process of "indigenization," a negotiation, interpretation and presentation of nationalistic and traditionalistic ideas serve as a basis for an imagination of (trans)local prehistoric and local national pasts— including a *golden age* myth, a "back to nature" worldview with attempts to reconstruct variously perceived traditions, as well as a development of utopian visions of a prospective *heaven on earth*—intended to widely spread future social projects. The findings are based on data obtained from fieldwork in 2005–2015, including participant observation and interviews with respondents in the Baltic countries and Russia.

Introduction

Contemporary representatives of alternative lifestyles and spirituality seekers are establishing communities, often as an opposition to popular culture and the values of a consumerist society. In the West, a disappointment with the progress of civilization revealed itself sharply in the second half of the twentieth century and in post-communist societies after the collapse of the Soviet Union. It induced a fragmentation of the cultural, political and religious centers and raised a focus towards localities and (re)construction of ethnicities, old and newly made customs and traditions, ideas of egalitarianism and anti-consumerism, search for alternative cultural forms and lifestyles, which were embodied in diverse avant-garde and anarchistic (anti-global, feminist, ecological, pacifist, etc.) movements, communitarian movements oriented to a search for spirituality, and other alternative youth subcultures (Pranskevičiūtė 2015, 183).

In this socio-cultural context, a focus on nature-based spiritualities,[1] a "back to nature"[2] worldview and the establishment of ecological or nature-based spirituality[3] settlements become visible among alternative subcultures of a wide range of worldviews and lifestyles (see Pranskevičiūtė 2015, 186).[4] The establishment of nature-based spirituality settlements is often under-

---

1. Here nature-based spirituality is understood as common to "the subset of such groups that perceive nature itself to be sacred" (Taylor 2001, 177).

2. "Back to nature" and harmonious life in nature narratives became popular from the works of Henry D. Thoreau and John Muir—early beginners of ecocentrism and the environmental movement in America (Pranskevičiūtė 2011, 77–78). In 1972, Norwegian philosopher Arne Naess (1973) consolidated a concept "deep ecology" expressing the intrinsic value of nature, which was widely used among environmentally minded social groups. A "back to nature" motive also appeared in sociocultural arenas and influenced a rise of diverse nature-based worldviews and lifestyles, as well as the emergence of communitarian movements, which established alternative social models, based in natural space.

3. Nature-based spirituality communities and settlements are considered to be communities and settlements with a broader scope of interests, values and lifestyles, which orientate toward nature and nature-based spiritualities. Ecological communities and settlements are understood as those which are strictly regulated in a particular society as standards of ecology (when these standards are not rarely established in a state level and legitimized by particular laws).

4. Contemporary anarchistic, pagan, secular, and religious (new and traditional) environmental movements with a spiritual outlook have formed as a response to environmental issues (Sessions 1994). According to Meera Nanda (2004), in the second part of the twentieth century, a contemporary eco-pagan spirituality established itself in ecological and nature-based spiritual movements. Lately, environmental and anti-globalist movements have been growing, which shows that more and more people are enchanted by a pagan vision of nature as a living, conscious, and sacred entity. Returning to pagan traditions is considered a phenomenon of counterculture in the West (Nanda 2004, 19). The inclination to a holistic lifestyle, alternative healing and ecological issues are also characteristic of New Age spirituality—a cultic milieu with a countercultural heritage (Geaves 2004). Environmental and spiritual ideas of alternative movements are also being implemented by the establishment of fast-spreading ecological communities and their settlements, such as eco-communities, ecovillages, green communities, and the like (Pepper 1991).

stood by participants as an effort to create *heaven on earth* in one or another way. The "back to nature" narrative often has the universalistic mode: it is believed that one day all humanity will return to nature and will create *heaven on earth* here. Secondly, the "back to nature" narrative may be as well related to traditionalistic moods and actions—reviving the imaginative archaic pasts, ancestral lifestyles, re-assembled traditions and "indigenous" existences. In this way, orientation to both universalistic and traditionalistic approaches opens a possibility for freely constructed "imagined indigenousness." Here, "imagined indigenousness" is related to both indigenizing and extending discourses, as summarized by Paul C. Johnson:

> *Indigenizing* discourses and practices have as their objective the configuration, at least imaginatively or discursively, of a pure group performing traditional practices on its original homeland. When outsider signs, symbols and practices are relied upon, they are quickly indigenized—given a culturally specific form that makes the outsider symbol "ours," even traditional.
>
> *Extending* discourses and practices take as their objective the lowering of social boundaries, the circulation of religious knowledge and symbols into wider availability, and the overt assimilation of new forms acknowledged to be from outside. (Johnson 2002, 312)

The groups of interest here, having worldviews based on the above focuses and ideas, tend to represent imagined and romanticized indigenousness, as it is often common within European contextual worldviews. They do this by reinterpreting ideas about "golden but oppressed and almost forgotten local religious pasts" (Tafjord 2018), recreating myths of glorious ancestors, etc. As Bjørn Ola Tafjord writes,

> Much like Johnson, I find it more interesting to notice, through the essays, how members of these new religious movements claim that they actually *represent* a pre-Christian European religion today. The religious or spiritual continuity from pre-Christian times to the present seems to be a key component in the movements' narratives about themselves, or a vital part of their myths. (Tafjord 2018)

Together with various sociocultural alternatives, diverse communities and their settlements, which implement alternative environmental and spirituality ideas, factually emerged in post-communist societies after the collapse of the Soviet Union, when a strong demand for spirituality and spirituality-oriented communities had arisen in its former territories. A major part of the ideas and movements related to alternative religiosity had reached the post-communist Eastern and Central Europe region from the West (North America (the United States) and Western Europe), while the formation of others is related to cultural specifics of particular Eastern and Central European localities (Pranskevičiūtė 2011, 34–36). One of the exceptional cases here is the Anastasia movements whose ground values (related to spirituality values, religious subjects, symbols, etc.) are taken from Russia.

The Anastasians do not use concepts such as "indigenous" or "indigeneity" in their daily vocabulary. Nevertheless, their other concepts like "ancestors," "homeland," "back to nature," "archaic," "prehistoric times," "past," "traditions" and "traditional," etc. point to Anastasian orientation to idealize the archaic past, to construct the imagined past and prospective *golden age* and "back to nature" narratives. The Anastasian movement has both universalistic and traditionalistic characteristics, and the Anastasians construct subcultural "imagined indigenousness" by using both indigenizing (emphasizing imaginative ancestral and local traditions) and extending (emphasizing universal relevance and prospective global engagement) discourses.

The Anastasia movement: General overview

The Anastasia movement is a New Age environmentalist phenomenon which began around 1997 and has its origins in the central part of Russia. The Anastasians can be seen as an outgrowth of the ideas narrated in the 10-volume collection called *The Ringing Cedars of Russia* (Megre 1998, 1999, 1999a, 2000, 2001, 2002, 2003, 2005, 2006, 2010). Various topics such as humankind's relationship with nature, God and the universe, the creation of the world, the power of thought, the ability to model the future, the relationships between men and women, the education of children, establishment of *love spaces,* are all developed and discussed in the series. The main hero of the books, Anastasia, is described as a young Siberian forest-based hermit, whose teachings are related to the concepts of naturalism, ecology and spirituality, which guide the principal Anastasian values.

The Anastasians move to nature-based family homesteads which are closely related to the Anastasians' understanding and definition of space—both secular and religious—resulting in the creation of *love spaces,*[5] namely, family homesteads about one hectare in size, which are conceived as linking "a person, nature, and cosmos" (Pranskevičiūtė 2015, 194). The *love space* provides a context for an alternative *system*, related to ecology, homeland, opposed to the eschatologically understood technocratic *system.*[6] These single homesteads

---

5. "Kin domain" (*Ru.:* rodovoe pomest'ye) is often synonymously used for a "family homestead," too.

6. The Anastasians interpret the social environment as a *system* that establishes obligatory behavior rules for people. It is believed, that "the *system* is a structure that is currently working by itself and is being directed towards distracting a man from Nature" (Inter-

or ecological settlements are set up around cities in various countries.

The beginning of the movement is linked with the series of the book series *The Ringing Cedars of Russia,* written by Russian Vladimir Megre from 1996. Diverse book readers' clubs, individual groups with various interests, family homesteads and their settlements, were all founded and developed around the ideas presented in these books. Even if the author does not lead the movement directly, he still has indirect influence on some processes related to the movement. Megre often participates in Anastasian events such as organized lectures (mostly in Russia), conferences, festivals, etc., and has also a family homestead in the Anastasian settlement "Zavetnoje" by the city Vladimir in Russia. In 1999, he established the Vladimir-based culture and creation support foundation "Anastasia"[7] which supports Anastasian activities, as well as family business related to the production and the international distribution of *The Ringing Cedars* book series and other derivatives.

The first nature-based spirituality settlements in the post-Soviet region were small individual communities. After the rise and spread of Anastasian ideas, this activity developed into the nature-based spiritual communitarian movement, a version of the establishment of nature-based spiritual settlements on a mass scale. Various Anastasian groups function in Russia and other post-Soviet countries, in Western Europe, Scandinavia, North America, Australia, the Republic of South Africa, etc. Quite amorphous and with their members belonging to a number of different organizations, Anastasian groups (including official clubs in the biggest cities, family homesteads and independent individuals) could be seen as counting about 1,000 in Lithuania, about 1,000 in Latvia, about 500 in Estonia, while the number of people, sharing Anastasian ideas in Russia is still vague.[8] In Lithuania, the beginning of the movement is linked with the establishment of the first book series readers club *"skambantys kedrai"* (*Lt.:* Ringing Cedars) in Kaunas, in 2002, February 20. The second Megre book readers club *"Gyvieji namai"* (*Lt.*: Living Home) has been established in Vilnius, in 2002. Similar clubs are established and in other cities and part of the people joining are involved in formation of family homesteads. According to the data of the Anastasians, at the end of 2019 there are forty family homesteads or their settlements in Lithuania, most of

---

view 2 with Algis, Anastasian, male, born in Lithuania in 1978).

7. Related to the website https://www.anastasia.ru/

8. The information about possible number of the Anastasians is presented in: Spisok deystvuy-ushchih poseleniy [List of Working Settlements]. Retrieved 18 October 2019 from http://www.eco-krug.ru/spisok-poseleniy; Rodovye pomestya, rodovye poseleniya, ekoposeleniya [Family homesteads, Settlements of Family homesteads, Eco-settlements]. Retrieved 18 October 2019 from http://poselenia.ru/search-rp?field_geo_taxonomy_country_value=59.

them consisting of one or a few families.[9] In Latvia, there have been a few unsuccessful attempts to establish Anastasian settlements in the 2000s. At the moment three family homestead settlements are still in a stage of formation. For example, the settlement "Dziesmas" (*Lv.:* Songs), existing from August 2002, has only one permanent resident and only four or five families live there during the summer period, although was initially intended to have about fifty families. The other settlements, "Ainavciems" (*Lv.:* Scenery of Village)[10] and "Gaismas Dārzi" (*Lv.:* Gardens of Light),[11] are in an early stage of development. The Estonian settlement "Raveda" (situated about 50 km from Tallinn) was established in 2005. Its existence is mainly based on the initiative of two families, although officially more families claim their participation in the life of the community. The other Estonian settlement "Mauri" (situated 35 km from Võru, 20 km to borders of Latvia and Russia) had eight people (six families) residing during the summer season in 2015.[12] Generally speaking of the Baltic states, the majority of settlements are established in Lithuania. In Latvia and Estonia, only single residents are in the settlements (also in individual nature-based spirituality or ecological homesteads), so the ideas of an alternative social project are still only at the theoretical level here. The number of individual family homesteads and settlements is not clear in Russia. According to different sources of the Anastasians and other enthusiasts of ecological settlements, there were 80 settlements in the winter, 2009–2010 (the same information dated 2009–2010 is presented on 18 October 2019),[13] or 201 settlements in 1 August 2011, 212 settlements in 22 June 2015, and 388 settlements in 18 October 2019,[14] or from 146 to 341 settlements in Russia (the website was accessed on 15 September 2011

---

9. The list of current family homesteads or their settlements in Lithuania, http://eko-gyvenvietes.wordpress.com/gimines-sodybu-gyvvenvieciu-sarasas/. The oldest settlements are considered to be established in Sidabriai, Maciūnai, Voskonys, Melkys by Vilnius, Braziūkai by Kaunas, Pakruostėlė and Sukiniai by Ukmergė, and Lamsodis by Klaipėda.

10. Latvian family homestead settlement "Ainavciems." Retrieved 6 October 2018 from https://www.facebook.com/ekociemats/.

11. Latvian family homestead settlement "Gaismas Dārzi." Retrieved 18 October 2019 from http://www.gaismasdarzi.lv/en.html.

12. Estonian family homestead settlement "Mauri." 18 October 2019 from http://anasta-sia.ee/content/mauri-puutalgud, 18 October 2019 from http://www.ecovillageroad.eu/user/10606.

13. Spisok deystvuyushchih poseleniy [List of Working Settlements]. Retrieved 18 October 2019 from http://www.eco-krug.ru/spisok-poseleniy.

14. Spisok poseleniy, sostoyashchih iz Rodovyh pomestiy [List of Settlements, Consisting of Family homesteads]. Retrieved 18 October 2019 from http://anastasia.ru/static/patri-mony_list.php.

and 9 November 2015 but the actual date of the record is unknown)[15] in Russia. These statistics show an increasing number of Anastasian settlements in Russia but, lacking dependable or official sources, they are not reliable.[16]

Baltic Anastasians individually and loosely interpret the ideas of the anthology, while the teaching is being adapted and changed by individuals in Russian groups, but the direction is common to almost all of them (Andreeva, Pranskevičiūtė 2010, 96). United by Anastasian ideas, people orientate to various activities, attribute themselves to various religious denominations, etc. However, they can be characterized as spirituality seekers, that is, they are united by the search of alternative spirituality, alternative lifestyle, also by Anastasian philosophy or some ideas of this philosophy (Pranskevičiūtė 2011, 57).

The Anastasia movement, which promotes subcultural values and lifestyles such as ecology, freedom, spirituality, and a possibility to have your own living space in nature receives rather positive estimation from societies in the Baltic states. However, the Anastasians in Russia are often treated negatively. Probably one of the reasons for the situation could be a negative approach of the Orthodox Church towards the Anastasia movement, actively presented in Russian mass media (Pranskevičiūtė 2012, 211–212).

The problem analyzed in this chapter concerns the process of Anastasian sacralization of natural space together with the romantic mode of a narrativization of a distant cultural past serving as a source for the formation of images of indigenousness in the movement. Belief in the sacredness of nature is one of the most important sources for the spirituality of Anastasians. For example, among the representatives, the conception of sacred nature often overlaps with cosmological pantheism, the personalization of nature and earth, treating humans as part of nature. Here, nature is considered to be a source of divinity, which also serves as a mediator for the communication between humanity and God (Pranskevičiūtė 2012). Such beliefs also influence the idea and establishment of alternative social projects based in natural spaces.

The subcultural "back to nature" worldview includes the ideas of coming back to the "right" world, sacralization of nature, the importance of harmony with people, the earth and God, ecological values and lifestyles in the movement. The implementation of ideas about alternative environmental and

---

15. Rodovye pomestya, rodovye poseleniya, ekoposeleniya [Family homesteads, Settlements of Family homesteads, Eco-settlements]. Retrieved 18 October 2019 from http://poselenia.ru/search-rp?field_geo_taxonomy_country_value=59.

16. Firstly, the data presented in three lists, is contradictory (different numbers of settlements are given). Secondly, in places, it does not give correct information (some settlements mentioned in the lists already do not exist, and some existing ones are not included).

spirituality are sought by forming nature-based communities and settlements while sacralizing space. The Anastasian "back to nature" worldview refers to the sources of sacred ancestral knowledge and authority, which are related to the narratives of a mythological *golden age* past, reconstruction of archaic traditions, emphasis of the importance of nature. Here, the Anastasian orientation to nature and search to reconstruct the past also correlates with contemporary pagan beliefs. For example, Sabina Magliocco considers contemporary paganism, a religion without sacred texts based on folklore and nature, which manifests itself via personal and direct experience (Magliocco 2014). According to the author, contemporary pagans use practices of reclamation for the construction of their own identity. Such practices reveal themselves by reconstruction of forgotten traditions or traditions which lost their meaning. "Reclamation, part of the process of tradition, encompasses revitalization and revival as well as the creation of new cultural forms out of what was previously rejected" (Magliocco 2014, 127). The Anastasians are in a similar way involved in a reclamation process of restoration of so called forgotten traditions, as well as in a creation of the forms of previously rejected lifestyles.

The main aim of this chapter is to discuss the process of Anastasian construction of "indigenous" and "indigenization"—to reveal how a process of Anastasian nature sacralization enhances "back to nature" worldview and lifestyles, which together with Anastasian negotiation, interpretation and presentation of traditionalistic ideas serve as a basis for an imagination of (trans) local prehistoric and local national pasts, nationalistic moods and attempts to reconstruct variously perceived traditions, as well as a development of utopian visions of a prospective *heaven on earth*.

As to the methods and scope of data, the data from fieldwork done in the Baltic countries and Russia in 2005–2015 comprise 60 semi-structured interviews with Lithuanian Anastasians[17] and 15 questionnaire-based inquiries with Lithuanian Anastasians (with 87 questions per questionnaire). It is important to mention that although it relates to fieldwork in the Baltic countries and Russia, this chapter refers only to Lithuanian Anastasian interviews, talks on internet forums, etc. Fieldwork in 2005–2008 was done during the FP6 project "Society and Lifestyles: Towards Enhancing Social Harmonization through Knowledge of Subcultural Communities (SAL)" (FP6 Prior-

---

17. Fourteen with members of the Vilnius (Lithuania) club *Gyvieji namai* (*Lt.:* Living Home), two with founders of the first Anastasia club in Lithuania *Skambantys kedrai* (*Lt.:* Ringing Cedars), which was established in 2002 in Kaunas, ten with representatives of various Lithuanian family homesteads, 18 with Anastasians in Saint Petersburg (Russia), five with Anastasians in family homesteads near Vladimir (Russia), eight with Anastasians in Riga (Latvia), and three with Anastasians in Tallinn (Estonia).

ity 7, STREP).[18] Data from documents of the researched groups and mass media, social networks and secondary sources was analyzed as well.

Nature, God and *Golden Age* Myth

The linkage with nature plays a crucial role in worldviews and lifestyles among the Anastasians. This linkage is related to a wish to (re)gain a spiritual connection (often explained as lost) with the environment—creating or restoring a harmonious relation with oneself, others, the earth and God—and the ecological values and lifestyles of the movement. Belief in the sacredness of nature is one of the most important sources for the Anastasian spirituality. Anastasians seek to get "back to nature,"[19] to (re)gain the lost personal spiritual connection with the environment and to restore the lost harmonious relation with oneself, others, the Earth, and God:

> One of the most important ideas of Anastasia is living in harmony with Nature, a life in Nature. According to the books of Megre, the ideal model of a man's life is a life in a homestead of at least one hectare. According to the books of Megre, it is like an opportunity to come back and create *heaven on earth*. Nature is conceived as the ideal piece of creation of God, and all technology as the imperfect result of ignorance and creativity of man.
> (Interview 3 with Jurgis, an Anastasian male, born in 1982 in Lithuania)

Ideas about a natural lifestyle in the Anastasian movement often overlap with cosmological pantheistic understandings ("God is everywhere"—that is, in Nature), personalizing nature ("Anastasia has told, plants react to a human, they can love or hate him, affect his health positively or negatively" [Megre 1998, 63]), equating God and nature ("God is Nature—a twitter of birds, wind, and rustle of trees…everything what is in Nature is the living book of sensual information, and much more: He touches us through Nature" (Interview 6 with Martynas, Anastasian male, born in 1981 in Lithuania), and the elements of nature-venerating pagan beliefs ("The books of Anastasia have changed my comprehension from a fear to a divinization of Nature. My way is to look for and to discover this divine system, where a man lives in a harmony with Nature" (Interview 3 with Jurgis, Anastasian male, born in 1982 in Lithuania). Equated with divine, nature also serves as a mediator for the communication between a man and God:

> Very important thing, Anastasia says about, that Nature is materialized thoughts of God. God has devised grass, trees, and animals. These are thoughts

---

18. Official website of the SAL project: http://sal.vdu.lt.

19. The word "Nature" is used to express the sacralization of nature by the Anastasians, and the word "nature" to express the author's ideas in the chapter. Nature is also synonymously identified with the Earth in the Anastasia movement.

of God and by communicating with them we communicate with God. And this is not an esoteric attitude. [...] The thoughts are being read with attention to a man and with a good imagination. You simply imagine what that or the other one man could think about at the moment. So it is also possible to talk with God in a such way.

(Interview 1 with Algis, Anastasian male, born in 1978 in Lithuania)

Such ideas are realized most visibly during the process of sacralization of (in the ideal case, natural) space (creating individual *love spaces*). Widely established Anastasian settlements are associated by Anastasians themselves with the formation of individual love spaces—instances of *heaven on earth*. Creating an individual *love space* is normally understood as a construction of a family homestead—a kind of individual project incorporating the diversity of an ecosystem, which is an ideal model not only for an alternative society, but also a model for a micro-cosmos that unites "a person, nature, and cosmos" (Pranskevičiūtė 2015, 194):

A *love space*, looking from a creative aspect, is inclusive: starting from planting trees, tending a private garden, keeping a house. Relations among people, neighbors would follow from this, even relations that are found among oneself, nature, and the cosmos.

(Interview 5 with Romas, Anastasian male, born in 1978 in Lithuania)

Perception of nature is closely related to the "back to nature" motive in the Anastasian ideology, as well as a mythological past and traditionalistic ideas in the movement. A "back to nature" motive often appears as an ecological form's reflection of a *golden age* myth—an imagination of a harmonious lifestyle of the archaic nations. Diverse variations of the *golden age* myth are related with a conception of happy and careless life of primeval humanity (*Encyclopedia of Mythology* 1997, 39–40). "Back to Nature" is often associated with coming back to God and archaic *golden age* period in the Anastasian movement:

"Back to Nature" means not only coming back to a physical Nature, living in Nature, but also coming back to such level of consciousness, which our archaic ancestors have had. Not those ancestors, which folklorists describe, but those archaic ones, who used to live twenty–thirty thousand years ago and in former times.

(Interview 1 with Algis, the Anastasian, male, born in 1978 [Lithuania])

It is possible to state that the "back to nature" motive is one of variations of the contemporary ecological *golden age* myth in the Anastasia movement.

The books of Anastasia present a narrative about the archaic period of humanity and degradation of the contemporary civilization. Vedic, Image and Occultic periods are excluded in the history division suggested by Megre.

The Vedic period is considered to be the *golden age* when people used to live like in Heaven: "Anastasia has told a lot about a particular *golden age* in the past, when people lived in a harmony with Nature" (Interview 2 with Jūra, the Anastasian, female, born in 1984 [Lithuania]).

Anastasia's philosophy provides inspiration for the spiritual quest for an individual's true self, and for this it is important the search of "one's roots." Therefore, one of the most important Anastasian values is described as "the return to your roots," which is often understood as the reconstruction of an (archaic) past lifestyle and raises issues of nationalism and of the revival of tradition, making these topics relevant to the movement.

The concept of the family homestead (*love space*) in the Anastasia movement is closely linked to the modernized ideas of the homeland, nationality and tradition. The family homestead (*love space*) itself is often equated with a homeland (more precisely, with an individually created homeland). It is believed that it is possible to form such a family homestead, which would unite generations (parents will fill the space with their love in such a way that their children will wish to stay there, grandchildren will live there, as well as it will be possible to communicate with their passed ancestors) and it will ensure the continuity of generations.

Nationalistic moods among Lithuanians are moderate: the aspiration here is more to sense, understand and get know the lifestyle of ancestors, individualistically and in communally reconstructed customs, traditions, rituals and interpreted folklore. A so-called national school (*Lt.:* tautinė mokykla) is being formed:

> Step by step, we are trying to rebuild our past feasts, to relate them again to the transformations of nature, to discover ancestral heritage. [...] Some [recent customs] have survived from ancient times. You will find links to celebrated ancestral holidays and rites told by Anastasia. What is exceptional, is that this heritage is still alive in our nation, still working today. Many things are perhaps not entirely understandable, but the preserved continuity allows you to trace again and revive what has been forgotten... Also, to recognize and to take away foreign elements, imposed distortions and to restore the legacy of the vedrusses. (From the social network discussion, 2018 October)

However, it is common for Russian Anastasians to refer strongly to nationalistic ideas (Andreeva 2009, 31–35). It is important to them to find a place where they can feel a connection with their own homeland and land (Andreeva and Pranskevičiūtė 2010). This should not be an abstract idea but relates to a personally formed space. In this case, the Lithuanian Anastasian perception of a homeland is wider: a homeland (more often "*love space*") may be anywhere (individual or 1 ha plot of land, an apartment in a city, a particular emotional state), where an individual wishes by himself to create a distinctive space:

> For me the words *love space* first of all are being associated with a safe environment, loved and close ones. This is not necessarily a hectare of land, it is first of all, I think, beautiful relations, satisfied need for security and being necessary in a family environment. These are important things, because only a person with such a foundation can feel as a full member of the society, communicate freely and create.
>
> (Interview 7 with Raminta, Anastasian, female, born in 1976 [Lithuania])

There are also and more direct expressions regarding the homeland and its role:

> By regaining our homeland, we are approaching God, the initial images of a human that our ancestors left for us. Our words, letters and sounds contain the meanings (codes) that bring together the most important features of the worldview of the nation. The disclosure of primordial meanings gives the access to the secret knowledge.
>
> (From the Anastasian social network discussion, 2018 October)

Traditionalistic ideas are also common for Russian Anastasians; the far and near past is being exalted, and the idea of the archaity of the Russian nation, which is related to the "myth of glorious ancestors" is being constructed in Megre books (Megre 2002, 97).

Exaltation of their own nation above others is also common for Russian Anastasians: it is believed that an extraordinary way of resurrection, opposite to Western ideology, is waiting for the Russian nation. Lithuanians, however, do not exalt themselves above other nations but orientate more towards reconstructions of the individualistic abstract archaic past and to old Lithuanian beliefs and traditions (Andreeva and Pranskevičiūtė 2010).[20] Nevertheless, there are some attempts to reconstruct the archaic past (or history) mentioned in the books:

> Yes, one should restore the true history step by step. And there are going to be many uncertainties. According to Anastasia, nations began to be divided by the messengers of wizards. Later, duchies joined to even larger derivatives—kingdoms, empires. They were served by great ideologists (servants of wizards)—they joined nations into religions. Diverse ideologies have been supported until today and if it is necessary they can be opposed and wars can be caused. For those ideologies, the armies are subordinate, such as, loyal to

---

20. However, a part of Lithuanian Anastasians refer to Russian Anastasian literature (written in Russian). They use Russian narratives on Russia, its great past and future mission to re-awake world.

the Pope crusaders who helped to destroy remaining vedrusses (vedras).
(From the Anastasian social network discussion, 2018 October)

"Back to Nature" is often associated with coming back to God and an archaic *golden age* period in this movement:

"Back to Nature" means not only coming back to a physical Nature, living in Nature, but also coming back to the level of consciousness our archaic ancestors had. Not those ancestors the folklorists describe, but those archaic ones, who used to live 20–30 thousands of years ago and in former times.
(Interview 1 with Algis, Anastasian male, born in 1978 in Lithuania)

The "back to nature" motive appears here as a reflection of a *golden age* myth, a vision of the harmonious lifestyle of archaic nations in the imagination of the representatives of the movement. Variations of *golden age* myth are usually related to conceptions about the happy and careless life of primeval humanity (*Mitologijos enciklopedija* [*Encyclopedia of Mythology*] 1997, 39–40).[21] It is possible to state that the "back to nature" motif is one of variations of the contemporary ecological *golden age* myth in the Anastasia movement, which presents a narrative about archaic period of humanity and degradation of the contemporary civilization. These include the Vedic, Image and Occultic periods as suggested by Megre's division into periods of history. The Vedic period is considered to be the *golden age* when people used to live like they were in Heaven[22]: "Anastasia has told a lot about a particular *golden age* in the past, when people lived in a harmony with Nature" (Interview 2 with Jūra, Anastasian, female, born in 1984, Lithuania).

The first wizards appeared in the Image period. It is stated in the Megre books that our world is being ruled by five wizards who have "occultic" archaic knowledge that they hide from other people. The contemporary Occultic period is considered to be a period of the intense degradation of human awareness. Vedrusses[23] have also fallen asleep during this period. This has happened because of the mistakes the vedrusses made in the Image period. If people solve the causes of these mistakes, a new *golden age* will emerge. Civilization is going to sleep until the last awakened one will solve the prin-

---

21. The linkage of orientation to ecology and religiosity is also noticed in the early works of of Henry D. Thoreau and John Muir (Pranskevičiūtė 2011a, 77–78). Ecological views of highly religious philosophers are overlapped with their identification of pantheistic God with nature (nature as a holiness), (Oelschlaeger 1991, 133–204).

22. Various references to Vedas are popular in contemporary Pagan beliefs (*Slavyano-Ariys-kiye Vedy* [*Slavic-Arian Vedas*] 2007; Shnirelman 2001).

23. Vedrusses, according to the books of Anastasia, are earlier widely spread archaic nations, which had sacral knowledge and was communicating directly with God.

ciple mistake of the Image period, which brought civilization to destruction, and will awaken others (Megre 2002). These ideas are expressed in the books written by the Anastasians:

> When we find our inner charms how to awake our inner ancestors inside of us,/ we will be born as young gods, like a man has told us/ through a dream, drowned in a mist, He has told a word when has decided./ He has chosen us, you and him, those who have not been created/ and has brought to a new truth, which we will have to irradiate. (*Veda prot̃eviai* [*Ancestors Lead*] 2009, 11)

In this case it is believed, that "awakened" Anastasians will be able to spread the lost "truth" to the rest of world.

Conclusion

This chapter has focused on the processes of Anastasian subcultural construction of "imagined indigenousness" with its universalistic and traditionalistic characteristics in the movement. These characteristics are related to Anastasian "indigenized" (emphasizing imaginative ancestral and local traditions) and "extended" (emphasizing relevance and prospective global engagement) discourses of nature-based spirituality, traditionalistic and nationalistic ideas influencing restoration of archaic pasts and *golden age* myth narratives.

Nature itself is experienced as "hierophany" (revealing the presence of transcendence) by the Anastasians, thus its sacralization in the movement prevails. The Anastasians consider nature as the best place for humanity's spiritual development. Here, the "back to nature" theme appears as a modern ecological variation of the *golden age* myth and as one of the most essential elements of Anastasian worldview. This ideal is related to the possibility of freeing oneself from the *system* and coming back to freedom and to the spiritual perfection of God by regaining one's lost spiritual link with Nature.

If to look at the impact of various sociocultural contexts, the cultural influence of Russia is different for Russian and Lithuanian Anastasians. Russocentrism (strong slavophile ideas) and (post)Soviet cultural heritage influences are common for Russian Anastasians. Moderate nationalistic and traditionalistic ideas are common for Lithuanian Anastasians (traditionalism is common for Russian Anastasians as well).

Looking from one side, the nationalistic question is related to an emphasis on their own nation, while from the other side it is related to the question of the spiritual revival of Russia and its future influence on the world (common for Russian Anastasians). Future research may show if the vision of Russia as a world leader in the researched subculture is an expression of a need to strengthen a national identity, or if it may reveal other reasons. It is also worth researching which ideas related to nationalism are common for Anastasians in other countries. Prospective research would contribute to the analysis of reasons of openness and attractivity of the Anastasia movement. During previous research it has been noticed that the Anastasia movement, which emphasizes nationalistic ideas, revival and individual recreation of customs and traditions, is growing globally. It is, therefore, a useful focus for considering the dynamic tension between what Johnson identifies as indigenizing and extending trajectories.

References

Andreeva, Julia. 2011. "Puteshestviye k pervoistokam: ezotericheskoye palomnichestvo anastasijcev k dol'menam Krasnodarskogo kraya" [A Journey to the Origins: Esoteric Pilgrimage to the Dolmens of the Region of Krasnodar]. In *Palomnichestvo i religioznyj turizm: mnogoobraziye interpretacij* [Pilgrimage and Religious Tourism: a Variety of Interpretations], edited by I. E. Vikulov, 4–20. Vladimir: VlGu.

———. 2009. *Proekt rodovogo poseleniya v soobschestve anastasiytsev.* [The project of family homestead's settlement in Anastasians' community]. Unpublished MA thesis, European University at St. Petersburg, Russia.

Andreeva, Julia and Rasa Pranskevičiūtė. 2010. "The conception of family homesteads in Anastasia movement: The cases of Russia and Lithuania." *Humanitāro zinātņu vēstnesis.* 18: 94–108.

Atnaujintas gyvenviečių sąrašas [Updated list of settlements], http://ekogyvenvietes. wordpress.com/gimines-sodybu-gyvenvieciu-sarasas. Retrieved 18 October 2019.

Geaves, Ron. 2004. "Contemporary Sufism." In *Encyclopedia of New Religions. New Religious Movements, Sects and Alternative Spiritualities*, edited by C. Partridge, 135–138. Oxford: Lion Publishing.

Johnson, Paul C. 2002. "Migrating bodies, circulating signs: Brazilian Candomblé, the Garifuna of the Caribbean, and the category of indigenous religions." *History of Religions* 41(4): 301–327. Reprinted in *Indigenous Diasporas and Dislocation*, edited by G. Harvey and C. D. Thompson, 63–81. London: Routledge.

Magliocco, Sabina. 2012. "Neopaganism." In *The Cambridge Companion to New Religious Movements*, edited by O. Hammer and M. Rothstein, 150–166. Cambridge: Cambridge University Press.

Mitologijos enciklopedija [Encyclopedia of Mythology]. 1997. Volume 1. Vilnius: Vaga.

Naess, Arne. 1973. "The shallow and the deep, long-range ecology movement: A summary." *Inquiry* 16: 95–100.

Nanda, Meera. 2004. "Eco-spirituality, Neo-paganism and the Hindu right. The dangers of religious environmentalism." *Women & Environments* 5: 19–22.

Oelschlaeger, Max. 1991. *The Idea of Wilderness: From Prehistory to the Age of Ecology.* New Haven, CT: Yale University Press.

Pepper, David. 1991. *Communes and the Green Vision. Counterculture, Lifestyle and the New Age.* London: Green Print.

Pranskevičiūtė, Rasa. 2015. "Communal Utopias within nature-based spiritualities: Vissarionites and Anastasians in the post-Soviet region." In *The Borders of Subculture: Resistance and the Mainstream,* edited by A. Dhoest, St. Malliet, J. Haers, B. Segaert, 183–200. Palgrave Macmillan.

———. 2012. "'Back to nature' philosophy in the Vissarion and the Anastasia movements." *Alternative Spirituality and Religion Review* 3(2): 207–224.

———. 2011. *Alternatyvių dvasingumo judėjimų tendencijos posovietinėje visuomenėje: visarionininkai ir anastasininkai* [Tendencies of alternative spiritual movements in a post-Soviet society: Vissarionites and Anastasians]. Unpublished PhD thesis, Vytautas Magnus University, Lithuania.

Sessions, George. 1994. "Deep ecology as worldview." In *Worldviews and Ecology: Religion, Philosophy, and the Environment,* edited by M. E. Tucker and J. A. Grim, 207–228. Maryknoll, NY: Orbis Books.

Shnirelman, Victor A., ed. 2001. *Neojazychestvo na prostorah Evrazii* [Neopaganism in the expanses of Eurasia]. Moskva: Biblejsko-Bogoslovskij Institut.

Taylor, Bron. 2001. "Earth and nature-based spirituality (Part I): From deep ecology to radical environmentalism." *Religion* 31(2): 175–193.

Tafjord, Bjørn O. 2018. "Romantic indigenizing of new religions in contemporary Europe: Critical methodological remarks." Paper presented at "Indigenising movements in Europe" panel at the conference of the European Association for the Study of Religions in Bern, Switzerland.

Other sources

Interviews with the Anastasians

1. Interview with Algis, male (b. 1978), the settlement of family homestead in Sukiniai (Ukmergė region, Lithuania), 12 October 2009 (joined the movement in 2002); stored in a private author's archive.

2. Interview with Jūra, female (b. 1984), Kaunas, Lithuania, 28 October 2008 (joined the movement in 2003); stored in a private author's archive.

3. Interview with Jurgis, male (b. 1982), Vilnius, Lithuania, 21 October 2008 (joined the movement in 2002); stored in a private author's archive.

4. Interview with Jurgis, male (b. 1982), Vilnius, Lithuania, 22 February 2010; stored in a private author's archive.

5. Interview with Romas, male (b. 1978), Vilnius and the settlement of family homestead near Vilnius (Lithuania), 2 December 2009 (joined the movement in 2002); stored in VMU SAL.

6. Interview with Martynas, male (b. 1981), Kaunas, Lithuania, 10 April 2012 (joined the movement in 2011); stored in a private author's archive.

7. Interview with Raminta, Anastasian, female, born in 1976 (Lithuania), 29 October 2008 (joined the movement in 2005); stored in a private author's archive.

VMU SAL—the electronic archive of the SAL project (Center for Cultural Studies (Vytautas Magnus University)); the address of the archive: http://salarchive.vdu.lt/filter/groups/anastasia.html.

Documents from the researched group, mass media and internet

Kupcova, Liudmila. 2009. *Obshcheniye s mudrecami dol'menov/ mesta sily, dol'meny i khramy sveta (gorod-kurort Gelendzhik, pos. Vozrozhdeniye, dolina reki Zhane)* [*Communication with Wisemen of Dolmens/ Places of Power, Dolmens and Shrines of World (City-resort Gelendzhik, village Vozrozhdeniye, valley of River Zhane*]. Krasnodar: (b.i.).

Latvian family homestead settlement "Ainavciems." https://www.facebook.com/ekociemats/. Facebook.com. Retrieved 18 October 2019.

Latvian family homestead settlement "Dziesmas." http://ekodziesmas.lv/ru/. Retrieved 18 October 2019.

Latvian family homestead settlement "Gaismas Dārzi." https://gaismasdarzi.wordpress.com/. Retrieved 18 October 2019.

Megre, Vladimir. 1998. *Anastasija. Esu tiems, kam esu* [Anastasia. I am for Whom I am]. Book 1. Vilnius: Asveja.

———. 1999. *Skambantys kedrai* [Ringing Cedars]. Book 2. Vilnius: Asveja.

———. 1999a. *Meilės erdvė* [Love Space]. Book 3. Vilnius: Asveja.

———. 2000. *Pasaulio sukūrimas* [Co-creation]. Book 4. Vilnius: Asveja.

———. 2001. *Kas mes?* [Who are We?]. Book 5. Vilnius: Asveja.

———. 2002. *Giminės knyga* [The Book of Kin]. Book 6. Vilnius: Asveja.

———. 2003. *Gyvybės energija* [Energy of Life]. Book 7. Vilnius: Asveja.

———. 2005. *Naujoji civilizacija* [New Civilization]. Book 8. Part 1. Vilnius: Asveja.

———. 2006. *Naujoji civilizacija. Meilės apeigos* [New Civilisation. Rites of Love]. Book 8. Part 2. Vilnius: Asveja.

———. 2010. Anasta. Moscow: Dilya.

Rodovye pomestya, rodovye poseleniya, ekoposeleniya [Family homesteads, settlements of family homesteads, ecosettlements]. http://poselenia.ru/search-rp?field_geo_taxonomy_country_value=59. Retrieved 18 October 2019.

Slavyano-Ariyskiye Vedy. Kniga pervaya. San'tii Vedy Peruna. [Slavic-Arian Vedas. Book First. Santhyas Vedas of Thunder God]. 2007. Asgard-Omsk: Tserkovnoye izdatel'stvo "ASGARD."

Spisok deystvuyushchih poseleniy [List of working settlements], http://www.eco-krug.ru/spisok-poseleniy. Retrieved 18 October 2019.

Spisok poseleniy, sostoyashchih iz Rodovyh pomestiy [List of settlements, consisting of family homesteads], http://anastasia.ru/static/patrimony_list.php. Retrieved 18 October 2019.

Veda protėviai. Gyvųjų sodybų bendruomenė [Ancestors Lead Community of Living Homesteads]. 2009. (Published diary of the Anastasian).

About the author

Rasa Pranskevičiūtė-Amoson is an anthropologist, based at Vilnius University, Institute of Asian and Transcultural Studies. Pranskevičiūtė-Amoson has experience of fifteen years (2004–2019) in applying qualitative social research methods. During this period, she has conducted fieldwork in Baltic countries, Russia, Sweden, Ukraine, Armenia, and India. She has published on the material collected during her fieldwork on post-Soviet and Soviet religiosity, alternative religious movements and subcultures. During 2014–2017, she was a book series editor in the field of New Religious Movements at De Gruyter Open. She has edited and co-edited journal issues (e.g., *Open Theology* (2017), *Journal of Lithuanian Anthropology* (to be published in 2019). Since 2016, she has been the correspondent for information concerning sociological and legal aspects of religion in Lithuania (French National Research Center (CNRS) and University of Strasbourg (France)). Since 2018, she has been President of the Lithuanian Society for the Study of Religions.

— 9 —

Modes of Indigenizing:
Remarks on Indigenous Religion as a Method

BJØRN OLA TAFJORD

Romanticisms, not colonialisms, drive the indigenizing and the religionizing in the cases described and analyzed in this special issue. In what follows, I shall explain what I mean by this observation and suggest ways to think about it critically. The task of this essay is to highlight entangled methodological and political contexts for the discussion about "indigenizing" that Graham Harvey opened in his introduction, a discussion that the different case studies then continued and exemplified. Inspired by Paul Christopher Johnson's theorizing about indigenizing (Johnson 2002a), Harvey asks whether it is useful to employ the concepts "indigenous" and "indigenizing" in studies of contemporary movements in Europe: British Druids (studied by Suzanne Owen), Italian shamans and witches (by Angela Puca), The English Bear Tribe (by Graham Harvey), Irish or Celtic Pagans (by Jenny Butler), English Powwow enthusiasts (by Christina Welch), Anastasians in Lithuania and Russia (by Rasa Pranskevičiūtė), and Goddess devotees in Glastonbury (by Amy Whitehead). These are movements (and scholars) that have been associated with the study of paganisms and the study of new religious movements, but usually not with the study of indigenous religions (except Harvey and Owen who have worked extensively in both fields of research).[1]

Introduction

In the seminal essay "Migrating Bodies, Circulating Signs: Brazilian Candomblé, the Garifuna of the Caribbean, and the Category of Indigenous Religions," Paul Christopher Johnson offers the following explication of his perspective:

---

1. In addition to their work in pagan studies, which is what they mainly draw and build on here, Harvey and Owen are widely known also for their studies of indigenous religions in other contexts (see, for example, Harvey 2000, 2013, 2016a, 2016b; Ralls-MacLeod and Harvey 2000; Harvey and Thompson 2005; Owen 2008, 2010, 2017).

Defining indigenous religions as the religions of those communities that imagine themselves in indigenous style—as organically bound to a land site—brackets the impasse between so-called romantic or essentialist and deconstructivist views of indigenous societies. Whether the Lakota actually emerged onto the surface of the earth from Wind Cave and are in an essential, primordial way the people of and from the Black Hills, versus historians' claims that they migrated into the region and conquered it after acquiring horses around 1700, is less important for my purposes than that their community makes itself imaginatively as of and related to that place. When the Garifuna say they were the first people to settle much of the coast of Honduras and Belize and forget that within a generation after their arrival in 1797 they drove the Miskito, already there, east to what is now Nicaragua, this historical fact is less important in this article than how the Garifuna understand and discursively present themselves to make community in the present. (Johnson 2002a, 306)

This is also the analytical stance that Graham Harvey, Suzanne Owen, Angela Puca, Jenny Butler, Christina Welch, Rasa Pranskevičiūtė, and Amy Whitehead have attempted to take with regard to the European cases they study. The outcome of their efforts makes me think it is time to revisit some of the issues that Johnson tries to bypass or bracket.

I propose that we, as analysts, try to distinguish, roughly, between three different poles or, better, different modes of indigenizing: between, first, indigenizing in colonial and anti-colonial modes, second, indigenizing in romantic modes, and, third, indigenizing in nationalist modes. There are both analytical and political reasons for making these distinctions and using this triadic scale. Below I shall make plain some of those reasons. Note first that the modes are heuristic ideal types, carved out by abstracting empirical observations of histories and identity politics.[2] They represent three different but related ideological currents. Deliberations on the meanings and uses of "indigenous" and "indigenizing" cannot escape historical and political realities. Scholarship is perhaps more entangled than ever before in broader ideological struggles that involve these concepts.

In practice, most cases of indigenizing are positioned somewhere in between the extremes of my triadic scale, and the qualities signaled by the different modes often overlap or mingle. But the preceding case studies of contemporary

---

2. Johnson (2002a, 311–313), too, presents his use of "indigenous" as an ideal type in the Weberian sense. Like Johnson, I do not intend to suggest that some modes of indigenizing are more authentic than other modes. I agree with his caution that "[w]e should take care that the category of indigenous religions, like the primitive and archaic before it, not serve as an epistemological and comparative anchor. [...] that the category not be used as our own [academic] crisis response, a fetish in a quixotian quest for stable, located meanings" (Johnson 2002a, 327; for comparable perspectives, see Clifford 2013; Johnson 2008).

European religious movements[3] produce notably different perspectives on what "indigenous" and "indigenizing" might entail than the one that Paul Johnson has developed in his study of the Garifuna in Honduras and Candomblé practitioners in Brazil (Johnson 2002a; see also Johnson 2002b, 2007). Whereas indigenizing in romantic modes can certainly be found also in Johnson's material, colonial and anti-colonial modes, which are fundamental as contexts for Candomblé practitioners and the Garifuna, are almost absent in these European cases. The difference between, on the one hand, indigenizing in colonial and anti-colonial modes and, on the other hand, indigenizing in romantic modes is most significant here, and I will focus on that first.[4]

Colonial and anti-colonial versus romantic modes of indigenizing

After reading the essays, my immediate thought was that they would have caused serious controversy if presented in Tromsø, the major town in the Norwegian part of Sápmi, or the Sami territory, where I live. The same would probably have happened if they were presented, say, at a meeting of the Native American and Indigenous Studies Association (NAISA) or the American Academy of Religion (AAR), instead of the 2018 meeting of the European Association for the Study of Religions (EASR) in Bern, Switzerland. Representatives of communities who are legally and politically recognized as "indigenous peoples" were largely absent in Bern. In comparison, in Tromsø, at NAISA, or at the AAR, there are always persons who self-identify as members of indigenous peoples attending panels on indigenous issues, and the scholar/activist interface is different from the EASR. In these places, it is very likely that some of the audience would have objected strongly to the attempts by European scholars to analyze these contemporary religious movements in Europe as "indigenous" or "indigenizing."

Among the Bribri in Talamanca, on the border between Costa Rica and Panama, where I have done fieldwork several times since the turn of the millennium, the claim that these European groups and their practices can be seen as *indígenas* or indigenous would probably be met with laughter. Most people there would have brushed this off as nonsense. But if one kept insist-

---

3. I call them "movements" because this is the descriptor that has been used in the discussions that the present essay is part of, but they could equally well be called "communities."

4. Indigenizing in nationalist modes is not prominent neither in Johnson's cases nor in most of the cases analyzed in this special issue (the exception is the Anastasians). Nonetheless, indigenizing in nationalist modes needs to be taken into serious account because reflections of it start appearing once we dig deeper into the cases and their contexts, and especially because it plays conspicuous roles in many political practices today both in Europe and elsewhere. I will address the relevance of this in a separate section below.

ing that Europeans and some of their practices are indigenous, many Bribris would take offense, because they regard themselves, and not foreigners, and especially not Europeans, as the authority when it comes to questions about whether someone or something is indigenous or not. From their perspectives, Europeans and European practices belong in a completely different category.[5]

In places like Tromsø and Talamanca, people have personal and communal experiences with colonialisms. Colonial histories and situations are also the base upon which a new globalizing movement of "indigenous peoples" has emerged in recent decades, supported by the United Nations and numerous other international organizations (see for example Clifford 2013; Niezen 2003, 2009).[6] These experiences and this movement have produced a strong anti-colonial discourse of indigeneity. This not only frames how many Samis, Bribris, and Native Americans now self-identify and recognize each other as indigenous, it also makes it unlikely that they would recognize as equally the indigenous groups or movements described in the essays of this special issue.

The international indigenous peoples' movement is a semi-coordinated act of resistance against historical and ongoing colonialisms (Clifford 2013; Niezen 2003, 2009). Some of these colonialisms have been and continue to be very violent, even deadly, in several cases to the point of extermination or near extermination of people as well as practices.[7] Religion, especially, is a sensitive topic because missionizing—the imposing of a new religion and attempts to eradicate an old one—has long been a significant component in most if not all of these colonialisms.[8] Even more important here, historically, the major-

---

5. On Bribris' uses of *indígena* and "indigenous," see Tafjord 2016a, 2016b. From Bribri perspectives, Europeans are *sikuapa*, originally made from a different substance and in a different way than *skowak*, *indígenas* or indigenous peoples (see also Bozzoli 1979; Nygren 1998).

6. The major institutional instruments of the international indigenous peoples' movement include the United Nations Permanent Forum on Indigenous Issues, the United Nations Declaration on the Rights of Indigenous Peoples (UNDRIP), and the International Labour Organization's Indigenous and Tribal Peoples Convention (ILO169).

7. The massive and relatively recent—but, by the broader public, largely ignored—genocide of "Indians," Native Americans, First Nations, or indigenous peoples in the territories that today are the USA and Canada, is a case in point. This has included the extermination of many of their practices, and deep transformations of their remaining practices. Systematic oppression and discrimination of Native Americans or First Nations continue in the USA and Canada today. See, for example, Deloria 1988; Nabokov 1999; Niezen 2000; Simpson 2014.

8. Missionizing has often contributed substantially to the altering of identities, sometimes weakening and sometimes empowering both indigenous identities and identities as "indigenous" (see for example Comaroff and Comaroff 1997; Longkumer 2018a, Tafjord 2016b).

ity of the colonizers have been Europeans and descendants of Europeans. In the perspectives of most members of the international indigenous peoples' movement, and in the political and legal frameworks sanctioned by the UN and other international institutions, indigenous peoples are those who have endured and resisted European colonialisms over the past five centuries.[9]

It is therefore critical to make a distinction between, on the one hand, indigenous peoples and indigeneity as this is articulated and understood by, say, Bribris in Talamanca, or Samis in Tromsø, or by those who congregate at NAISA or at UN meetings, and, on the other hand, the indigenousness claimed by or attributed to the religious movements described in the essays of this special issue: British Druids, Italian shamans and witches, the English Bear Tribe, Irish Pagans, European Powwow enthusiasts, Anastasians in Lithuania and Russia, and Goddess devotees in Glastonbury.

One of the clearest commonalities of these contemporary European movements, as we get to know them through the essays, is their salient romanticisms. They all represent indigenousness—or "imagined indigenousness"—in European romantic modes. Each in their own way, they recycle old and invent new ideas about golden but oppressed and almost forgotten local religious pasts, about grand religious ancestors or rare noble Others who can serve as exemplary guides to (post)modern seekers, and about nature worship and nature religion that can be revived or imported. They locate what they see as the ideal—that which they try to rescue and revitalize—either in a different and more glorious time or, as in the case of the Powwow enthusiasts, in a different and more glorious community and place. Primordialism and primitivism are positively valued parts of their ideologies, ethically as well as aesthetically. It is common to interpret the history of romantic ideas and movements in Europe as driven by complex reactions to modernity, including colonialism (see for example, Bauman and Briggs 2003; Geertz 2004; Lincoln 1999; Penny 2014).

Presumably, most adults are members in these romantic religious movements voluntarily. Thereby, insofar as they represent marginalized minorities in the larger societies, they have put themselves in this position by adopting particular identities, ideas, and practices. Regardless of how wholehearted

---

9. To accommodate the Garifuna and the Candomblé practitioners, who Johnson writes about, in the hegemonic discourse on indigeneity and coloniality is much easier (although not straightforward) than to do the same with the European movements analyzed in this special issue. Note that references to the Garifuna as indigenous (see for example Anderson 2009; Johnson 2002a, 2007; Palacio 2007) occur more often than references to Candomblé practitioners as indigenous. Frequently, members of both these groups are also described as African-Americans, African diaspora, or descendants of Africans. In now dominant international discourses on indigenous peoples, they represent neither prototypical indigenous Americans nor prototypical indigenous Africans.

their commitment and how difficult the discrimination that they face may be, this marks a major difference from indigenous peoples who have not joined their communities by voluntary action, who have been subjugated or marginalized against their own will, and who cannot freely abandon the positions that they are held in by colonial actors and structures.

Due to all of the above, it is crucial that scholars do not copy uncritically, and turn into academic analytical strategies, the ways in which some members of these religious movements in Europe today compare themselves to indigenous peoples around the world. Nor should we duplicate naively, as scholarly analyses, how members of the international indigenous peoples' movement now compare themselves to each other and to others.[10] Yet we must take very seriously the comparisons and the analyses that the members of these movements make.

Complicating intersections

But are not some of these European movements also engaging in colonial and anti-colonial modes of indigenizing? Consider, for example, the Powwow enthusiasts who, when they mimic Native Americans, elevate a community that has suffered from colonization and, in the process, offer an implicit critique of the dominant society of which they are a part.[11] I would argue that they do this, too, in a predominantly romantic mode. They celebrate the figure of the noble Indian. Their appropriation of Plains Indian practices and aesthetics comes across as an example of the kind of caricature that many Native Americans and members of other legally recognized indigenous peoples have termed neo-colonial and reacted to with indignation (see for example, Deloria 1988; Hilleary 2017, 2018; Owen 2008).

What about the critical stances of these European religious movements with regard to contemporary Christianity and their ideas about the historical Christian colonization of Europe? If the propagation and rule of Christianity in Europe can be seen as colonization, then it was arguably a different colonial project than the ones that people elsewhere in the world were subjected to by European powers from the 16th century onwards. The spread of Christianity in Europe was conducted by Europeans in a remoter past. Moreover, by applying Johnson's perspective without further qualifying it, one could

---

10. Needless to say, scholars should not adopt colonial or nationalist ways of comparing and analyzing either.

11. As shown by H. Glenn Penny (2014), in his study of a comparable German movement, many participants see what they do also as a celebration of values that are indigenous both to their own community and to Native Americans. Some Native American persons have participated in these gatherings and embraced this perspective.

easily argue that if any religion has become indigenous or indigenized in Europe in the past millennium, it is Christianity.[12] When looking beyond Europe from this vantage point, it becomes conspicuous how, over the past 500 years, as part of their colonial practices, Europeans and their descendants have—with relative but often remarkable success—tried to overthrow other indigenous religions in order to establish their own indigenous religion as a universal religion.[13] Without such contextual considerations, the comparison of contemporary religious movements in Europe with the communities that in recent centuries have been most marginalized by European colonialism, through the analyses of the former as "indigenous" or "indigenizing," might become an invitation to anachronistic thinking. It also risks relativizing the brutal colonial histories and structures that many members of the international indigenous peoples' movement are facing, and that provide a legal basis for the recognition of indigenous peoples internationally. This, however, does not mean that the druids, the shamans, the witches, the bear tribe, the pagans, the Anastasians, and the goddess devotees may not be marginalized too.

As I have argued elsewhere (Tafjord 2013, 2017; see also Tafjord and Alles 2018), "indigenous religion" does not always mean the traditional religion of an indigenous people. This phrase has been used in different ways also by scholars. For sure, to introduce general restrictions on uses of categories does not advance serious scholarship. For example, if we, for analytical purposes, employ "indigenous religion" as a historically and geographically contingent relational concept (as the opposite of "exogenous religion"), then we might appreciate, from a vast historical distance, reports about druids and paganism as descriptions of elements of pre-Christian European indigenous religions (for example Tacitus' reports, see Woolf 2013). Sound critique of the historical sources is a prerequisite for this approach, which quickly discloses that the contemporary religious movements in Europe are very different from the ancient communities who they purport to revive. Such a historical-critical approach furthermore reveals that these religious movements are relatively new and that they have emerged and become socially embedded somewhere in Europe. But beyond laying bare these rudimentary facts, this approach has little to offer the analysis of the cases.

Much like Johnson, I find it more interesting to notice, through the essays, how members of these new religious movements claim that they actually *rep-*

---

12. This resonates with the ideas of some contemporary European nationalists. See below.

13. Over the course of the past century, in the study of religion, it has become common to refer to Christianity as a "world religion" (see for example Masuzawa 2005; Smith 1998), a classification which suggests that it is different from and even more than an indigenous religion (see also Cox 2007).

resent a pre-Christian European religion today. The religious or spiritual continuity from pre-Christian times to the present seems to be a key component in the movements' narratives about themselves, or a vital part of their myths. What I would have liked to see even more of in the case studies is detailed descriptions and analytical unpacking of *how* different actors discursively connect with distant local religious pasts. What I miss, except in Welch's study of the Powwowers, is deeper discussions of the histories of their ideas, which would have led us to European Romanticism. I also wonder how the authors reflect on their own analyses in relation to this ideological current.

Of course, heavily colonized and widely recognized indigenous peoples are also often romantic and imaginative in their dealings with their past (see, for example, Gill 1987). In fact, now and then, everyone seems guilty of romanticism in some shape and degree. But colonial situations and structures, as well as colonial and anti-colonial histories and horizons, catalyze and condition romanticizing in critical ways. Experiences of discrimination, violence, and loss make the imagining and idealizing of bygone times, and of a community without the colonizers, a key tool for resilience and endurance.

To inscribe oneself in some of the romantic images of the colonizers, for example by joining forces with environmentalists who envision indigenous peoples as ecological sages living in harmony with nature (see for example, Conklin and Graham 1995; Ødemark 2017), is one strategy that members of indigenous peoples have sometimes used. Widespread romantic stereotypes about indigenous peoples have been effective also in and for the international indigenous peoples' movement, by offering informal criteria for mutual identification between otherwise very different peoples, and by providing international organizations and states, which are still strongly influenced by colonial gazes, with platforms for intuitive as well as formal recognition of certain communities as indigenous (see, for example, Hodgson 2014). "Strategic essentialism" (see, for example, Bell 2014; Spivak 1996) is a term that leaders in this movement often use when they talk about this.

When members of the contemporary religious movements in Europe try to indigenize by comparing themselves to indigenous peoples, what they tap into are usually romantic stereotypes developed first by European colonizers and later—now appropriated and deployed more or less strategically—by indigenous peoples themselves.[14] The essays show remarkably few examples of direct and deliberate dialogue between members of the European movements and members of indigenous peoples from other continents. The most

---

14. See, for example, Longkumer 2015 for an instructive case study of how an indigenous community has appropriated and taken advantage of once colonial stereotypes about themselves.

influential sources for these European religious movements' ideas about indigenous peoples seem to be travel reports and fiction—films as well as literature—but also scholars and academic texts. For the English Bear Tribe, for example, Graham Harvey's work plays a vital role.[15]

Nationalist affinities

A lack of firsthand engagement with internationally recognized indigenous peoples comes through also in the anthology *Contemporary Pagan and Native Faith Movements in Europe: Colonialist and Nationalist Impulses* edited by Kathryn Rountree (2015), which contains thirteen case studies of comparable European groups.[16] Surprisingly, although Rountree's book has "colonialist impulses" in its subtitle, there is hardly any mentioning of European colonialism and its consequences for indigenous peoples, not even in her introduction called "Context is everything." Insofar as she and the other contributors speak about colonialism, they mean something very different, namely how mainly British and North-American pagan leaders of different stripes influence local pagans in places like Malta and Flanders.

Many of the case studies in Rountree's anthology focus on overt nationalists. In comparison, only some of the groups described in the present volume, most notably the Anastasians in Russia, openly express support of political nationalism. Yet, the fact that others, like the British Druids, on their webpages and elsewhere, repeatedly must underscore that they do not back nationalist and racist ideas, indicates that they attract sympathies from the far right and that their teachings to some extent have affinity, at least structurally, with current right-wing ideologies.

In Europe today, nationalist movements are expanding rapidly and many of them thrive on a rhetoric of indigenousness. They, too, indigenize in romantic modes as they link national culture and peoplehood to territory and religion while imagining, idealizing, and wanting to restore a more pure and glorious society of the past. In Norway, where I live, the most extreme and infamous examples of attempts to indigenize religions in romantic nationalist

---

15. They also report being inspired by bear poetry and traditions from Finnish, Sami, Khanty Mansi, Ainu, and Nivkh peoples. See the English Bear Tribe's homepage http://www.ancientmusic.co.uk/bear_tribe/about.html (accessed 8 October 2018).

16. A notable exception is shown by Siv Ellen Kraft (2015) in her study of Sami neo-shamanism in Norway. Whereas the other case studies in Rountree's anthology all fit comfortably in the academic box of neo-paganism, Kraft's study fruitfully disturbs the customary boundary between the study of neo-paganism and the study of indigenous religions. Kraft sheds light on a conceptual and empirical middle ground, or "third space," where complex interaction between not only indigenous traditions and neo-pagan movements but also scholarship takes place. This middle ground deserves much more attention from scholars.

modes are those of the convicted individuals Anders B. Breivik, with his ideas about Christendom (see, for example, Juergensmeyer 2017, 20–23; Bangstad 2014), and Varg Vikernes, with his ideas about pre-Christian Norse traditions (see for example, Hagen 2011).[17] But they are far from alone in their ways of thinking. Much like Breivik, the Nordic as well as the British Defense League cast Christianity as the indigenous religion of Europe in opposition to Islam, which they portray as alien and invasive (see, for example, Meleagrou-Hitchens and Brun 2013). Viktor Orbán's political and ideological movement in Hungary does the same (see for example, Fekete 2016; Orbán 2007), as do several other comparable movements across Europe today.[18]

I must underscore immediately that neither the British druids nor the Italian shamans and witches, the Bear Tribe, the Irish pagans, the Powwow-enthusiasts, or the Goddess devotees do seem xenophobic or obsessed with nationhood. On the contrary, in the essays, they come across as cultural introverts, or in the case of the Powwowers, as dedicated fans of a foreign culture. Instead of being concerned with the policing of borders, they seem occupied with a search for insights in what they regard as the heart of their own traditions or, again in the powwowing case, in what they regard as the core of a spiritually superior civilization. They are depicted as seekers who are open-minded towards other societies and cultures, contemporary as well as historical ones, and who are mostly inclusive in their practices and attitudes. Nevertheless, it is evident that many of the arguments that inspire them also inspire right-wing nationalists, and both these camps align their own discourses with international discourses on and of indigenous peoples.

In their struggles for sovereignty, and against continuing colonization, many of those who are recognized as indigenous peoples in UN fora practice some sort of nationalism linked with religion, too.[19] Naga movements in Northeast India is one obvious example (see, for example, Longkumer 2018a; 2018b), and some Native Hawaiian movements is another (see, for example, Goodyear-Ka'ōpua, Hussey and Wright 2014; Johnson 2017). However, these practices

---

17. For more examples of groups who idealize and practice what they see as pre-Christian European religions, and who are hostile to Christianity, see Rountree 2015.

18. Examples of comparable movements with similar strategies abound also outside of Europe. To mention just two, take Christian nationalists in the USA (see, for example, Whitehead, Perry and Baker 2018), or the Hindutva movement in India (see, for example, Longkumer 2017). Evidently, these two cases, one in a colonial settler state, the other in a post-colonial state, further complicate the issue of relations between indigenizing in colonial and anti-colonial, romantic, and nationalist modes in ways that are beyond the scope of this essay.

19. Due to the colonial history and ring of "religion," in many communities the preferred term for practices that would otherwise fit in scholarly definitions of religion is "spirituality."

are, in most cases, reactive and secondary to indigenizing in colonial and anti-colonial modes.[20] Therefore, analytically, it is crucial to consider the explicit or implicit nationalisms of different indigenous peoples' rights and sovereignty movements as visionary assemblages of alternative orders, advanced in long-lasting and at times violent struggles against coloniality. Then we can also examine how they draw on and conjure up (often romanticized) memories of pre-colonial or early contact institutions, and how they imagine (often in romanticized fashion) new collective paths towards a decolonized future.

As all of the above suggests, in practice, the boundaries between indigenizing in colonial and anti-colonial modes versus romantic modes versus nationalist modes are far from clear-cut. Yet I do think it is important for scholars to take into account the differences between these three modes of indigenizing. I will return to this toward the end of this essay, but first I shall tackle Harvey's question about the usefulness of the concepts "indigenous" and "indigenizing" from another angle.

Useful for whom, for what, and in which contexts?

Harvey's invitation to test the utility of the concepts "indigenous" and "indigenizing," and the responses that have come in the foregoing essays, call for three clarifying questions: Useful for whom? Useful for what? Useful in which contexts?

To the first question: The case studies have demonstrated that scholars, as well as the folks whom they study, can and do use the term "indigenous" successfully, or creatively, in their differing projects, which in spite of diverging purposes (see below) all contribute to an indigenizing of certain European people, practices, objects, and ideas. Actually, there is a larger lexicon of indigeneity doing effective work for the scholars as well as for the communities studied. "Native," "tribe," "spirituality," and "shamanism" are just some among the many other concepts that circulate in and travel between scholarly language and the religious, political, or otherwise ideological and pragmatic rhetoric of the people populating the studies.

The second question draws attention to the particular ends that "indigenous" and the related concepts here serve. Obviously, detailed uses are best described and contextualized in the case studies. However, on a more general level, sev-

---

20. Fifteen years ago, the anthropologist Adam Kuper started a heated debate with the publication of the essay "The Return of the Native" (2003). In it, he claims that the indigenous peoples' movement promoted by the UN thrives on old notions of primitive peoples and "exploits the very general European belief that true citizenship is a matter of ties of blood and soil" (Kuper 2003, 395). Numerous responses critical of Kuper's critique followed, among them Ramos 2003; Kenrick and Lewis 2004; Saugestad 2004; and Barnard 2006.

eral sorts of uses may be observed. First, note how these concepts are used for *analysis*. They are employed as theoretical tools, either heuristically or with more fixed meanings and results. Scholars use them for analysis all the time, and so do others.[21] Those who scholars study (with) do their analyses, too, often with the same concepts that scholars use. What Arthur Pendragon, one of the leaders of the British Druids, offers in the BBC interview quoted by Owen where he says that "We are looking at the indigenous religion of these isles—it's not a new religion but one of the oldest," is clearly also an analysis that parallels (and competes with) scholarly analyses. To make his claim, he has sought, observed and interpreted data, and theorized based on his findings.

The same concepts are used for *politics*, that is, for making and influencing agendas, decisions, programs, and projects. For example, as Owen notes, Pendragon seeks not only official recognition of Druidry as a historical British religion but also special access to Stonehenge, and he wants a reburial of the human remains found there to take place. Furthermore, the concepts are used for making *history*, either to tell alternative histories or to authenticate a more or less established narrative about the past, or to give an account located somewhere in between alternative and established versions. Puca, for example, reports how those who identify as witches and shamans in Italy today speak about the continuous existence of persons like themselves in their families or local communities throughout history.

Another field of usage for "indigenous" and the related concepts is *ethics*. They are deployed to sanction particular kinds of behavior, for instance in the English Bear Tribe where an emphasis on humans' place in the food chain generates critical reflections about and ritual protocols for the treatment of animals and eating. There, indigenous foodways become synonymous with ethical foodways. The concepts are used also for *aesthetics*, to convey or create certain expressions, impressions, expectations, gazes, emanations, auras, appreciations, or sensations. Feathers, ponchos, and moccasins are not the only things that the English Powwow enthusiasts put on; they also dress up in concepts like "Indian," "native," "indigenous," and "spiritual." Moreover, the concepts are used frequently for doing *theology* or theologizing, for instance, in Glastonbury, in order to think about a Goddess in particular ways. *Sociality* and *identification* are yet other uses of the concepts, including the formation and maintenance of social groups, or of "Us" and "Others," through inclusion and exclusion, association and disassociation. Take, for example, Butler's Irish or Celtic Pagans. By making "Celtic" a central node in their articulations of indigeneity, they are able to bypass troubled connotations of Irishness, and

---

21. For an overview of various ways in which scholars use "indigenous religion(s)," see Tafjord 2017.

include people beyond Ireland in their group, as well as practices that others would see as Catholic in their activities. At the same time, they distinguish themselves from those who are not Celtic and their activities from those with a Christian and not Celtic pedigree. Hence they attain senses of both sharedness and specialness. *Legal recognition* is sometimes sought and made possible by uses of these concepts. The context of Pendragon's claim to BBC was the British Charity Commission's official classification of Druidry as a religion. The concepts are also making certain *economies* thrive, as they brand and add value to products, including religious objects or practices, and make them more attractive on some markets. They are handy, for example for the Anastasians, when they make efforts to spread, grow, and root their ideas and practices in different Slavic and Baltic communities. Not to forget, the use of "indigenous" and related concepts also make the study of paganisms (and its scholars) more interesting on a larger academic marketplace. These are just some of the sorts or fields of uses that can be observed in and generalized from the foregoing case studies.[22] It is important to note that in practice, it is rarely if ever possible to speak about only one such usage without leaving out important aspects of an enterprise or an event. Multiple simultaneous uses—some more conscious or foregrounded than others—seems to be the rule.

The third question, about contexts, is impossible to answer in general terms. The successfulness of the deployment of "indigenous" and "indigenizing" is contextually contingent. Like I have pointed out above, uses of "indigenous" and "indigenizing" that may be welcomed in some scholarly contexts, for example in the study of paganisms, may be met with criticism in other scholarly contexts, for example in indigenous studies. The case studies in this special issue demonstrate a bewildering array of situations in which indigenizing is efficacious, often in various ways at the same time, both for scholars and for others. Comparable selections of case studies of indigenizing of religions among legally recognized indigenous peoples, or among nationalists, would have provided insights into significantly different contexts, where the usefulness of the concepts would have played out in other ways.

Indigenizing and religionizing

In addition to shedding light on indigenizing, the case studies in this special issue provide glimpses of processes that we might think of as "religionizing"

---

22. By all means, scholars of religion are engaged not only in analysis and the commodification of their products and services. Either individual scholars recognize it or not, their work and their uses of "indigenous religion" may interfere in politics, history making, ethics, aesthetics, theology, sociality, identities, legal recognition, as well as in numerous other institutions and domains of life.

(or "religionization," or "religionification," see Dressler 2013, 2019; Tafjord 2016a, 2016b). By religionizing, I mean the assembling and translation of practices, practitioners, objects, and ideas into representations or instances of "religion" or "religiosity." The treatment of these contemporary European movements as religions or religious depends on such procedures. Even if the authors of the essays do not address this issue explicitly, they all engage in religionizing in this sense, as do many of the members of the movements that they study. Those who take for granted that they study or participate in religion do this unconsciously. If we think of indigenizing in parallel terms, we become attentive to the double translational move—the indigenizing and religionizing—that is required to constitute something as "indigenous religion."

As we might deduce, for example from Amy Whitehead's study of the Goddess movement in Glastonbury, there are different degrees of indigenizing and religionizing going on. Whereas some—the scholars here in particular—translate practices, practitioners, objects, and ideas *all the way into* "indigenous religion," that is, articulate them with these precise words, others translate them only part of the way, *toward* "indigenous religion."[23] Different paths or registers are available for partial translations toward indigenous religion. As we have seen in the foregoing case studies, instead of speaking about indigenous "religion," many actors prefer indigenous "spirituality" or indigenous "tradition." Instead of "indigenous," some favor "native" or "tribal." Terms like shaman and shamanism, or animist and animism, may in many contexts index or hint at both indigeneity and religion. In other words, special vocabularies—alongside special repertoires of symbols, gestures, and other actions—are available for anyone who wants to represent or frame particular practices, practitioners, objects, and ideas as more or less indigenous and more or less religious, and thereby as strongly or loosely associated with an indigenous religion.

The translation of something or someone towards or into "indigenous religion" might be mindful, strategic, and heuristic, as is the case for the researchers in this special issue. The members of the movements that they study may also be mindful, strategic, and heuristic with their translations. Still, most translations are part of a tradition, that is, they refer to and build on previous translations and demonstrate various degrees of so-called "path

---

23. Scholars of religion are among the most eager to translate things all the way into religion, often even if the informants do not do this themselves. Since to study phenomena as "religion" is the basic business idea of our discipline, this observation should not come as a surprise. In fact, for this special issue, the authors have been given the explicit task to translate their cases into indigenous or indigenizing religion, in order to test the fruitfulness of this particular translation.

dependence."[24] Over time, many translations have become naturalized and taken for granted. There are long colonial histories and genealogies of both indigenizing and religionizing (see, for example, Chidester 1996, 2014; Todorov 1982; Wenger 2009). The indigenizing and religionizing of certain practices, practitioners, objects, and ideas are historically particular European enterprises (see also Balagangadhara 1994; Mandair 2009). Others have taken up such translations in reaction to European practices. Only in recent decades, with the emergence of the relatively influential international indigenous peoples' movement, has a reconstitution of indigenous religion as a mostly positive formation taken place, at least in some contexts, partly supplanting earlier and usually pejorative ideas about primal religion, primitive religion, superstition, and idolatry (see for example, Cox 2007; Johnson 2002a, 309). For indigenous peoples, the new positive recognition of indigenous religions has been hard-fought, and in many settings, they continue to face entrenched negative and even demonizing attitudes as missionaries and modernizers keep targeting their practices. This is why representatives of indigenous peoples are often zealous when it comes to protecting the new status that they have won through a partial conquest and recalibration of a conceptual apparatus that used to be controlled by their colonizers. Presumably, this increasingly positive status of indigenous religion is also part of the explanation of why members of some new movements in Europe now want to sail under this flag. Moreover, I believe it is one of the reasons why some scholars now choose this concept for their analyses of new religious movements who are otherwise often marginalized both in scholarship and in society at large.

Indigenous religion as a method

If we follow the anthropologist Marisol de la Cadena's lead, we can think of concepts as methods (de la Cadena 2015; Taguchi 2017; see also de la Cadena and Blaser 2018). In this perspective, the translating of subjects and objects into indigenous religion—the combined indigenizing and religionizing—becomes an act of "thinking conceptually." It becomes a reflexive, creative, critical, constructive, and sometimes systematic method for (re)assembling, (re)framing, (re)connecting, comparing, and transforming entities: histories, groups, and practices. Conceiving of indigenous religion as a method foregrounds the question: What do different actors *do* with "indigenous" and "religion," or, what do they achieve with their indigenizing and religionizing? The same question ought to be asked of everyone, scholars included. While the useful-for-what question above made us aware of several generalized fields of uses, thinking about indigenous religion as a method encourages us to

---

24. On the concept of "path dependence," see for example, Mahoney 2000.

scrutinize individual speech acts and the particular situations in which they are performed, and hence to appreciate more in detail the work that the concepts are employed to do in each instance.

Instead of constructing a test of the usefulness of a concept based on a universalized measure, such an approach requires that we follow Wittgenstein's recommendation to look for the job that a concept is put to do in different "language games" (Wittgenstein [1953] 2009). In order to identify what "indigenous" (or indigenizing) and "religion" (or religionizing) are achieving in each instance, we need to detect what the game played is all about. We need to consider the double move—the indigenizing and the religionizing—in relation to the "rules" and the "world" of the game. Take, for example, the Standing Rock Sioux scholar Vine Deloria's move (in Deloria 2003), that Owen mentions in her essay. Deloria suggested that Europeans and their descendants go study their own indigenous religion, Paganism. They should do that instead of bothering or intruding on Native Americans. With this move he was (re)creating and emphasizing a "we" and an "other"—and making a distinction between "ours" and "theirs" or "yours." To understand Paganism was not Deloria's project here. In this occasion, he was not interested in the details of Paganism, and he did not care much about what Europeans and their descendants did, as long as they did their own thing instead of interfering in Native American practices. His "game" was all about the distinction—the drawing and policing of a border. The momentary establishment of an equivalence, the making of the comparison, between Native American indigenous religion and European indigenous religion, was pragmatic and served an overarching task. Apart from being ancient and belonging to particular people in particular places, and sharing a role in Christian doctrine, Deloria was not saying that Native American practices and Paganism are similar, comparable, or exchangeable—quite the opposite.[25]

Now, how does indigenous religion as a method help different actors achieve different things in the case studies that make up this special issue? Due to the complexities of each case, and the limited space available here, I can only mention a few of their many accomplishments. Here are some of the most obvious: Harvey, Owen, Puca, Butler, Welch, Pranskevičiūtė, and Whitehead all use this method to create a new angle from whence to approach and ana-

---

25. Deloria's argument, and the language game that he plays, is reminiscent of arguments and language games that I have heard numerous times among the Bribri in Talamanca (see, for example, Tafjord 2016a, 2016b). Bribris, too, tend to recommend—and even demand—that *sikuapa* ("foreigners") do their own things; that what is right for foreigners, is not necessarily right for Bribris, and vice versa, especially but not only with regard to religion.

lyze their materials. British Druids use this method to relate to land, a place, and its history, as well as to connect and identify with something (imagined as) pre-Christian. Members of the English Bear Tribe use it to compare themselves to both pre-Christians and contemporary indigenous peoples, and to imagine certain things as nature and natural. So do the Anastasians, who also use it to claim superiority. Some use this method to import and export practices like witchcraft and shamanism, or Powwowing. Almost everyone who uses it do so to accommodate something or someone in one's own group, culture, place, or practice. The Powwow enthusiasts use it to play Indians, but also to deal with colonial guilt. Anastasians and Bear Tribe members use it to imagine and deal with the future. The Goddess devotees in Glastonbury and Celtic Pagans in Ireland use it to construct a new past, or—as they see it—to reconstruct and revitalize almost forgotten practices from the past, and to mark space and (re)draw borders. Practically all the practitioners described in the essays use it to contest the dominant religion in their broader home societies, which in all these cases is some version of Christianity. And, importantly, the authors of the essays use it to contest the marginality of the movements they describe, by suggesting that they are comparable to indigenous religions elsewhere in the world.

Indigenous religion as a figure of power

Let us return to the observation that "indigenous religion" has become an increasingly positive figure across a number of academic, political, cultural, and religious discourses in recent years.[26] We might even say that, in some contexts, especially where multiculturalism and liberal democracy are influential ideologies, indigenous religion has become a figure of power (Tafjord and Alles 2018; cf. Povinelli 2016; Comaroff and Comaroff 2009). Relatively widespread international recognition—if not always in practice then at least formally—of indigenous peoples' rights and of religious rights, sponsored by powerful institutions like the United Nations, the International Labour Organziation, international legislation, numerous nation-states, and countless NGOs, has made indigenous religion not just part of the vocabulary but also part of the functional apparatuses of contemporary politics, law, economy, education, healthcare, and theology. In short, sometimes it has leverage in powerful institutions and muscle against mighty opponents (see Tafjord and Alles 2018; Johnson and Kraft 2018; Årsheim 2018; McNally 2017;

---

26. Yet we must not forget that, simultaneously, in other discourses, for example in Christian mission networks, "indigenous religion" is often associated with primitivism and superstition, negative associations that often have real consequences for the practices and the practitioners who become assembled and targeted under and by means of this figure.

Tafjord 2016a). In many contexts, it offers some protection for ideas, practices, places, and groups, and it might pave the way for benefits or privileges.[27]

This has made it attractive to many actors, and, in principle, the figure is available for anyone who wants to try to inscribe his or her own group, or some other group, and the group's practices in it. To start benefitting from such inscriptions, one need not gain the recognition of everyone. It is enough to convince the right audiences in each context. Not entirely unlike how clever representatives of indigenous peoples with long colonial histories and an anti-colonial agenda have managed to appropriate and change to their own advantage what was once a colonial method and figure, representatives of new religious movements in Europe, and the scholars who study them, now try to adopt and adapt the method and the figure of indigenous religion for their own purposes.

The groups addressed in this special issue are relatively small and marginal. Their influence is quite limited, so, at first glance, it might not seem to matter much politically that they compare themselves to, and that scholars do not distinguish them clearer from, those who today indigenize and religionize themselves and their practices, objects, and ideas in anti-colonial modes. However, because these romantic new religious movements in Europe and their ethnographers are not alone in challenging the meanings and borders of indigenous religion, but joined by other much larger movements that also indigenize and religionize in romantic modes, namely right-wing nationalist movements both within and beyond Europe, they do contribute seriously to a diluting and potential jeopardizing of the fragile anti-colonial project of the internationally recognized indigenous peoples' movement. What will this do to the future utility of this method and this figure for people who continue to be heavily caught up in colonial or colonializing structures? And how do we as scholars contribute to that future?

Acknowledgments

A short version of these remarks was presented in response to two panels titled "Indigenizing movements in Europe" at the 2018 conference of the European Association for the Study of Religions in Bern, Switzerland. Thanks to Graham Harvey for inviting me to comment critically on the panels and on the essays, and to the authors of the essays for their sharing of drafts and ideas. Also thanks to May-Lisbeth Brew, Sam Gill, Monica Grini,

---

27. Concepts like "indigenous religion" (see Tafjord 2016a) and "indigenous knowledges" (see Whyte 2018) have become efficient foreign relations tools for many indigenous peoples today. Furthermore, like Whyte (2018) points out, in many cases, such concepts may now have what he calls "governance-value" also in the internal affairs indigenous communities.

Rosalind Hackett, Helen Jennings, Greg Johnson, Siv Ellen Kraft, Arkotong Longkumer, Liudmila Nikanorova, Nils Oskal, and Håkan Rydving for their critical and encouraging comments to my remarks.

References

Anderson, Mark. 2009. *Black and Indigenous: Garifuna Activism and Consumer Culture in Honduras*. Minneapolis: University of Minnesota Press.

Årsheim, Helge. 2018. "Including and excluding indigenous religion through law." *Numen* 65(5–6): 531–561. https://doi.org/10.1163/15685276-12341511

Balagangadhara, S. N. 1994. *"The Heathen in His Blindness…": Asia, the West and the Dynamic of Religion*. Leiden: Brill. https://doi.org/10.1163/9789004378865

Bangstad, Sindre. 2014. *Anders Breivik and the Rise of Islamophobia*. London: Zed books.

Barnard, Alan. 2006. "Kalahari Revisionism, Vienna and the 'indigenous peoples' debate." *Social Anthropology* 14(1): 1–16. https://doi.org/10.1111/j.1469-8676.2006.tb00020.x

Bauman, Richard and Charles L. Briggs. 2003. *Voices of Modernity: Language Ideologies and the Politics of Inequality*. Cambridge: Cambridge University Press. https://doi.org/10.1017/CBO9780511486647

Bell, Avril. 2014. "Strategic essentialism, indigenous agency and difference." In *Relating Indigenous and Settler Identities: Beyond Domination*, 116–136. London: Palgrave Macmillan. https://doi.org/10.1057/9781137313560_5

Bozzoli de Wille, María E. 1979. *El nacimiento y la muerte entre los bribris*. San José: Editorial Universidad de Costa Rica.

Chidester, David. 1996. *Savage Systems: Colonialism and Comparative Religion in Southern Africa*. Charlottesville: University of Virginia Press.

———. 2014. *Empire of Religion: Imperialism and Comparative Religion*. Chicago, IL: University of Chicago Press. https://doi.org/10.7208/chicago/9780226117577.001.0001

Clifford, James. 2013. *Returns: Becoming Indigenous in the Twenty-First Century*. Cambridge, MA: Harvard University Press.

Comaroff, John L. and Jean Comaroff. 1997. *Of Revelation and Revolution, Volume 2: The Dialectics of Modernity on a South African Frontier*. Chicago, IL: University of Chicago Press. https://doi.org/10.7208/chicago/9780226114675.001.0001

———. 2009. *Ethnicity, Inc.* Chicago, IL: University of Chicago Press. https://doi.org/10.7208/chicago/9780226114736.001.0001

Conklin, Beth A. and Laura R. Graham. 1995. "The shifting middle ground: Amazonian indians and eco-politics." *American Anthropologist* 97(4): 695–710. https://doi.org/10.1525/aa.1995.97.4.02a00120

Cox, James L. 2007. *From Primitive to Indigenous: The Academic Study of Indigenous Religions*. Aldershot: Ashgate.

de la Cadena, Marisol. 2015. *Earth Beings: Ecologies of Practice across Andean Worlds*. Durham, NC: Duke University Press. https://doi.org/10.1215/9780822375265

de la Cadena, Marisol and Mario Blaser. 2018. "Pluriverse: Proposals for a world of many worlds." In *A World of Many Worlds*, edited by M. de la Cadena and M. Blaser, 1–22. Durham, NC: Duke University Press. https://doi.org/10.1215/9781478004318

Deloria, Vine, Jr. 1988 [1969]. *Custer Died for Your Sins*. Norman: University of Oklahoma Press.

———. 2003 [1973]. *God Is Red: A Native View of Religion*. Golden, CO: Fulcrum.

Dressler, Markus. 2013. *Writing Religion: The Making of Turkish Alevi Islam*. Oxford: Oxford University Press. https://doi.org/10.1093/acprof:oso/9780199969401.001.0001

———. 2019. "Modes of religionization: A constructivist approach to secularity." Working Paper Series of the HCAS "Multiple Secularities—Beyond the West, Beyond Modernities" 7, Leipzig University. https://www.multiple-secularities.de/media/wps7_dressler_religionization.pdf (accessed September 14, 2019).

Fekete, Liz. 2016. "Hungary: Power, punishment, and the 'Christian-National idea'." *Race and Class* 57(4): 39–53. https://doi.org/10.1177/0306396815624607

Geertz, Armin W. 2004. "Can we move beyond primitivism? On recovering the indigenes of indigenous religions in the academic study of religions." In *Beyond Primitivism: Indigenous Religious Traditions and Modernity*, edited by J. K. Olupona, 37–70. London: Routledge.

Gill, Sam D. 1987. *Mother Earth: An American Story*. Chicago, IL: University of Chicago Press.

Goodyear-Ka'ōpua, Noelani, Ikaika Hussey and Erin K. Wright, eds. 2014. *A Nation Rising: Hawaiian Movements for Life, Land, and Sovereignty*. Durham, NC: Duke University Press. https://doi.org/10.1215/9780822376552

Hagen, Ross. 2011. "Musical style, ideology, and mythology in Norwegian Black Metal." In *Metal Rules the Globe: Heavy Metal Music Around the World*, edited by J. Wallach, H. M. Berger and P. D. Greene, 180–199. Durham, NC: Duke University Press. https://doi.org/10.1215/9780822392835-008

Harvey, Graham and Charles D. Thompson Jr, eds. 2005. *Indigenous Diasporas and Dislocations*. Aldershot: Ashgate.

Harvey, Graham, ed. 2000. *Indigenous Religions: A Companion*. New York: Cassell.

Harvey, Graham. 2013. "Why study indigenous religions?" In *Critical Reflections on Indigenous Religions*, edited by J. L. Cox, 19–28. Farnham: Ashgate.

————. 2016a. "Performing indigeneity and performing guesthood." In *Religious Categories and the Construction of the Indigenous*, edited by C. Hartney and D. J. Tower, 74–91. Leiden: Brill. https://doi.org/10.1163/9789004328983_006

————. 2016b. "Indigenising in a globalised world: The re-seeding of belonging to lands." *Worldviews: Global Religions, Culture, and Ecology* 20(3): 300–310. https://doi.org/10.1163/15685357-02003007

Hilleary, Cecily. 2017 (May 4). Native Americans decry appropriation of their history, culture. *Voice of America News*. https://www.voanews.com/a/native-americans-decry-appropriation-of-their-hist/3837209.html (accessed September 21, 2018).

————. 2018 (March 7). #DearNonNatives: What Native Americans want non-natives to know. *Voice of America News* https://www.voanews.com/a/dear-non-natives-what-native-americans-want-us-to-know/4284194.html (accessed September 21, 2018).

Hodgson, Dorothy L. 2014. "Culture claims: Being Maasai at the United Nations." In *Performing Indigeneity: Global Histories and Contemporary Experiences*, edited by L. R. Graham and H. G. Penny, 55–82. Lincoln: University of Nebraska Press. https://doi.org/10.2307/j.ctt1d9nmw6.7

Johnson, Greg. 2008. "Authenticity, invention, articulation: Theorizing contemporary Hawaiian traditions from the outside." *Method and Theory in the Study of Religion* 20(3): 243–258. https://doi.org/10.1163/157006808X317464

————. 2017. "Materialising and performing Hawaiian religion(s) on Mauna Kea." In *Handbook of Indigenous Religion(s)*, edited by G. Johnson and S. E. Kraft, 156–175. Leiden: Brill. https://doi.org/10.1163/9789004346710_010

Johnson, Greg and Siv E. Kraft. 2018. "Standing rock religion(s): Ceremonies, social media, and music videos." *Numen* 65(5–6): 499–530. https://doi.org/10.1163/15685276-12341510

Johnson, Paul C. 2002a. "Migrating bodies, circulating signs: Brazilian Candomblé, the Garifuna of the Caribbean, and the category of indigenous religions." *History of Religions* 41(4): 301–327. https://doi.org/10.1086/463690

————. 2002b. *Secrets, Gossip and Gods: The Transformation of Brazilian Candomblé*. Oxford: Oxford University Press. https://doi.org/10.1093/0195150589.003.0008

————. 2007. *Diaspora Conversions: Black Carib Religion and the Recovery of Africa*. Berkeley: University of California Press.

Juergensmeyer, Mark. 2017. *Terror in the Mind of God: The Global Rise of Religious Violence*. Oakland: University of California Press.

Kenrick, Justin and Jerome Lewis. 2004. "Indigenous peoples' rights and the politics of the term 'indigenous'." *Anthropology Today* 20(2): 4–9. https://doi.org/10.1111/j.0268-540X.2004.00256.x

Kraft, Siv E. 2015. "Sami Neo-shamanism in Norway: Colonial grounds, ethnic revival and pagan pathways." In *Contemporary Pagan and Native Faith Movements in Europe: Colonialist and Nationalist Impulses*, edited by K. Rountree, 25–42. New York: Berghahn. https://doi.org/10.2307/j.ctt9qctm0.6

Kuper, Adam. 2003. "The return of the native." *Current Anthropology* 44(3): 389–395. https://doi.org/10.1086/368120

Lincoln, Bruce. 1999. *Theorizing Myth: Narrative, Ideology, and Scholarship*. Chicago, IL: University of Chicago Press.

Longkumer, Arkotong. 2015. "'As our ancestors once lived': Representation, performance and constructing a national culture amongst the Nagas of India." *Himalaya* 35(1): 51–64.

———. 2017. "Is Hinduism the world's largest indigenous religion?" In *Handbook of Indigenous Religion(s)*, edited by. G. Johnson and S. E. Kraft, 263–278. Leiden: Brill. https://doi.org/10.1163/9789004346710_017

———. 2018a. "'Along Kingdom's Highway': The proliferation of Christianity, education, and print amongst the Nagas in northeast India." *Contemporary South Asia* 27(2): 160–178. https://doi.org/10.1080/09584935.2018.1471041

———. 2018b. "Bible, guns, and land: Sovereignty and nationalism amongst the Nagas of India." *Nations and Nationalism* 24(4): 1097–1116. https://doi.org/10.1111/nana.12405

Mahoney, James. 2000. "Path dependence in historical sociology." *Theory and Society* 29(4): 507–548. https://doi.org/10.1023/A:1007113830879

Mandair, Arvind-Pal S. 2009. *Religion and the Specter of the West: Sikhism, India, Postcoloniality, and the Politics of Translation*. New York: Columbia University Press. https://doi.org/10.7312/mand14724

Masuzawa, Tomoko. 2005. *The Invention of World Religions: Or, How European Universalism Was Preserved in the Language of Pluralism*. Chicago, IL: University of Chicago Press. https://doi.org/10.7208/chicago/9780226922621.001.0001

McNally, Michael D. 2017. "Religion as peoplehood: Native American religious traditions and the discourse of indigenous rights." In *Handbook of Indigenous Religion(s)*, edited by G. Johnson and S. E. Kraft, 52–79. Leiden: Brill. https://doi.org/10.1163/9789004346710_004

Meleagrou-Hitchens, Alexander and Hans Brun. 2013. *A Neo-Nationalist Network: The English Defence League and Europe's Counter-Jihad Movement*. London: ICSR.

Nabokov, Peter, ed. 1999. *Native American Testimony: A Chronicle of Indian-White Relations from Prophecy to Present, 1492–2000*. London: Penguin.

Niezen, Ronald. 2000. *Spirit Wars: Native North American Religions in the Age of Nation Building*. Berkeley: University of California Press.

————. 2003. *The Origins of Indigenism: Human Rights and the Politics of Identity*. Berkeley: University of California Press.

————. 2009. *The Rediscovered Self: Indigenous Identity and Cultural Justice*. Montreal: McGill-Queen's University Press.

Nygren, Anja. 1998. "Struggle over meanings: Reconstruction of indigenous mythology, cultural identity, and social representation." *Ethnohistory* 45(1): 31–63. https://doi.org/10.2307/483171

Ødemark, John T. 2017. "Timing indigenous culture and religion: Tales of conversion and ecological salvation from the Amazon." In *Handbook of Indigenous Religion(s)*, edited by G. Johnson and S. E. Kraft, 138–155. Leiden: Brill. https://doi.org/10.1163/9789004346710_009

Orbán, Viktor. 2007. "The role and consequences of religion in former communist countries." *European View* 6: 103–109. https://doi.org/10.1007/s12290-007-0003-9

Owen, Suzanne. 2008. *The Appropriation of Native American Spirituality*. London: Continuum.

————. 2010. "Production of sacred space in the Mi'kmaq Powwow." *Diskus* 11. http://jbasr.com/basr/diskus/diskus11/owen.htm

————. 2017. "Unsettled natives in the Newfoundland imaginary." In *Handbook of Indigenous Religion(s)*, edited by G. Johnson and S. E. Kraft, 221–233. Leiden: Brill. https://doi.org/10.1163/9789004346710_014

Palacio, Joseph. 2007. "How did the Garifuna become an indigenous people? Reconstructing the cultural persona of an African-Native American people in Central America." *Pueblos y Fronteras* 4. https://doi.org/10.22201/cimsur.18704115e.2007.4.226

Penny, H. Glenn. 2014. "Not playing indian: Surrogate indigeneity and the German hobbyist scene." In *Performing Indigeneity: Global Histories and Contemporary Experiences*, edited by L. R. Graham and H. G. Penny, 169–205. Lincoln: University of Nebraska Press. https://doi.org/10.2307/j.ctt1d9nmw6.11

Povinelli, Elizabeth A. 2016. *Geontologies: A Requiem to Late Liberalism*. Durham, NC: Duke University Press. https://doi.org/10.1215/9780822373810

Ralls-MacLeod, Karen and Graham Harvey, eds. 2000. *Indigenous Religious Musics*. Aldershot: Ashgate.

Ramos, Alcida R. 2003. "Comments." *Current Anthropology* 44(3): 397–398. https://doi.org/10.1086/344652

Rountree, Kathryn, ed. 2015. *Contemporary Pagan and Native Faith Movements in Europe: Colonialist and Nationalist Impulses*. New York: Berghahn. https://doi.org/10.2307/j.ctt9qctm0

Saugestad, Sidsel. 2004. "On the return of the native." *Current Anthropology* 45(2): 263–264. https://doi.org/10.1086/382253

Simpson, Audra. 2014. *Mohawk Interruptus: Political Life across the Borders of Settler States*. Durham, NC: Duke University Press. https://doi.org/10.1215/9780822376781

Smith, Jonathan Z. 1998. "Religion, religions, religious." In *Critical Terms for Religious Studies*, edited by M. C. Taylor, 269–284. Chicago, IL: University of Chicago Press.

Spivak, Gayatri C. 1996 [1985]. "Subaltern studies: Deconstructing historiography." In *The Spivak Reader*, edited by D. Landry and G. MacLean, 203–236. New York: Routledge.

Tafjord, Bjørn O. 2013. "Indigenous religion(s) as an analytical category." *Method and Theory in the Study of Religion* 25(3): 221–243. https://doi.org/10.1163/15700682-12341258

———. 2016a. "How talking about indigenous religion may change things: An example from Talamanca." *Numen* 63(5–6): 548–575. https://doi.org/10.1163/15685276-12341438

———. 2016b. "Scales, translations, and siding effects: Uses of *indígena* and *religión* in Talamanca and beyond." In *Religious Categories and the Construction of the Indigenous*, edited by C. Hartney and D. J. Tower, 138–177. Leiden: Brill. https://doi.org/10.1163/9789004328983_009

———. 2017. "Towards a typology of academic uses of 'indigenous religion(s),' or, eight (or nine) language games that scholars play with this phrase." In *Handbook of Indigenous Religion(s)*, edited by G. Johnson and S. E. Kraft, 25–51. Leiden: Brill. https://doi.org/10.1163/9789004346710_003

Tafjord, Bjørn O. and Gregory D. Alles. 2018. "Introduction: Performances and mediations of indigenous religion(s)." *Numen* 65(5–6): 457–466. https://doi.org/10.1163/15685276-12341508

Taguchi, Yoko. 2017. "An interview with Marisol de la Cadena." *NatureCulture*. http://natureculture.sakura.ne.jp/an-interview-with-marisol-de-la-cadena/#more-140

Todorov, Tzvetan. 1982. *La conquête de l'Amérique: La question de l'autre*. Paris: Editions du Seuil.

Wenger, Tisa. 2009. *We Have a Religion: The 1920s Pueblo Indian Dance Controversy and American Religious Freedom*. Chapel Hill: University of North Carolina Press. https://doi.org/10.5149/9780807894217_wenger

Whitehead, Andrew L., Samuel L. Perry and Joseph O. Baker. 2018. "Make America Christian again: Christian nationalism and voting for Donald Trump in the 2016 Presidential Election." *Sociology of Religion* 79(2): 147–171. https://doi.org/10.1093/socrel/srx070

Whyte, Kyle. 2018. "What do indigenous knowledges do for indigenous peoples?" In *Traditional Ecological Knowledge: Learning from Indigenous Practices for*

Environmental Sustainability, edited by M. K. Nelson and D. Shilling, 57–82. Cambridge: Cambridge University Press.

Wittgenstein, Ludwig. 2009 [1953]. *Philosophische Untersuchungen*. Malden, MA: Wiley-Blackwell.

Woolf, Greg. 2013. "Ethnography and the Gods in Tacitus' *Germania*." In *Ancient Ethnography: New Approaches*, edited by E. Almagor and J. Skinner, 133–152. London: Bloomsbury.

About the author

Bjørn Ola Tafjord is Professor of Religious Studies at UiT The Arctic University of Norway and co-director of the research group "Indigenous Religion(s): Local Grounds, Global Networks" (INREL). His research is primarily ethnographic and historiographic. He has done fieldwork in Talamanca (Costa Rica) regularly since the year 2000, and taught in Tromsø (Northern Norway and Sápmi) since 2007. Most of his essays address methodological issues, for example "Indigenous Religion(s) as an Analytical Category" (in *Method and Theory in the Study of Religion* 2013), "How Talking about Indigenous Religion May Change Things" (*Numen* 2016), "Scales, Translations, and Siding Effects" (in *Religious Categories and the Construction of the Indigenous* 2016), and "Towards a Typology of Academic Uses of 'Indigenous Religion(s)', or Eight (or Nine) Language Games that Scholars Play with This Phrase" (in *Handbook of Indigenous Religion(s)* 2017).

Index

Index

Index

Index

CPSIA information can be obtained
at www.ICGtesting.com
Printed in the USA
JSHW031211240520
5810JS00001B/7